FAMILY REUNIFICATION IN THE EU

This monograph examines the intricate legislative and jurisprudential scenario of family reunification between EU citizens and third country nationals that has developed in the European Union over the last 50 years. Focusing on family residence rights granted to third country national family members of EU citizens, it examines one of the largest sectors affected with over two hundred thousand permits granted each year. In addition to its practical significance, the field has been the object of a lively debate which has yet to be systematically analysed. Using a historical approach, it illustrates the development of the legislation and of the case law on the issue considering the factors that influenced the choices of the EU Legislator and of the Court over the years. It also suggests what future path the Court could take when deciding on cases in the field in order to reinforce the protection of families. This important research ensures full understanding of the EU legislation and of the Court's jurisprudence and allows for its correct application by Member States.

Volume 73 in the Series Modern Studies in European Law

Modern Studies in European Law
Recent titles in this series:

Uniformity of Customs Administration in the European Union
Kathrin Limbach

The Impact of Union Citizenship on the EU's Market Freedoms
Alina Tryfonidou

Equal Citizenship and Its Limits in EU Law
Päivi Johanna Neuvonen

European Law on Unfair Commercial Practices and Contract Law
Mateja Durovic

The European Union's External Action in Times of Crisis
Edited by Piet Eeckhout and Manual Lopez-Escudero

The Legitimacy of Family Rights in Strasbourg Case Law: Living Instrument or Extinguished Sovereignty?
Carmen Draghici

Strengthening the Rule of Law in Europe: From a Common Concept to Mechanisms of Implementation
Edited by Werner Schroeder

The Pluralist Character of the European Economic Constitution
Clemens Kaupa

Exceptions from EU Free Movement Law
Edited by Panos Koutrakos, Niamh Nic Shuibhne and Phil Syrpis

Reconceptualising European Equality Law: A Comparative Institutional Analysis
Johanna Croon-Gestefeld

Marketing and Advertising Law in a Process of Harmonization
Edited by Ulf Bernitz and Caroline Heide-Jörgensen

The Fundamental Right to Data Protection: Normative Value in the Context of Counter-Terrorism Surveillance
Maria Tzanou

Republican Europe
Anna Kocharov

Family Reunification in the EU
Chiara Berneri

For the complete list of titles in this series, see
'Modern Studies in European Law' link at
www.bloomsburyprofessional.com/uk/series/modern-studies-in-european-law

Family Reunification in the EU

The Movement and Residence Rights of Third Country National Family Members of EU Citizens

Chiara Berneri

•HART•
PUBLISHING
OXFORD AND PORTLAND, OREGON
2017

Hart Publishing
An imprint of Bloomsbury Publishing Plc

Hart Publishing Ltd
Kemp House
Chawley Park
Cumnor Hill
Oxford OX2 9PH
UK

Bloomsbury Publishing Plc
50 Bedford Square
London
WC1B 3DP
UK

www.hartpub.co.uk
www.bloomsbury.com

Published in North America (US and Canada) by
Hart Publishing
c/o International Specialized Book Services
920 NE 58th Avenue, Suite 300
Portland, OR 97213-3786
USA

www.isbs.com

First published 2017

British Library Cataloguing-in-Publication Data
A catalogue record for this book is available from the British Library.

ISBN: HB: 978-1-50990-478-5
ePDF: 978-1-50990-480-8
ePub: 978-1-50990-481-5

Library of Congress Cataloging-in-Publication Data

Names: Berneri, Chiara, author.

Title: Family reunification in the EU : the movement and residence rights of third country national family members of EU citizens / Chiara Berneri.

Description: Oxford ; Portland, Oregon : Hart Publishing, an imprint of Bloomsbury Publishing Plc, 2017. | Series: Modern studies in european law ; volume 73 | Based on author's thesis (Doctoral-City Law School, London, 2013) issued under title: The movement and residence rights of third country national family members of EU citizens : a historical and jurisprudential approach. | Includes bibliographical references and index.

Identifiers: LCCN 2016058795 (print) | LCCN 2016059675 (ebook) | ISBN 9781509904785 (hardback : alk. paper) | ISBN 9781509904815 (Epub)

Subjects: LCSH: Emigration and immigration law—European Union countries. | Freedom of movement—European Union countries. | Family reunification—Law and legislation—European Union countries.

Classification: LCC KJE6044 .B474 2017 (print) | LCC KJE6044 (ebook) | DDC 342.2408/2—dc23

LC record available at https://lccn.loc.gov/2016058795

Typeset by Compuscript Ltd, Shannon
Printed and bound in Great Britain by Lightning Source UK Ltd

To find out more about our authors and books visit www.hartpublishing.co.uk. Here you will find extracts, author information, details of forthcoming events and the option to sign up for our newsletters.

Acknowledgements

I would like to express my sincere gratitude to all the people that directly and indirectly helped me in writing this book.

First of all, I would like to thank my PhD supervisors, Professor Daniel Wilsher and Professor Steve Peers. They have been a true source of inspiration, support and guidance during and after my PhD. I have benefited immensely from their help since the very beginning of this project. I am very lucky to have found two great *maestri*. I would also like to thank my PhD examiners, Professor Elspeth Guild and Doctor Nicholas Hatzis, for their comments and precious advice on how my thesis could be turned into a monograph.

In addition to my supervisors and PhD examiners I would like to thank Professor Jo Shaw and Professor Niamh Nic Shuibhne, who ignited in me a passion for this area of the law during my LLM at the University of Edinburgh. Without their teaching and feedback I would have never contemplated the idea of writing a PhD thesis on this topic, let alone a book.

I would also like to express my gratitude to Professor Joseph Weiler, whom I had the honour to meet in 2011 in Edinburgh, for his suggestions and, most of all, for his kind words of encouragement when I was just a young, clueless PhD student.

I would like to thank Judge Marta Cartabia too for her constant mentoring and encouragement over these years.

Many thanks go to the people that have allowed me to write this book by helping me on a daily basis. In particular, my sincere gratitude goes to our nanny Felicia Lovin for her immense dedication and for taking care of my family and me so well over the last year. My immense gratitude goes also to my grandmothers Clementina Grugni and Maria Stragliati, who are now looking after us from heaven, for their love and their daily prayers for me, to my parents Carla Mazzocchi and Enrico Berneri for their help, constant support and unconditional love, to my children Patrick Francesco Larcom and Raffaele Douglas Larcom who, with their smiles and affection, always remind me that life is much bigger than a book, and most of all to my husband Shaun Larcom. Without his love and care, patience and priceless advice I would have never finished, and probably not even started, this book.

AMDG

Contents

Table of Cases

Alphabetical list

Chronological list

Table of Legislation

Primary Legislation

Secondary Legislation

Soft Law

Introduction

THE EUROPEAN UNION (henceforth the EU or the Union)[1] has developed complex legislation concerning family reunification[2] of third country national EU family members.[3] For the purpose of simplicity it is possible to subdivide the group of families affected by this legislation into three main categories. The first category includes those third country nationals already residing within the territory of one of the Member States wishing to live with a third country national family member. In accordance with the power granted by the Treaty at Article 79(2)(a)(b) TFEU[4] in the area of immigration, the EU released Directive 2003/86/EC on the right to family reunification, which sets minimum standard conditions for the exercise of

[1] For the purpose of simplicity, in this book the terms European Union, EU or Union will be used also when referring to the European Economic Community (EEC).

[2] The family reunification legislation does not simply encompass the right of residence of a third country national family member within the EU but also all the other rights connected to it such as employment rights, education rights, right to stay after death or divorce from the EU citizen etc.

[3] The necessity of protecting families was understood far back in the past, since the *ius commune* era. On this point see M Antokolskaia, 'The "better law" approach and the harmonization of family law', KB Woelki (ed), in *Perspective for the Unification and Harmonization of Family Law in Europe*, (Oxford, Hart Publishing, 2003) 159, 169–70. After the Second World War, protection was granted to families at international level. State family law is subject to both private international law conventions and public international law. Under the first group we can list the Hague Convention on Child Abduction (25 October 1980, entered into force 1 December 1983), the Hague Convention on Inter-country Adoption (29 May 1993, entered into force 1 May 1995), the Convention on the Law Applicable to Maintenance Obligations towards Children (24 October 1956, entered into force 1 January 1962) and the Hague Convention on the International Recovery of Child Support and Other Forms of Family Maintenance (23 November 2007, entered into force 1 January 2013). These treaties are binding on state parties and in many states they become enforceable through implementing legislation. As far as public constitutional law is concerned, the major pieces of legislation affecting family law are the Universal Declaration of Human Rights (art 16, 10 December 1948), the European Convention on Human Rights and Fundamental Freedoms (ECHR, Art 8, Art 14 and Protocol 1 Art 1, 4 November 1950, entered into force 3 September 1953), International Covenant on Civil and Political Rights (ICCPR, Art 7, 16 December 1966, entered into force 23 March 1976), the International Covenant on Economic, Social and Cultural Rights (ICESCR, Art 10, 16 December 1966, entered into force 3 January 1976). The first treaties that, at international level, recognised the right to family reunification were Convention on the Elimination of Discrimination Against Women (signed 18 December 1979, entered into force 3 September 1981), the Convention on the Rights of the Child (adopted 20 November 1989, entered into force 2 September 1990) and the Convention on the Protection of the Rights of All Migrant Workers and Members of Their Families (approved 18 December 1990, entered into force 1 July 2003). Nevertheless, even when these provisions started to be protected internationally, the treaties and conventions that contained them did not envisage a clear system of enforcement. For example the Convention on the Protection of the Rights of All Migrant Workers and Members of Their Families established, at Art 72, a Committee for the Rights of Migrant Workers. However, this body functions as a body of political pressure and is not able to enforce sanctions.

[4] Several directives were adopted by taking this article as a legal ground (or the previous Art 63(3)(4) TEC): Dir 2003/86/EC on the right of family reunification; Dir 2003/109/EC concerning the status

the right to family reunification by third country nationals residing lawfully in the territory of the Member States.[5] This Directive has consequentially shaped national legislation that has to be applied to this category of family members. The second category covers EU workers or citizens residing in another Member State wishing to live with a third country national family member. Also in this case the right of entry and residence of the third country national is granted in accordance with EU law, although this time owing to Directive 2004/38/EC[6] on the right of free movement of EU citizens and their family members. Finally, the third category concerns those nationals residing in their EU Member State of origin wishing to live with a third country national family member. The legislation applying to this category is still national. In other words, it is up to the state to decide the conditions and the modality of admission of these specific third country nationals. However, in accordance to the recent jurisprudence of the Court of Justice of the European Union (henceforth the CJEU or the Court), third country national family members of EU non-moving citizens should be allowed to reside in the national Member State of their EU sponsor if the denial of this right would force the latter to leave the territory of the EU. In these cases, family reunification rights are granted not via national rules but by EU law.

This book focuses on the issue of family reunification rights granted to third country nationals within the EU and, in particular, on the two last categories of potential applicants listed above. Leaving aside the numerical importance of this phenomenon,[7] it is worth focusing on this specific issue because it has been the

of third-country nationals who are long-term residents; Dir 2004/81/EC on the residence permit issued to third-country nationals who are victims of trafficking in human beings; Dir 2004/114/EC on the conditions of admission of third-country nationals for the purposes of studies, pupil exchange, unremunerated training or voluntary service; Dir 2005/71/EC on a specific procedure for admitting third-country nationals for the purposes of scientific research; Dir 2009/50/EC on the conditions of entry and residence of highly qualified workers.

5 Council Dir 2003/86/EC [2003] OJ L 251/12. For an account of this Directive see K Groenendijk, 'Family Reunification as a Right under Community Law' (2006) 10 *European Journal of Migration and Law* 215. Apart from freedom of movement legislation and Dir 2003/86/EC, family reunification provisions can be found in several Association Agreements with third countries. In addition, there are also several special EU law regimes of family reunion with regard to special categories of third country nationals such as Refugees and Blue Card Directive holders. The special rules for refugees are set out in Chapter V of the general Family Reunion Directive. The special rules for Blue Card Directive holders are instead contained in Council Dir 2009/50/EC [2009] OJ L 155/17. For a detailed explanation of these exceptions see S Peers, *EU Justice and Home Affairs Law* (Oxford, Oxford University Press, 2011) 473–78.

6 Council Dir 2004/38/EC [2004] OJ L 158/77.

7 Family reunification between third country nationals and EU citizens, be they either moving or static, is not an irrelevant phenomenon. In 2010 the total numbers of permits released by the 27 Member States to third country nationals willing to reunite with non-EU citizens was 508,325 (see Green Paper on the right to family reunification of third-country nationals living in the European Union (Dir 2003/86/EC) COM (2011) 735 final, 10) whilst the total numbers of permits released for family reasons to third country nationals regardless of the nationality of the sponsor amounted roughly to 775,000 (see file 'First residence permits issued in the EU-28 by reasons, 2008, 2009, 2010, 2011, 2012, 2013 and 2014.png', data collected from Eurostat available at ec.europa.eu/eurostat/statistics-explained/index.php/File:First_residence_permits_issued_in_the_EU-28_by_reasons,_2008,_2009,_2010,_2011,_2012,_2013_and_2014.png). These data, once combined, suggest that in 2010 roughly 226,675 third country nationals applied for family reunification with EU sponsors.

object of a lively debate, which is still ongoing. Indeed over the years, particularly with regard to cases concerning EU moving citizens and third country nationals, Member States[8] have often tried to deny family reunification rights to third country national EU family members,[9] despite the clear indications of the EU Legislator. Moreover, the Court's answer to the challenges that have been raised concerning this issue have not been completely consistent, swinging between liberal and austere positions,[10] and often utilising reasoning that is difficult to reconcile with others.

The object of this book is to analyse the intricate legislative and jurisprudential development of the phenomenon of family reunification between EU citizens and third country nationals. In order to fulfil this aim, the book endorses a historical approach. Through historical analysis the book will show how the phenomenon of family reunification between EU citizens and third country nationals is the fruit of a development that, starting from the legislation of the first post-Second World War era, reached its peak in the more recent judgments of the CJEU. Using a historical perspective, it will be shown that family reunification legislative provisions, their more recent CJEU interpretation and the new application of the concept of EU citizenship to family reunification cases involving EU citizens and third country nationals find their grounds on different but concrete historical trends that influenced the development of the EU approach on this issue.

It is common knowledge that, since its beginning, the main aim of the EU has been the creation of a common market. The Treaty of Rome, in establishing the

[8] It is worth pointing out that just some Member States raised issues concerning third country national family members. From the cases that will be analysed we can note that those involved in these kinds of dispute most often are Germany, the Netherlands, the UK, Belgium and Ireland, to which one should add also Denmark, Greece, Austria and Poland, which are often listed among the intervening states in the post *Zambrano* cases.

[9] See Chapters 3 and 4 for an account of the Member States' approach.

[10] A Tryfonidou, 'Family Reunification Rights of (Migrant) Union Citizens: Towards a More Liberal Approach' (2009) 15 *European Law Journal* 634, 634. It was also argued that the Court 'must either endeavour to weave its case law logically together or, if there are good reasons to push the law in a different direction, articulate its reasoning as clearly and explicitly as possible': N Nic Shuibhne, 'Case Law: (Some) of the Kids Are all right' (2012) 49 *Common Market Law Review* 349, 379. As far as family reunification between EU static citizens and third country nationals is concerned, it was also argued that the post-*Zambrano* cases are good examples of how the Court conjured rights, and limits to them, out of nowhere: A Dashwood, 'Judicial Activism and Conferred Powers—Is the CJEU Falling into Bad Habits?', paper presented at the 10th IEL (Institute of European Law) Annual Lecture, Birmingham University, 27 June 2012. On the academic debate addressed by the Court see also in particular S Acierno, 'The *Carpenter* judgment: fundamental rights and the limits of the Community legal order' (2003) 28 *European Law Review* 398, 407; E Spaventa, 'From Gebhard to Carpenter: Towards a (Non-) Economic European Constitution' *Common Market Law Review* (2004) 41 743, 767; A Tryfonidou, 'Jia or "Carpenter II": the edge of reason' (2007) 32 *European Law Review* 908, 917 (in this case comment the author underlined how the Court did not succeed in making explicit whether it was willing to depart from the previous *Akrich* case and to endorse a new family reunification approach); JB Bierbach, 'European citizens' third-country family members and Community law' (2008) 4 *European Constitutional Law Review* 344, 356–57 (in this case comment the author underlines how the CJEU's reasoning was far from providing legal certainty); NG Foster, *Foster on EU Law* (Oxford, Oxford University Press, 2011) 353.

EU, recognised that certain matters had necessarily to be free from any regulation that would restrict their movement among the Member States. The aim of developing the right of free movement of workers was immediately endorsed by the Court. The CJEU, through its restless activity, immediately from the early sixties started to interpret broadly the provisions on free movement of workers and, later on, to apply the deterrence test to free movement of labour cases in order to eliminate all the obstacles that could hinder Member States' workers from taking advantage of such a crucial right.[11] Furthermore, in 1992 the concept of European citizenship (from now on also EU citizenship) was finally introduced in the Maastricht Treaty. The Court interpreted this new concept not only as a way to extend free movement rights to non-economically active people but also as a source of self-standing rights occurring without the presence of a real cross-border element. However, the action of the EU and of the Court soon began to clash with immigration policies adopted by some Member States. Over the last 40 years immigration has become a particularly prominent issue in Europe and it has often generated vehement national political debate. Since the oil crisis of the seventies, passing through the fall of the Berlin Wall, followed by the 9/11 terrorist attacks, the more recent Arab spring and the current immigration crisis stemming from the Syrian civil war, many European states have begun to fear waves of legal and illegal third country nationals and have acted to keep them from crossing their borders.[12] For these reasons the signing of the Schengen Treaty as well as the introduction of the concept of EU citizenship and the enhancement of free movement of workers, which have eased the movements of people throughout the EU, have had a deep impact on the perception of immigration, to the extent that the greater internationalism of Europeans has simultaneously triggered strong Eurocentrism, fear of third country nationals and xenophobia.[13] The development of the EU approach over family reunification between EU citizens and third country nationals, both legislative and jurisprudential, will be analysed considering these factors in the background. Adopting this approach will allow us to offer a realistic account of this phenomenon relying on factors that clearly influenced the choices of the Legislator and of the Court.

To this end, the book is organised as follows. Chapter 1 focuses on the post-Second World War bilateral agreements period up until the signing of the Treaty of Rome and the creation of the Common Market. This chapter shows that family reunification provisions were introduced within the free movement legislation for the purpose of matching the post-war lack of manpower of Northern European states with the Italian surplus of labour through the establishment of the right

[11] On this point see Chapter 2.

[12] Among others see the UN High Commissioner for Refugees, interview of Antonio Guterres, 20 March 2012, available at www.epc.eu/events_rep_details.php?cat_id=6&pub_id=1430.

[13] D Cesarani and M Fulbrook, *Citizenship, Nationality and Migration in Europe* (London, Taylor & Francis, 2002) 3.

of free movement of people.[14] By looking at the connections between bilateral agreements and the Common Market the book will show how family reunification was introduced not for humanitarian reasons but as an incentive to encourage Italian workers to move towards northern European Member States in order to fill their lack of manpower.

Chapter 2 focuses on the move towards stricter immigration that occurred after the oil crisis. This chapter will show how the sudden drop in economic activity pushed some states to endorse protectionist measures, which included reducing immigration. The 'other' started to be stigmatised as a potential threat[15] for the economy and society by the media and within the political arena[16] and this has become part of the common mentality that continues to the present day.

Chapter 3 focuses on the analysis of the secondary legislation and the first case law over the issue of family reunification between EU citizens and third country nationals. It will be shown how the provisions contained in these pieces of legislation found their roots at the interface between free movement of workers and citizens and Member States' concerns over immigration and how these two currents ended up shaping the reasoning of the Court in applying them. In particular, the chapter is subdivided in three subsections. The first subsection is dedicated to the development of the secondary legislation provisions concerning residence rights of third country national family members and on how the Court applied and interpreted them. The second subsection is dedicated to further provisions inserted since the first secondary legislation such as the requirement, to be fulfilled by the EU worker, of having proper housing available for himself and his family, the consequences faced by EU workers and their family members in case the former cease to work through physical incapacity, retirement age or death, the condition of dependency of the third country national upon the EU worker, the conditions under which EU workers and their family members can be expelled for breach of public policy, public security and public health and the working status, education rights and social and tax advantages of EU workers' family members. The third subsection is finally dedicated to some provisions inserted in more recent secondary legislation such as the condition on sickness insurance and sufficient economic resources that the EU worker has to fulfil in order to reunite with his family in the host Member State, provisions on the rights of family members in case of separation or divorce from the EU worker and the provision on the right of permanent residence of family members of EU workers. Overall, it will be shown how the approach of the Legislator and of the CJEU has been particularly

[14] Among others see F Pastore and G Sciortino, *Tutori Lontani: il Ruolo degli Stati d'Origine nel Processo di Integrazione degli Immigrati* (2001) Ricerca svolta su incarico della Commissione delle politiche di integrazione degli immigrati presso Centro Studi di Politica Internazionale (Cespi) 10–11, available at www.cespi.it/PASTORE/tutori-lontani.PDF.

[15] KJ Bade, *Migration in European History* (Oxford, Blackwell Publishing, 2003) 280.

[16] ibid.

open towards third country national family members' residence rights although not completely free from the influence of Member States' immigration concerns which have, at times, determined the outcome of the cases.

Chapter 4 will show how the Court's reasoning in cases involving EU static citizens was mainly built around the immigration concerns of some Member States, this time however at the interplay with the development of the EU citizenship status as a source of self-standing rights. Unlike the previous chapter, however, it will be shown that overall the outcome of these cases was shaped around the immigration concerns of the Member States, as is evident in the post *Zambrano*[17] cases up until *Alokpa*.[18]

Finally, Chapter 5 will be dedicated to some conclusions. It will focus on the potential development of the concept of EU citizenship as a status that protects not just the right to move but also the right to reside. It will be shown that, potentially, an enhanced concept of EU citizenship could reinforce the protection of families composed of EU citizens and third country nationals, both in cases involving EU static and moving citizens.

[17] Case C-34/09 *Ruiz Zambrano v Office national de l'emploi (ONEm)* EU:C:2011:124.

[18] Case C-86/12 *Alokpa and Others v Ministre du Travail, de l'Emploi et de l'Immigration* EU:C:2013:645.

1

Family Reunification at the Time of Bilateral Agreements and the Common Market

1. INTRODUCTION

THE FIRST EU law provision granting family residence rights to family members of EU workers can be found in Council Regulation 15/1961/EEC[1] on free movement of workers. This was the first regulation of a three-step phase that culminated with Regulation 1612/1968/EEC and the full liberalisation of manpower.[2] Article 10(1) of the latter regulation provided that the spouse, the descendants who are under the age of 21 years or dependants and the dependent relatives in the ascending line of the worker and his spouse have the right, irrespective of their nationality, 'to install themselves with a worker who is a national of one Member State and who is employed in the territory of another Member State'.

It has been argued that, originally, these provisions were not introduced for humanitarian concerns[3] but for economic reasons concerning the Common Market.[4] As the goal of the EU was in fact the creation of a market in which factors of

[1] Council Reg 15/1961/EEC [1961] OJ L 1073/6. This measure was also accompanied by the Directive of 13 December 1961 on the administration practices concerning settlement, employment and residence OJ 80 1513–16.

[2] The second step of this three-step phase started with the introduction of Council Reg 38/1964/EEC [1964] OJ L 965/64. The third and last one started in 1968 with Council Reg 1612/1968/EEC OJ Sp Ed 1968, L 257/2. Council Reg 1612/68/EEC was repealed in 2011 by Council Reg 492/2011/EU [2011] OJ L 141/1. The subdivision in different phases was meant to introduce gradually the concept of freedom of movement of workers in order not to negatively affect the domestic markets. For instance, in the first two phases, the priority to take up job offers was given to national workers (if the competent authorities did not propose the name of a national worker within three weeks, only then could the offer be taken up by the worker of another Member State). This limitation was eliminated with Council Reg 1612/68/EEC.

[3] A sign that the EU did not intend to create a general legislative protection for family reunifications consists in the fact that these rights were considered residual. Indeed, family members who had the nationality of a Member State and were economically active could rely directly on the free movement provisions in order to have access to the host Member State. On this point see J Handoll, *Free Movement of Persons in the EU* (New York, Wiley, 1995) 249.

[4] G Barret, 'Family Matters: European Community Law and Third Country National Family Members' (2003) 40 *Common Market Law Review* 369, 375–76.The first to explicate this idea was AG Darmon in the *Demirel* case (Case C-12/86 *Demirel v Stadt Schwäbisch Gmünd* EU:C:1987:232.

production (goods, services, capital and labour) could move where the requirements of supply and demand dictated,[5] residence rights of family members were built as an instrument to avoid hindrances to the free movement of the European worker.

This chapter will look at the origins of the phenomenon of family reunification between European workers and their family members. The chapter will start this historical overview by looking at family residence rights from the time of bilateral agreements between Italy and northern European countries and will show how they played a role in creating an incentive for workers to migrate towards the receiving state. It will then highlight also that the provisions inserted in the first secondary free movement legislation were drafted as a way to create incentives for unemployed Italians to move to the northern European Member States. Finally, it will be noted that the openness of the EU provisions was not just directed towards family members born in one of the EU Member States but also towards third country national family members.

The message conveyed in this chapter is fundamental in order to clarify the background that brought about the first provisions on family reunification and to highlight the reasons behind their development both in terms of legislative changes and jurisprudential interpretation.

2. MOVEMENT RIGHTS OF WORKERS AND THE ROLE OF ITALY: FROM BILATERAL AGREEMENTS TO THE TREATY OF ROME AND THE COMMON MARKET

The years from 1945 to the late sixties were characterised by an increased inflow of immigrants to different European states and from outside and inside Europe.[6] The rise in the number of immigrants coming to Europe was triggered by two main factors: on one side, strong economic growth in the old continent, on the other, a shortage of workers and the process of decolonisation.[7] With regard to economic growth, nothing in the history of Europe resembles the experience of the post-war years. The standard of living of all social classes increased continually and rapidly

He pointed out that 'family reunification for example is treated by community law as a necessary element in giving effect to the freedom of movement of workers and does not become a right until the freedom which it presupposed has taken effect'. On this point see also E Guild, *The Legal Elements of European Identity, EU Citizenship and Migration Law* (The Hague, Kluwer Law International, 2004) 98.

[5] Barret, above n 4 at 375–76.

[6] KF Zimmerman, 'Tackling the European Migration Problem' (1995) 9 *The Journal of Economic Perspectives* 45, 46–47.

[7] In particular France and England opened the doors to immigration from some of their colonies (Algeria, the Caribbean, India and Pakistan) and encouraged immigration of ex-colonials back to their motherland. On this point see M Martiniello, 'The new migratory Europe: Towards a proactive immigration policy', in CA Parsons and TM Smeeding (eds), *Immigration and the Transformation of Europe* (Cambridge, Cambridge University Press, 2006) 301.

for more than two decades.[8] As far as the shortage of workers is concerned, data show that immediately after the war the number of displaced people was around 20 million.[9] This circumstance made the Federal Republic of Germany (henceforth Germany) and many other states of continental Europe realise that their labour requirements could not be satisfied by their own nationals alone.[10] The realisation that some of the northern states needed labour engendered a significant rise in migration.[11] This lack of labour then started to be filled both by immigrants coming from ex-colonies and immigrants coming from southern Europe (Spain, Portugal, Greece, Italy and the Balkans) and North Africa and Turkey.[12] The need for immigrant workers went hand in hand with the relaxation of borders. Indeed, some European states such as Belgium, Luxembourg and the Netherlands began to adopt more friendly policies on immigration like eliminating the stringent passport controls inherited from the inter-war period.[13]

This chapter is only focused on the role of Italy. This is because Italy was the only southern European country involved both in negotiating bilateral agreements and in the drafting of the Common Market and, therefore, it is the link through which it is possible to discover potential connections between the two projects in terms of family reunification policies. From the end of the Second World War, Italy's vast population and lack of capital enhanced a widespread political consensus on the necessity of developing new efficient migration policies. With an official level of unemployment of 2,000,000 people[14] the Italian government considered the emigration of national workers to be a vital necessity.[15] The migratory outflow had to be rapid and as vast as possible and the government's own diplomatic initiatives

[8] AS Milward, *The European Rescue of the Nation State* (London, Routledge, 1992) 21. The author explains the uniqueness of this period underlining the role of the state as the crucial and most important factor. The successful institutional management of the economy of that time, in his view, was one of the main explanatory factors of the new European economic expansion.

[9] Zimmerman, above n 6 at 46. On this point see also KJ Bade, *Migration in European History* (Oxford, Blackwell Publishing, 2003) 215.

[10] R Hansen, 'Migration to Europe since 1945: its History and its Lessons' (2003) 74 *The Political Quarterly* 25, 25.

[11] LP Moch, 'Foreign Workers in Western Europe: The "Cheaper Hands" in Historical Perspective' in J Klausen and L Tilly (eds), *European Integration in Social and Historical Perspective: 1850 to the Present* (New York, Rowman & Littlefield, 1997) 111.

[12] See Martiniello, above n 7 at 7.

[13] J Torpey, *The Invention of the Passport* (Cambridge, Cambridge University Press, 1999). The author underlined how, in spite of the generally liberal attitude toward freedom of movement during the late 19th century, governments became increasingly oriented to making distinctions between their own citizens and others on the basis of documents such as ID cards or, more commonly, passports (at 93).

[14] To this critical scenario one has to add nearly one million people, just from the north of Italy, that were previously employed in the war industry and, after the war ended, were left without a job. See C Besana, 'Accordi Internazionali ed Emigrazione della Manodopera Italiana tra Ricostruzione e Sviluppo' in Sergio Zaninelli and M Taccolini (eds), *Il lavoro come fattore produttivo e come risorsa nella storia economica italiana: atti del Convegno di studi, Roma, 24 novembre 2000* (Milano, Vita e pensiero, 2002) 4.

[15] F Romero, 'Migration as an issue in European interdependence and integration: the case of Italy' in AS Milward, F Lynch, R Ranieri, F Romero and V Soresen (eds), *The Frontier of National Sovereignty: History and Theory, 1945–1992* (London, Routledge, 1993) 37.

had to be focused on the pursuit of this goal. Hence, the promotion of emigration became the primary purpose of Italy's foreign policy.[16] The exigency of several states to recruit workers and the corresponding need of Italy to find employment for its nationals made everyone realise the necessity of agreeing on an intelligent inter-state policy that had to be capable of allowing workers to move from one part of Europe to another in order to take up employment.[17] This common purpose opened up the golden era of bilateral treaties. As Schmitter highlights, these treaties were the trigger and guidance of Europe after the Second World War.[18] From 1946 onwards Italy signed bilateral agreements with all the European countries that experienced labour shortages, including Belgium, France, Germany, Luxembourg, the Netherlands and the UK. These agreements organised the co-operation between different states' employment services with the aim of promoting the recruitment of specific types of worker. An overall ceiling was usually set to limit the number of immigrant workers that could be admitted every year. The decision on recruitment was left to the expressed demand of the receiving state. Depending on the country, sometimes the concrete process of recruitment was either managed directly by a government agency or left to the employer.[19]

Despite their crucial role in finding a temporary answer to the problems of labour shortages and unemployment after the Second World War, it is important to note that bilateral agreements were no more than an appendage to the employment policy, as they did not encompass any vision for a long-term integration of immigrant workers. For example, workers were given work and accommodation for a limited stay, the labour market was limited just to some sectors such as mining, iron and steel, and the recruitment process was only focused on young male workers.[20] Moreover, bilateral agreements never really led towards a permanent opening of the foreign markets because the receiving states always used them as 'turn on and off' solutions to immigration. 'When demand (for labour) was very high the economic priorities of the host countries could occasionally coincide with the needs of the sending countries, but the agreements did not assure any irreversible right to the latter.'[21]

The volatility of the northern European demand and the temporary nature of employment offered by the host states triggered many returns and soon made Italy realise that these agreements were an inadequate instrument for the solution of the Italian migratory problems. The Italian government therefore became increasingly persuaded that national barriers to the circulation of manpower had to be brought down another way. The only way to circumvent the problem of national

[16] ibid.

[17] F Pastore and G Sciortino, *Tutori Lontani: il Ruolo degli Stati d'Origine nel Processo di Integrazione degli Immigrati*, Ricerca svolta su incarico della Commissione delle politiche di integrazione degli immigrati (2001), available at www.cespi.it/PASTORE/tutori-lontani.PDF, 10–11.

[18] BS Heisler, 'Sending Countries and the Politics of Emigration and Destination' (1985) 19 *International Migration Review* 469, 474.

[19] Romero, above n 15 at 40.

[20] Martiniello, above n 7 at 310.

[21] Romero, above n 15 at 39–40.

barriers was to internationalise the issue of Italian unemployment and deal with it at a multilateral level. The issue of full employment had to transcend national state borders and be placed in the broader backdrop of the economic co-operation within Western Europe.[22] Italy, under pressure from the United States, proposed to the OEEC[23] Member States a complete liberalisation on the circulation of manpower. This would have allowed a more efficient utilisation of the available workforces through the total opening of European borders within 10 years. This solution, however, found criticism in some states. In particular France, Belgium and the UK were very much concerned about losing their sovereignty on labour and immigration policies and the proposal was not taken up.[24]

In the early fifties the French Prime Minister Robert Schuman, tired of the hesitations of the European intellectual environment,[25] proposed that the market for coal and steel, of which Europe was witnessing a shortage, had to be controlled by a new supranational authority, which became on 18 April 1951 the European Coal and Steel Community (ECSC).[26] During the negotiations, the Italian delegates took the opportunity to argue that, in order to achieve a completely integrated market for coal and steel, freedom of circulation for workers had to be encompassed within the treaty provisions. However, France and Germany made it clear that free circulation could be contemplated just for workers with proven qualifications. The strict Franco-German formulation was finally accepted in the ECSC Treaty.[27] Article 69 committed Member States to lift every employment restriction based on nationality, just for a restricted category of workers, by stating that 'Member States bind themselves to renounce any restriction based on nationality against the employment in the coal and steel industry of workers of proven qualifications for such industries who possess the nationality of one of the Member States; this commitment shall be subject to the limitations imposed by the fundamental needs of health and public order'. The Franco-German approach to the issue of freedom of movement left the Italian diplomats, aiming for a wider interpretation of the ECSC Treaty,[28] unsatisfied. Owing to this limited progress, bilateral

[22] ibid, 40.

[23] OEEC stands for Organization for European Economic Co-operation. It was founded in 1948 with the aim of continuing a joint economic recovery programme within Europe after the end of the Second World War. Originally the OEEC had 18 participants. In September 1961 the OEEC was superseded by the Organization for Economic Co-operation and Development (OECD), a worldwide body.

[24] L Tosi, 'La tutela internazionale dell'immigrazione' in P Bevilacqua, A De Clementi and E Franzina (eds), *Storia dell'immigrazione italiana, vol 2, arrivi* (Roma, Donzelli Editore, 2001) 453–56.

[25] See DW Urwin, *The Community of Europe, A History of European Integration since 1945* (New York, Longman, 1995) 1–3.

[26] Treaty Establishing the European Coal and Steel Community, expired 23 July 2002.

[27] Romero, above n 15 at 43.

[28] ibid. Italy argued that freedom of circulation had to entail the full harmonisation of all the factors and procedures regulating access to the labour market of the six Member States. However, this attempt did not find the approval of the other Member States. France and Luxembourg conceived the free movement of workers within Europe as an aim that had to be achieved when the problem of unemployment in Europe had been completely solved. On the other side Belgium and the Netherlands did not agree to a mutual recognition of qualifications and to harmonisation of social legislation.

agreements still seemed the only way to achieve suitable advantages for the Italian workers. In 1955 Italy signed its last migration bilateral agreement with Germany which, up until then, had been reluctant to engage with Italy.[29] With the signing of the German-Italian Treaty all the industrial regions of Western Europe were completely engaged in bilateral migratory schemes with Italy as a counterpart.[30]

The issue of freedom of movement took an explicit and fuller shape with the negotiations for the Common Market, which began in 1955 in Messina.[31] On that occasion the Benelux countries suggested that the target to achieve was the creation of a new comprehensive economic community. Surprisingly, they suggested that this new economic community should not encompass limited economic areas of integration[32] but had to pursue the aim of achieving a complete common market of goods, services, capital and labour. It is interesting to note how the Benelux countries moved from an initial scepticism to a belief that that a common market was the path to pursue. The forerunner in this change of attitude was the Netherlands. Up until 1955 the Netherlands was a firm opponent of common market schemes. The view that prevailed among the Dutch was that they needed to pursue an Atlantic co-operation with the US rather than belonging to a small continental bloc that had, in their view, very little to offer.[33] The change occurred in 1955 following American pressure on the Netherlands to participate in the European Defence Community, a project that, if it did not fail due to the lack of ratification by the French Parliament, would have established a pan-European military force. On that occasion the Netherlands started to demand economic and not just military co-operation.[34] Later on Germany too joined the Netherlands and Italy in asking for a gradual introduction of the free circulation of workers. As a matter of fact, the serious objections put forward by Germany[35] on the Common Market project became counterbalanced by the simplified access that they would have

Finally Germany agreed on a common European approach to unemployment but foresaw its solution in a future co-ordination of economic policies and not in the move towards free movement of labour.

[29] For example the German government was, for some years, quite reluctant to sign a bilateral migration agreement with Italy. On this point see JD Steinert, 'L'accordo di emigrazione italo-tedesco e il reclutamento di manodopera italiana negli anni cinquanta' in J Petersen (ed), *L'emigrazione tra Italia e Germania* (Bari, Piero Lacaita Editore, 1993) 142–60.

[30] Romero, above n 15 at 43.

[31] ibid, 52–58. On this point see also Urwin, above n 25 at 74. Some pushes to liberalise the job market came particularly from Nato. Straight after the Korean War Nato started to look suspiciously at the imbalance between countries with full employment and localised shortages of skilled workers and other nations with large groups of available manpower. Initially the US asked the OEEC to liberalise work in Europe. Later on, they started to push for the creation of the Common Market.

[32] Jean Monnet was the one who strongly suggested for further sector integration in the field of transport and energy. See Urwin, above n 25 at 62–67.

[33] See Milward, above n 8 at 173.

[34] ibid.

[35] One of these objections was the fact that German exports were not just concentrated on the market of the six but targeted also Austria, Denmark, Norway, Sweden, Switzerland and the UK. A customs union that would introduce an external tariff higher than the one applied so far by Germany was going to be regarded by these states with suspicion. ibid, 196.

had to the French and Italian markets, which were the biggest importers from Germany at the time.[36]

At the end of the conference the freedom of movement of workers was incorporated among the aims to pursue for the creation of the Common Market in order to launch 'a fresh advance towards the building of Europe'.[37] These aims took the concrete form of an embryonic Common Market proposal, owing to the restless work of the Belgian Prime Minister of the time, Henry Spaak. His first *ad interim* report issued in 1956, known as the Spaak Report,[38] referred to unemployment not as a hindrance but rather as a resource for European growth. According to it, unemployment could be better tackled by common action.[39] To this end, Chapter III, Title III was completely dedicated to free movement of labour and particular attention was also given to the avoidance of discrimination between nationals and non-nationals when taking up job positions.[40]

The indications contained in the Spaak Report were finally crystallised in the EEC Treaty.[41] Workers were subdivided into salaried, service providers and self-employed[42] and their right to freely move within the territory of the Union was encompassed in the part of the Treaty dedicated to the Foundations of the Community.[43] With regard to salaried workers, Article 48(2) stated that free movement 'shall entail the abolition of any discrimination based on nationality between workers of the Member States as regards employment, remuneration and other conditions of work and employment'. Likewise, with regard to the freedom of establishment, Article 53 stated that Member States 'shall not introduce any new restrictions on the right of establishment in their territories of nationals of other Member States, save as otherwise provided in this Treaty'. Finally, Article 59 on service providers prohibited 'restrictions on freedom to provide services within the Community'.

The EEC Treaty also set out the basis for the implementation of free movement of workers through secondary legislation. The EEC Treaty stated in fact that 'for the purpose of establishing a Common Market the activities of the Community shall include … c) the abolition as between Member States, of obstacles to freedom of movement for persons, services and capital' and that 'as soon as this Treaty enters

[36] ibid.

[37] Messina declaration, 3 June 1955.

[38] Comité Intergouvernemental créé par la Conférence de Messine, Rapport des Chefs de délégation aux Ministres des Affaires Etrangères, Brussels, 21 April 1956, available at www.cvce.eu/obj/rapport_des_chefs_de_delegation_aux_ministres_des_affaires_etrangeres_bruxelles_21_avril_1956-fr-52a08e74-02f5-4912-a667-2ea34b9dcdea.html

[39] ibid, 91.

[40] ibid.

[41] Treaty Establishing the European Economic Community, 25 March 1957. On the same day the Treaty Establishing the European Atomic Energy Community (Euratom or EAEC Treaty) was also signed.

[42] EEC Treaty provisions from Art 48 to Art 66.

[43] See Art 3 EEC Treaty. This article lists the fundamental policies of the Community. Its paragraph C includes among these policies 'the abolition, as between Member States, of obstacles to freedom of movement for persons, services and capital'.

into force, the Council shall, acting on a proposal from the Commission and after consulting the Economic and Social Committee, issue directives or make regulations setting out the measures required to bring about, by progressive stages, freedom of movement for workers, as defined in Article 48'. The secondary legislation concerning free movement of workers, adopted soon after the entry into force of the EEC Treaty and culminating in Council Regulation 1612/68/EEC, worked on a long 'step-by-step' process in order to abolish the limits that could be perceived as a strain on the right of workers to move freely within the Union.[44] With the three successive community regulations the national priorities for employment were reduced and eventually abolished for all EEC workers and family members.

Despite having avoided the option of an integrated system and having preferred a sort of gradual easing of their interdependence, at no point did any of the Member States obstruct the process of gradual liberalisation of the market. Interestingly, despite all the Italian claims in order to achieve a common market, full integration only came about when its impact on the Italian nation was no longer so crucial.[45]

3. BILATERAL AGREEMENTS AND FAMILY MEMBERS' RESIDENCE RIGHTS

Having pictured the historical background from the bilateral agreements to the Common Market, the book will now focus on the approach of granting family residence rights adopted in the bilateral agreements concluded between northern European states and Italy. This section is divided into five sub-sections. The first four of these will describe the approach adopted by the bilateral agreements concluded by some states with Italy. The last sub-section will explain the reasons why the open approach towards granting residence rights to workers' family members was probably adopted in order to create extra incentives to the Italian movement of labour towards northern Europe.

Before starting this analysis a clarification of method is necessary. As mentioned above, given the fundamental role of Italy both in the drafting of bilateral agreements and in the pursuit of the Common Market this analysis is going to focus just on the bilateral agreements that see this country as one of the counterparts. The northern European states with which Italy concluded bilateral agreements and on which the analysis is going to be focused are Belgium, France, Germany and

[44] Secondary legislation soon followed the EEC Treaty provisions on freedom of movement. In the first phase, Council Reg 15/1960/EEC tempered the normal priority given to national workers when taking up a job position with a temporal limitation. Art 1 provided that, once passed three weeks from the registration of a vacancy without a national worker having responded to it, the position had to be granted to a worker of another Member State at equal conditions. This provision was completely abolished in the second phase by Council Reg 38/1964/EEC, although even with this second regulation priority was still given to national workers. A complete abolition of any restriction occurred with Council Reg 1612/68/EEC.

[45] Milward, above n 8 at 59. Towards the end of the 60s Italian migration changed. Figures for departure decreased dramatically. Rates of return grew higher than ever. In the 1970s migration from Italy stopped.

Luxembourg. This choice is triggered by the fact these countries and Italy were not just involved in bilateral agreements but became also the founding fathers of Europe. This coincidence will allow us to draw similarities and connections between the bilateral agreements and the Common Market approach as far as family reunification is concerned. The Netherlands has been left out of this account. The reason lies in the fact that, despite also being one of the six founding fathers of Europe, it had a later history of bilateral agreements with Italy[46] and therefore the origins of EU provisions on family residence rights cannot be really traced back in the bilateral agreement relationship between Italy and the Netherlands.

3.1. Belgium

From the eighteenth century the economy of 30 municipalities in the Borinage, a region of southern Belgium, was founded on coal mining. After the Second World War this region was a valuable resource, in the worldwide coal shortage, for the rebuilding of Europe. There was no more striking example anywhere in Europe of the post-war concern for employment than the re-establishment and maintenance of the production of coal in the mines of southern Belgium. In fact during the world coal shortage of 1945, when the only coal available on world markets were allocations from the United States, it appeared logical to avoid any sort of reduction in the size of Belgian industries.[47]

The necessity of re-establishing the coal industry made mining a protected occupation during the war and even after. For example, even the lowest skilled group of mining workers were granted good salaries and good pension schemes.[48] Moreover, the necessity of finding workers in order to revitalise the coal industry convinced the Belgian government to approve a 'statute' for coal miners. This statute provided exceptional advantages to them such as the right to retire before 30 years of work, supplementary holidays and up to 4,200 kg of free coal per year.[49] Despite such advantages, Belgian citizens still showed little desire to work

[46] The Netherlands was the last northern European state to start concluding bilateral agreements with southern European and northern African states. The Dutch government concluded bilateral recruitment agreements with Italy, Spain, Portugal, Turkey, Greece, Morocco, Yugoslavia and Tunisia between 1960 and 1970. On this point see S Castles, 'The Guest-Worker in Western Europe—An Obituary' (1986) 20 *International Migration Review* 761, 765. The reason could be rooted in the fact that, unlike the other northern European states, the Netherlands had a very accelerated economic growth to the extent that, by the early fifties, Dutch industry had largely recovered from the Second World War and unemployment reached a very low level (see SK van Walsum, *The Family and the Nation: Dutch Family Migration Policies in the Context of Changing Family Norms* (Newcastle-upon-Tyne, Cambridge Scholar Publishing, 2008) 26–27).

[47] Milward, above n 8 at 51.

[48] For all the economic advantages applied to the miners see A Martens, *Les Immigrés: Flux et reflux d'une main-d'oeuvre d'appoint, La politique belge de l'immigration de 1945 à 1970* (Louvain, Presses Universitaires de Louvain, 1976) 64.

[49] ibid.

underground.[50] Moreover, many citizens were still displaced because of the war and Belgium had labour shortages.[51] In order to fill these gaps, initially Belgium retained 64,000 German prisoners for its mines. However, when the prisoners were released in 1947, the crucial question was about who could replace them. Given its structural lack of workers, Belgium looked for men in the country in which it was sure to find them: Italy.[52]

The first bilateral agreement between Belgium and Italy was signed on 20 June 1946.[53] Belgium agreed to supply to Italy five tons of coal per month for each Italian worker. Italy, on its side, agreed to provide Belgium with 2,000 workers per week.[54] After 1947 immigrants made up about three-quarters of the total underground labour force; of them about three-quarters were Italian.[55] Apart from this exchange between men and primary resources, the agreement also encompassed some other provisions on the rights of Italian workers. The agreement stated that the Belgian government had to provide Italian workers with appropriate housing, food, employment conditions and a salary that had to be equal to that of Belgian miners.[56] Despite the attempt to give Italian migrants enhanced protection on certain issues, the legislation remained silent on family residence rights. This is not surprising since the first Belgian national legislation that mentions the concept of family reunification is the Belgian Aliens Act of 15 December 1980.[57] However, like France, Belgium perceived itself as a country of immigration, needing families to settle both for economic and demographic reasons.[58] To this aim, the famous French demographer Alfred Sauvy in his report[59] underlined how Belgium had to adopt, in order to improve production and solve its demographic

[50] Milward, above n 8 at 51.

[51] Bade, above n 9 at 204. Even five years after the world war ended, Europe's total population was 531 million, about 6 million less than in 1940.

[52] Milward, above n 8 at 51.

[53] The text of this agreement was modified on 23 June 1947. The Italian text of the Bilateral Agreement between Italy and Belgium can be found in Atti Parlamentari dell'Assemblea Costituente, Doc No 42, 22 October 1947.

[54] Section 11 of the Protocol of the Agreement. On this point see A Canovi, 'L'Immagine degli Italiani in Belgio: Appunti Geostorici' (2011) 5 Dossier: Italia altre. Immagini e Comunita' Italiane all'Estero, available at www.studistorici.com/2011/01/29/canovi_numero_5/2.

[55] For detailed data see Besana, above n 14 at 26. According to their data, Italian migrants working in Belgian mines numbered 26,000 in 1946 and by 1948 this figure had reached 46,000.

[56] See Art 3 Bilateral Agreement Belgium–Italy, 20 June 1946. Despite this provision in reality the working and living conditions of Italian miners were quite precarious. On this point see F Cumoli, 'Dai campi al sottosuolo. Reclutamento e strategie di adattamento al lavoro dei minatori italiani in Belgio' in (2009) 5 *Storicamente*, available at www.storicamente.org/07_dossier/emigrazione-italiana-in-belgio.htm.

[57] Art 10(4) Loi du 15 décembre 1980 sur l'accès au territoire, le séjour, l'établissement et l'éloignement des étrangers, available at dofi.ibz.be/sites/dvzoe/FR/Documents/19801215_F.pdf.

[58] A John, 'Family Reunification For Migrants and Refugees: a Forgotten Human Right?' *A comparative analysis of family reunification under domestic law and jurisprudence, international and regional instruments, ECHR case law and the EU* (2003), available at www.fd.uc.pt/hrc/working_papers/arturojohn.pdf, 6.

[59] A Sauvy, *Le rapport Sauvy sur le problème de l'économie et de la population en Wallonie*, Liège, 1962, Conseil Economique Wallon.

problems, a policy of integration and assimilation of the families of the migrant workers. As Belgium had a strong interest for Italian workers to stay in order to develop its coal industry, the authorities made efforts through campaigns[60] such as its brochures 'Vivre et travailler en Belgique' rather than through legislation, to encourage prospective immigrants to bring their families along. In their view this would have allowed families to lead a normal life, overcome any difficulties in settling in[61] and finally establish themselves in Belgium. According to the chronicles of the time, in many public squares in Italy it was possible to find posters declaring the advantages granted by Belgium to foreign miners, among which there was also the possibility soon to reunite with their families.[62] One of these advantages granted by the Belgian government, for instance, was the covering of 50 per cent of the travel expenses of the family.[63] From 1946 to 1957 140,469 Italian workers, followed by 46,364 family members, reached Belgium.[64]

3.2. France

France has a long tradition of immigration. Since the second half of the nineteenth century thousands of foreigners had been recruited or granted admission in the hope of compensating for the country's insufficient labour supply and low birth rate.[65] The real problem of immigration arose in France in 1945, in conjunction with the issues of demography and its labour force. To understand their importance as post-war concerns, one must appreciate the situation that existed at the end of the Second World War. As result of the war, France lost a large part of its population.[66] On top of this issue, France was also experiencing a severe decline it its birth rate. It was again Alfred Sauvy, the eminent demographer who

[60] Campaigns to recruit Italian workers were organised by the Belgian trade unions. For a deeper account see F Micelli, 'L'emigrazione dal Friuli Venezia Giulia in Belgio' available at www.ammer-fvg.org/ita/paesi/index_tree_d.asp?CCat_ID=BE&CCatS_ID=&Cont_ID=262.

[61] John, above n 58 at 6.

[62] This was the original content of the poster: 'Approfittate degli speciali vantaggi che il Belgio accorda ai suoi minatori. Il viaggio dall'Italia all'estero e' completamente gratuito per i lavoratori italiani firmatari di un contratto annuale di lavoro per miniere. Il viaggio dall'Italia al Belgio dura in ferrovia solo 18 ore. Compiute le semplici formalita' d'uso la vostra famiglia potra' raggiungervi in Belgio'. See 'Dimensioni e caratteristiche del fenomeno occupazionale della popolazione immigrata in provincia di Latina', available at www.progettostima.it/public/articoli/29/Files/Rapporto%20finale%2009%2006%202010.pdf, 28.

[63] Western Europe's Migrant Workers (1974) report 28, 21.

[64] Micelli, above n 60 at 10. The fact that family reunification was just stimulated through political campaigns and not through the legislation leaves uncertainties on which family members could effectively join the Italian workers and what were effectively the rights granted to them by the host Member State.

[65] G Verbunt, 'France' in T Hammar (ed), *European Immigration Policy: A Comparative Study* (Cambridge, Cambridge University Press, 1985) 127. For a detailed account on this issue see Y Lequin, *Histoire des étrangers et de l'immigration en France* (Paris, Larousse, 1992) 313 *et seq.*

[66] Apparently 1,500,000 military and civilians died during the First World War. In the second conflict figures were around 2,100,000.

would advise Belgium some years later, who suggested that in order to overcome the post-war economic stagnation a programme of permanent, large-scale immigration was a top priority.[67]

On 2 November 1945, with an *ordonnance*, the National Immigration Office (ONI) was created.[68] This institution was given a monopoly over the recruitment of foreign labour into France. Although ONI was meant to become the most highly organised system of recruitment for migrants coming to France from every foreign state, within some years after its creation it was left responsible only for migrants coming from Europe.[69] When the Commissariat Général du Plan[70] set France the objective of increasing production to 25 per cent above that in 1929 by 1950[71] ONI, with the support of the then Minister of Labour Ambroise Croizat, concentrated all its efforts on Italy. All of a sudden Italy became the cornerstone of the new French migration policy. Geographic and cultural proximity, the presence of former Italian migrants and the absence of political obstacles made Italy the perfect candidate to supply the French with much-needed labour.[72]

The bilateral agreement between France and Italy was ratified on 21 March 1947.[73] According to this agreement, France had to grant the recruitment of 200,000 Italian workers per year.[74] Prior to leaving, workers had to be subjected

[67] On this point see A Sauvy, 'Evaluation des besoins de l'immigration française' (1946) 1 *Population* (French edition) 91.

[68] For more details about ONI see Castles, above n 46 at 763, and G Tapinos, *L'immigration étrangère en France 1946–1973, Travaux et Documents* Cahier n 71 (Paris, Presses Universitaires de France, 1975) 22–23. Before the creation of ONI the recruitment process of immigrants was not state led but private. In particular, it was controlled by the Société générale d'immigration, a consortium of big firms comprising mainly mines and steel companies. On this point see in particular C Wihtol de Wenden, 'The case of France' in G Zincone, R Pennix and M Borkert (eds), *Migration Policy Making in Europe* (Amsterdam, Amsterdam University Press, 2001) 67.

[69] Castles, above n 46 at 764.

[70] It was created in 1946 and lasted until 2006. Its main purpose was to plan the economy of France, mainly through five-year plans.

[71] Tapinos, above n 68 at 16.

[72] ibid, 19.

[73] The text of the Bilateral Treaty between Italy and France can be found at Atti parlamentari dell'Assemblea Costituente, Doc No 45, 20 November 1947. Soon after, other bilateral agreements were signed by France with other countries which were experiencing excess of manpower, such as Spain in 1956, Morocco in 1963, Portugal in 1964, former Yugoslavia in 1965, Tunisia and Turkey in 1964 (and came into force in 1969). On this point see H de Lary, 'Bilateral Labour Agreements Concluded by France' in *Migration for Employment: Bilateral Agreements at a Crossroads* (Paris, OECD Publishing, 2004) 43. Each of these agreements specified the number of workers to be admitted each year, the conditions of work guaranteed and the requirements for entry. Every nationality group had its own set of legal rights and duties and its own limits on numbers. On this point see GP Freeman, *Immigrant Labor and Racial Conflict in Industrial Societies: The French and British Experience 1945–1975* (Princeton NJ, Princeton University Press, 1979) 68–74.

[74] Art 1: 'En vue d'assurer pendant l'année 1947 le recrutement en Italie et la mise au travail en France de 200,000 travailleurs destinés à l'industrie et l'agriculture et désireux de se rendre en France, les deux Gouvernements prendront les mesures nécessaires, chacun en ce qui le concerne, pour que le départ en France de ces immigrants et leur mise au travail aient lieu à la cadence de 17,000 personnes par mois, en moyenne.' The recruitment had to happen with monthly quotas of 17,000 workers each. To this end the Office national d'immigration opened an Italian branch in Milan. Welcome centres were also placed close to the borders between the two states.

to medical checks by the Italian health authorities.[75] Italian workers could not choose the job position they were going to take, nor the place to which they would be assigned.[76] Also, unlike the Belgian agreement, in the French one it was not possible to find provisions binding the French government to provide Italian workers with appropriate housing. Despite less generous general terms, a special regime was applied to Italian workers who had families. In fact, in this Treaty it was possible to find provisions that explicitly referred to the possibility of transferring family members to France,[77] instead of simply granting workers the right of sending allowances to their relatives back in Italy.[78] Article 14 stated that a special agreement had to determine the conditions under which families of Italian workers could travel to France. The French government, on its side, had to facilitate the arrival of these families to the territory of France by taking up some of their travel expenses. The explicit mention of the issue of family reunification is not surprising because family reunification provisions were already present at national level via Ordonnance no. 45-2658,[79] showing that France had early sensitivity over such issues. From 1947 to 1949 the total number of families recorded by the ONI included approximately 58,000 people, 48 per cent of which were Italian.[80]

3.3. Germany

Until 1885 Germany was mainly an emigration country.[81] The peak of emigration was reached between 1881 and 1885 when 857,000 migrants left Germany.[82] After the economic expansion began, the number of emigrants dropped rapidly and, as a consequence, during the late nineteenth century overseas German migration was massively replaced by internal migration from rural to industrialised parts of the country.

After the Second World War, Germany slowly started to turn into an immigration country. During this period Germany began to face massive immigration flows. The first people that entered the country were either refugees from Eastern Europe or expelled persons from the former German territories.[83] These voluntary migrants practically covered the vacant places that, during the war, were

[75] Arts 3, 4, 5.

[76] Art 7.

[77] Art 18.

[78] With regard to the faculty to send allowances back in Italy see Arts 12, 13, 14.

[79] Art 5(1) Ordonnance No 45-2658 du 2 novembre 1945 relative aux conditions d'entrée et de séjour des étrangers en France, available at www.legifrance.gouv.fr/affichTexte.do?cidTexte=JORFTEXT000000699737&dateTexte=19860911.

[80] Tapinos, above n 68 at 31.

[81] H Esser and H Korte, 'Federal Republic of Germany' in T Hammar (ed), *European Immigration Policy: A Comparative Study* (Cambridge, Cambridge University Press, 1985) 165. Germans emigrated mainly to the United States and, to a lesser extent, to Canada, Australia and South America.

[82] ibid,166.

[83] See T Liebig, 'Recruitment of Foreign Labour in Germany and Switzerland' in *Migration for Employment: Bilateral Agreements at a Crossroads* (Paris, OECD Publishing, 2004), 158.

occupied by war prisoners[84] and ended up functioning as a large labour reserve. Nevertheless, the almost immediate efforts begun by the allies after the cessation of hostilities to reconstruct the industrial capacity of Germany, together with the currency reform of 1948, triggered such a deep and fast economic recovery that all the labour surpluses were soon absorbed.[85]

West German employers started actively importing foreign labour from 1948. Despite the delay compared to other European countries, the outcome was probably the most organised state recruitment apparatus anywhere in Europe, known as the guestworker system.[86] Initially, the Federal Labour Office of Germany set up recruitment offices all around the Mediterranean countries. German employers in need of foreign labour had to apply to the Labour Office, which, after receiving payment of a fee, had the task of recruiting suitable workers. Workers had to pass a test that allowed the Labour Office to evaluate their occupational skills. Moreover, workers were subjected to medical tests and police record checks. If all the prerequisites were fulfilled, they were all accompanied in groups to Germany, where employers had to provide them with proper accommodation.[87]

The first bilateral recruitment agreement was concluded with Italy in 1955.[88] As early as 1953 Italy had expressed its will to sign a bilateral agreement with Germany. However, it was only in April 1954 that the negotiations started and, after a period of stalemate,[89] the agreement was signed. The decision to sign this agreement was dictated by economic and historical circumstances. In the early fifties Germany, in order to develop its economy, pushed for a strong liberalisation of international trade. At that time Germany traded intensely with Italy, one of its major coal importers.[90] At the same time the Italian economy, as previously mentioned, was characterised by high levels of unemployment. When Italy pressured Germany to hire seasonal Italian workers, threatening to adopt a more restrictive importation policy in case of a negative answer, Germany accepted the Italian conditions. This decision was moved surely out of fear of losing its biggest importer of coal[91] and, presumably, also because Germany desperately needed new labour to keep pace with its continuously growing economy.[92]

[84] Esser and Korte, above n 81 at 167–69.

[85] RC Rist, *Guestworkers in Germany: The Prospects for Pluralism* (New York, Praeger Publishers, 1978) 61.

[86] Castles, above n 46 at 768.

[87] ibid.

[88] The text of the Treaty can be found in Diritto Internazionale, vol XVII, 1963, 280. Further recruitment agreements were concluded later on by Germany with Spain (1960), Greece (1960), Turkey (1961), Portugal (1964) and Yugoslavia (1968). See Esser and Korte, above n 81 at 170.

[89] G Prontera, 'L'emigrazione italiana verso la Repubblica Federale Tedesca. L'accordo bilaterale del 1955, la ricezione sulla stampa, il ruolo dei centri di emigrazione di Milano e Verona' (2008) 4 *Storicamente* available at www.storicamente.org/07_dossier/migrazioni-prontera.htm.

[90] ibid.

[91] ibid.

[92] ibid. In September 1955 the unemployment of German workers nearly disappeared. In fact German unemployment reached 2.7% by September 1955.

According to the agreement, Germany had to indicate the number of workers that needed to be recruited and for what kind of jobs.[93] Practically, the Federal Labour Office, acting jointly with the Italian Labour Ministry, was responsible for recruitment. From Nuremberg all job requests from German employers had to be sent to the local offices of the Italian Labour Ministry, which was in charge of viewing and choosing the workers.[94] Once the worker was accepted, he was granted a bilingual job contract[95] and an authorisation to work, which was the prerequisite to have a work permit issued once in Germany.[96] The German government also covered the visa and travel expenses for the Italian workers.[97] They were also granted the same work and housing conditions as German workers.[98]

Looking at the content of the agreement it is also clear how the presence of Italian workers on German territory was meant to be limited in time.[99] In fact, probably because of the nation's self-perception of not being a country of immigration, German bilateral agreements[100] were characterised by the creation of a rotation system which intended to frequently replace the previous generation of temporary guestworkers with a new one.[101]

Despite the German temporary job policy towards immigrants and lack of a broader legislation concerning protecting family residence rights[102] the agreement, surprisingly, made reference to family rights and adopted quite an open position on family reunification. Article 15 stated that all the Italian workers that wished to be accompanied by their families had to prove that they were living in

[93] Art 4(2).
[94] Art 5(1)
[95] Art 9(1).
[96] Arts 9(3) and 11.
[97] Art 16.
[98] Steinert above n 29 at 142–60.
[99] P Borruso, 'Note sull'emigrazione clandestina italiana 1876–1976' in M Sanfilippo (ed), *Emigrazione e Storia d'Italia* (Cosenza, Luigi Pellegrini Editore, 2003) 265. Art 4(2) of the Treaty shows how Germany looked at the Italian permanence within its territory as temporary. As a matter of fact it states that the job offers had to indicate clearly how long the job would have lasted.
[100] See John, above n 58 at 5.
[101] Among all the reasons why importing temporary foreign workers seemed to be the best solution there was the fact it was considered less risky, considering the still uncertain economic recovery of Germany. See H Werner, 'From the German "Guestworker" Programmes of the Sixties to the Current "Green Card" Initiative for IT Specialists' (2001) 43 Institut für Arbeitsmarkt-und Berufsforschung der Bundesanstalt für Arbeit (IAB), available at www.ilo.org/wcmsp5/groups/public/---ed_protect/---protrav/---migrant/documents/publication/wcms_201876.pdf, 7.
[102] See RR Marin, *Immigration as a Democratic Challenge: Citizenship and Inclusion in Germany and the United States* (Cambridge, Cambridge University Press, 2000) 12. The legal regime of aliens reflected this conception of immigrants as temporary guests. During the first years of guestworkers immigration the old Nazi legislation was still applied to govern aliens' presence within the country. In 1965 this regulation was replaced by the Aliens Act (Ausländergesetz), which was presented as a break from the past and an expression of liberal policy towards foreigners (on this point see P Gassert and AE Steinweis, *Coping with the Nazi past: West German debates on Nazism and generational conflict*, (New York, Berghan Books, 2006) 111–12). However, despite this manifesto, this statute did not grant permanent residence permits but simply temporary rights to stay. Moreover, this statute did not create any provision on family residence rights. Indeed detailed rules for reuniting foreign families were not instituted until 1981.

proper housing. Workers, when issues of public safety or public order were not occurring, were given residence permits for their families in the shortest possible time. Moreover, requests for residence permits for relatives not belonging to the core family unit were also accepted.[103] The same article states explicitly that the competent offices also had to examine 'benevolently' the admission requests of other family members.[104] Finally, although the bilateral agreement between Italy and Germany did not specify it in any provision, the policy of Germany was that the family member (generally the woman) who was allowed to enter with the foreign worker was also entitled to take up a job position.[105]

3.4. Luxembourg

The first migration flows to Luxembourg can be traced back to the last quarter of the nineteenth century. That period was characterised by the industrialisation of the country and the beginning of mining activities. The fast development of the mining and steel industry created the need to import a huge amount of manpower since the need for labour could not be supplied entirely by the native population. Both low- and high-skilled workers were required.[106]

The first wave of immigrants to be employed in the steel and coal industry was, once again, Italian.[107] The first Italian wave of migration to Luxembourg occurred in between the last decade of the nineteenth century and the beginning of the First World War. Italian workers used to move to Luxembourg mainly from the northern and central regions of Italy. This first migration flow was characterised by extreme temporariness. Workers stayed for limited periods and generally returned to Italy in winter.[108] Temporariness, with some exceptions in the period before the First World War, continued to characterise the presence of Italian migrants in Luxembourg up until the post-Second World War period.[109] At the end of the

[103] See Art 15. These provision was applied also to workers that were meant to remain in Germany for a period no longer than nine months.

[104] ibid.

[105] The job market was in such need of recruitment that the family member was also encouraged to apply for jobs. See M Mattes, 'Gender and Migration in Germany: the case of female labour migration from the 1950s to the 1970s' (2009) available at migrationeducation.de/fileadmin/uploads/Mattes-GenderMigration_01.pdf, 4. The author underlines how, during the 1960s, the German recruitment agencies promised that Italians would receive preferential treatment if they decided to move with or to be joined by their wives. On migration of women after the Second World War see also E Kofman, 'Female "Birds of Passage" a Decade later: Gender and Immigration in the European Union' (1999) 33 *International Migration Review* 269, 274.

[106] M Valentova and G Berzoza, 'Attitudes towards immigrants in Luxembourg: do contacts matter?' CEPS/INSTEAD working paper (2010) available at www.ceps.lu/pdf/3/art1547.pdf, 3.

[107] ibid.

[108] ML Caldognetto, 'Per una storia dell'emigrazione dal Montefeltro al Lussemburgo: temi, problemi, prospettive' (2010) 32 Studi Montefeltrani, Pesaro, Societa' di Studi Storici per il Montefeltro, available at www.cdmh.lu/resources/pdf/_base_documents/9983156792.pdf 505, 506.

[109] ibid.

war Luxembourg was on its knees. One third of the country was destroyed. Its infrastructure and railways had to be totally rebuilt. Agriculture stopped together with the steel and coal industry.[110] Luxembourg realised that, in order to face its economic problems, migration had to be enhanced. In 1948 the first bilateral agreement between Luxembourg and Italy was signed. Luxembourg needed Italians to work in the mines to rebuild the country.[111] On the other side Italy, once again, needed to reduce its national unemployment rate. The last bilateral agreement concluded between Luxembourg and Italy before the creation of the European Communities was signed on 16 January 1957.[112] All requests to hire Italian employees had to be sent first to the Office National du Travail in Luxembourg and, from there, to the Italian Embassy, which had the task of transmitting them to the competent Italian office.[113] The Italian Labour Offices had to make sure that all the workers fulfilled all the health, sanitary and professional conditions required.[114] The Government of Luxembourg had to make sure that Italian workers were granted the same work conditions that applied to national workers[115] and that they were given proper housing and food in compliance with their eating habits.[116]

Like Germany, Luxembourg continued to have a preference for temporary immigration. Indeed, the Italy–Luxembourg bilateral agreement envisaged two kinds of contract for Italian migrant workers: contract A, the contract concerning workers hired for a limited period of time, and contract B, the contract that was utilised for workers engaged in a permanent position. From the text of the bilateral agreement it is evident that preference was given to temporary workers. In fact Article 3 stated that all the Italian workers coming to Luxembourg after 31 December 1956 would have been given a contract of type A whereas contracts of type B could be only issued in accordance with the quotas agreed by the two contracting states.[117] In this context family residence rights could surely be granted in cases in which the worker was hired with a contract classified as B, when he could prove that he could fulfil the requirement of proper housing. However, even in cases in which an Italian worker was issued with a type A contract he could still obtain family residence rights for his family in cases where he was authorised by the Luxembourg Ministry of Justice. Finally, as far as family reunification is concerned, according to the bilateral treaty, the concept of family encompassed the spouse and children until 18 years old or of any age if they were unable to work. The Luxembourg government also had to facilitate the reunion of other dependent family members who

[110] JM Kreins, *Histoire du Luxembourg: des origines à nos jours* (Paris, Presses Universitaires de France, 1996) 104.
[111] Caldognetto, above n 108 at 510.
[112] Text of the Treaty can be found in Diritto Internazionale, vol XIII, 1959, 347.
[113] Art 2.
[114] Art 3.
[115] Art 8.
[116] Art 7.
[117] Art 2.

did not belong to the core family unit.[118] This open approach towards granting family residence rights, despite the clear preference for the temporariness of the workers' stay, is not surprising. Indeed, as a sort of reaction to the booming economy and the declining birth rate, the government did endorse a policy of family-based immigration from 1960 onward but without passing any general laws apart from its guestworker agreements with Portugal and Italy.[119]

3.5. The Role of Provisions on Family Residence Rights in the Bilateral Agreements

Some scholars have tried to analyse the advantages and disadvantages triggered by bilateral agreements on migratory waves. Among others, the very interesting article by Martin and Miller showed that, if on one hand it is true that without the manpower supplied by guestworker programmes the post-war economic recovery probably could not have been possible, on the other hand this short-term benefit was diluted by long-term economic problems such as dependence on foreigners for growth, delays in the receiving countries on rationalisation of industries and restructuring of the labour force, deteriorating working conditions of national low-skilled workers, social service expenses and governmental infrastructure expenditure and increasing social problems such as discrimination and xenophobia.[120] To this dark side of the bilateral agreements system one should also add the often precarious working and living conditions that the guestworkers had to face. As far as the Belgian experience is concerned, chronicles of the time spoke about 'men worn out by silicosis, widows of miners, young people crippled from injuries suffered at work and families still housed in barracks'.[121] Similar experiences were also witnessed in France and Germany.[122]

Despite the prospect of facing these precarious conditions, the signing of bilateral agreements increased the influx of Italian workers towards the above-mentioned northern European states. As far as Belgium is concerned from 1947, the same year in which the bilateral agreement with Italy was signed, the Italian population started to grow and from 84,134 in 1947 it reached a peak of 200,086

[118] Art 3, final notes.

[119] See in particular S Kollwelter, 'Immigration in Luxembourg: New Challenges for a New Country', Migration Policy Institute, available at www.migrationpolicy.org/article/immigration-luxembourg-new-challenges-old-country. The first immigration legislation was passed in Luxembourg in March 1972.

[120] PL Martin and MJ Miller, 'Guestworkers: Lessons from Western Europe' (1980) 33 *Industrial and Labor Relations Review* 33 315, 327–28.

[121] Canovi, above n 54 at 4.

[122] While in France many migrant workers ended up living in *bidonvilles*, Germany had special workers' camps. 'Long barrack-like quarters clean and characterless. Three men to a small, twelve foot by six foot room, for which they each pay 30DM a week.' For a deeper account see Western Europe's migrant workers above n 63 at 19.

in less than 15 years.[123] Likewise, in France the wave of Italian immigrants began in 1946, once again in the same year in which the bilateral agreement between the two countries was signed, and from 1950 until 1956 77 per cent of all the permanent immigrant workers were Italians.[124] Finally also in Germany and Luxembourg the wave of Italian migrants increased dramatically after the bilateral agreements were signed. As a matter of fact in Germany between 1955 and 1956, the number of Italian migrants moved from none to 15,600 people. In Luxembourg after the signing of the bilateral agreement with Italy Italian migrants increased immediately to more than 2,000 people, reaching a peak of 8,100 working permits issued to Italian workers in a year.[125] In the light of these data it seems evident that for many, the prospect of finding a job, as opposed to being unemployed in an Italian country village, was stronger than the thought of all the difficulties that they had to face.

It has been mentioned previously how the bilateral agreements reached between Italy and other northern European states already acknowledged some concerns towards granting family residence rights and dealt with them.[126] Professor Boyd of the University of Ottawa made a point on the role of family networks in migration movements.[127] In her work she underlined the fact that families are migratory units.[128] This means that a family may either migrate together or, as happens in the majority of cases, individuals may be sent out with the expectation that other members of the family will be allowed to be sent for in the future. Consequently, the increment of the scale of migration in certain regions is connected to the abolition of limitations to family reunifications, which can be perceived as a deterrent from moving into another state.[129] In this backdrop, therefore, it is plausible that the possibility of pursuing family reunification in the new host state was also an incentive for the decision of the Italian workers to move abroad. This incentive

[123] J Leman, *From Challenging Culture to Challenged Culture: The Sicilian Cultural Code and The Socio-Cultural Praxis of Sicilian Immigrants in Belgium* (Leuven, Leuven University Press, 1987) 74.

[124] JR McDonald, 'Labour Immigration in France, 1946–1965' (1969) 59 *Annals of the Association of the American Geographers* 116, 119.

[125] The data on Germany and Luxembourg can be found on the report of the Committee for Social Affairs, 5 October 1960, Doc No 67, 4.

[126] Although the bilateral agreement between Belgium and Italy did not expressly encompass family reunification provisions, the Belgian government adopted very favourable policies towards family reunification. See Section 3.1 above.

[127] M Boyd, 'Family and Personal Networks in International Migration: Recent Development and New Agendas' (1989) 23 *International Migration Review* 638, 638. In this paper the author suggests that the role of chain migration in providing information is the key factor that allows the evolution of linkages between sending and receiving countries.

[128] ibid, 643.

[129] ibid, 646. Professor Boyd also highlighted how, most of the time, 'friendly' family reunification norms are motivated by state opportunistic reasons. The state in fact, being in need of manpower, intentionally removes the psychological deterrent of the worker of not being able to enjoy the company of his relatives in the new state. Therefore the choice of the migrant cannot ultimately be considered totally free, as it is highly conditioned and dependent on the regulations and the objectives that are set by the states. On this point see also R Penninx, 'International Migration in Western Europe Since 1973: Developments, Mechanism and Controls' (1986) 20 *International Migration Review* 951, 961.

is so effective that one may as well wonder whether the protection of family residence rights guaranteed by bilateral agreements was moved by the selfish perspective of some receiving states that enough Italian workers would arrive there rather than real concerns for preserving the unity of families.

4. EEC FAMILY RESIDENCE RIGHTS PROVISIONS AND APPROACH TOWARDS THIRD COUNTRY NATIONALS

In the previous section of this chapter it was suggested that residence rights for family members seem to have been guaranteed in order to encourage Italian workers to move towards northern European states. The necessity of enhancing the decisions of the Italian workers to move abroad as much as possible was the result of the high Italian unemployment rate and the lack of manpower of northern European states. Nearly 10 years from the signing of the first bilateral agreement with Belgium, the social and economic conditions of Italy and of northern Europe were not drastically different. As a matter of fact, at the time of the signature of the Treaty of Rome, the unemployment rate of Italy was still quite high while the other northern founding father states still suffered of a high shortage of manpower. As the Parliamentary Committee for Social Affairs reported in 1960: 'Italy is the only country that still has at its disposal sufficient reserve of labour force not only to avoid the danger of internal penury but also enough to satisfy the demand of other states.'[130] In this similar historical background, considering the existing Italian particular employment needs both during the bilateral treaties era and during the negotiation and drafting of the Common Market project, the family members residence rights provisions contained in the EU free movement legislation and the provisions contained in the bilateral treaties seem both to have strong historical roots in the post-Second World War backdrop and in the necessity of pushing Italian workers to migrate towards states affected by a lack of labour.

The idea that family residence rights provisions were inserted in order to create an incentive or, in the language to which we are more used, remove all the obstacles, for the workers to move is evident in particular from the way in which they were drafted. The more open the provisions are, the fewer the obstacles for the sponsor to move abroad. The openness of these provisions can be easily noted in their approach towards the EU sponsor's relatives. In Council Regulation 15/1961/EEC,[131] at Article 11(1), it was stated that the spouse and descendants under the age of 21 years could rejoin their EU national worker relative who was regularly employed in another Member State. Article 11(2) stated also that every host Member State had to 'facilitate' the entrance of 'other' family members who do not belong to the core family household but, nevertheless, were totally or partially

130 Committee for Social Affairs, above n 125 at 5.

131 As mentioned in the introduction, the first provisions on family residence rights can be found in this regulation. Family provisions were encompassed in Title II, named 'Workers' Family'.

dependent on the worker and lived under the same roof in the Member State of origin. The same provision could be found in Council Regulation 38/1964/EEC at Article 17 and in Council Regulation 1612/1968/EEC at Article 10(1) which, in addition, added a new category of family members who were entitled to join the EEC relative. Indeed, Article 10(1) provided that the spouse, the descendants who are under the age of 21 years or dependants and the dependent relatives in the ascending line of the worker and his spouse had the right 'to install themselves with a worker who is a national of one Member State and who is employed in the territory of another Member State'.

Another interesting aspect that suggests the capacity of family residence rights provisions to create incentives for the workers to move is their openness to third country national family members. It was initially Regulation 38/1964/EEC that, at Article 17, specified that the spouse, dependants under 21 years old and ascendants or descendants who were dependent either on the European worker or his spouse were admitted to the host Member State regardless of their nationality. This was later on confirmed in Regulation 1612/1968/EEC that, at Article 10, emphasised the equality between nationals and third country nationals by stating that 'irrespective of their nationality', the spouse and their descendants had the right to move in with the European worker in the Member State. Finally, also Article 11 of the same regulation stated that the spouse of the European worker, children under 21 years old or children who were dependent on the worker had 'the right to take up an activity as an employed person throughout the territory of that same state, even if they are not nationals of any Member State'.

However, it is important to note that the Member States' apparent openness towards third country nationals cannot be explained as a genuine concern for their well being. The openness of family residence rights provisions towards third country nationals shows a glimpse of the disingenuous European attitude toward immigration in the immediate years following the Second World War. Until the oil crisis, immigration was not seen as a threat but as an economic resource to be mobilised according to precise labour requirements.[132] This is because, first of all, immigration was supposed to be temporary and therefore immigrants could cause no threat to the nation state: in the case of unfavourable economic conditions, immigrants were expected to go home.[133] Second, the kind of immigration that the EU experienced in those years was very different from the one that started to develop in the seventies, when immigration concerns started to break out. Indeed, the *travaux préparatoires* of the Messina conference show the majority of immigrants residing within the territory of the states that then became the founding fathers of the EU were either French nationals of Algerian origin or Italians.[134] The minimum exposure to people coming from 'exotic' places probably reinforced the

[132] See Martiniello, above n 8 at 303.

[133] ibid.

[134] K Eisele, *The external dimension of the EU's migration policy: different legal positions of TCN in the EU: a comparative perspective* (Leiden, Brill Nijhoff, 2013) 74.

first EU Member States' conviction that immigration was something that they did not need to worry about.[135] In the next chapter we will see how the antagonistic approach of the Member States towards third country nationals was soon revealed when the immigration situation started to rise in prominence at the outbreak of the oil crisis.

To conclude, in this section it has been shown that the provisions on family reunification inserted in the secondary legislation on free movement were characterised by the aim of enhancing free movement of workers and, like the previous bilateral agreements, found their roots in the post-Second World War needs of matching the Northern Europe shortage of labour with the Italian surplus of labour. The way in which these provisions were drafted demonstrates how efforts to encourage the movement of Italian workers were achieved in a concrete fashion.

5. CONCLUSIONS

This chapter has provided the background underpinning the introduction of the first provisions on family reunification. It has been shown how it seems that in the bilateral agreements signed by Italy and other northern European states, family reunification was introduced in order to encourage Italian workers to move towards the receiving northern European states. Likewise, the first EU provisions on family reunification seem willing to fulfil the same aim.

The next chapter presents further relevant historical developments of Europe from the mid seventies until now. It will point out that after the oil crisis the approach towards immigration changed drastically. Member States moved from a favourable approach, although disingenuous, to a strict one and rapidly began to seal their borders. This change of attitude towards immigration highly influenced the application and development of the EU family reunification provisions concerning EU citizens and third country nationals over the years, as both the legislation and case law will show.

[135] ibid, 37. The fact that third country national immigration was not considered a threat in those years is supported by the fact that Art 69 ECSC referred specifically to 'workers who are nationals of a Member State' whereas the drafters of the Rome Treaty did not use the same phraseology but referred simply to workers. Hence, the argument goes that the drafters of the Rome Treaty probably meant to create a common policy for all workers regardless of their nationality.

2

Foreigners Become Enemies: The New Immigration Approach since the Oil Crisis of 1973

1. INTRODUCTION

THE PREVIOUS CHAPTER looked at the origins of the provisions granting residence rights to family members during the bilateral agreements era up until the Common Market. It suggested that family residence rights were drafted as ancillary rights in order to create incentives for Italian workers to move towards the other Member States which were experiencing a lack of manpower.

This chapter will continue focusing on what happened after the oil crisis. Indeed, from the middle of the 1970s, a significant change occurred in terms of the way migrants were perceived in Europe. At the time of the oil crisis employment opportunities for workers were drastically reduced. European States began to strengthen their borders and to look at immigrants as potential enemies. Moreover, they started to endorse a defensive attitude toward foreigners. At first the measures took the shape of stricter national immigration legislation, on both legal and illegal immigrants. Later on, for those states that were already part of the European Union, stricter EU measures on border controls against citizens of non-Member States—the third country nationals—were endorsed. This was the beginning of a tougher approach towards immigration that is continuing and characterises the many immigration measures adopted by the EU.

The aim of this chapter is to show why concerns about third country nationals started to grow and how the Member States and the EU reacted to these fears. This chapter is particularly useful in order to give a more realistic explanation later on in the book of the approach adopted by the EU Legislator and by the CJEU when dealing with the issue of family reunification between EU citizens and third country nationals. The chapter is divided into four sections. After this brief introduction, Section 2 will be dedicated to analysing the approach of the Member States on third country nationals and will focus on the reasons why the 'other' started to be stigmatised. Section 3 will be dedicated to looking at the process of border strengthening at the EU level. Finally Section 4 will offer some conclusions.

2. THE STIGMATISATION OF FOREIGNERS

As mentioned in the previous chapter, the economic expansion of Western Europe throughout the 1960s was remarkable. This led to an enormous increase in immigration[1] towards and within Europe. Such immigration was seen as a short-term phenomenon, capable of satisfying the state's immediate labour needs without long-term consequences.[2] However, in the 1970s things started to change. It was in 1973–1974 when the first oil crisis struck the economies of Europe. This crisis particularly affected the labour market. Almost overnight oil became scarce and very expensive.[3] This large macroeconomic shock led to reduced economic output and higher rates of unemployment. This particularly affected the once-prosperous coal and heavy industries which, due to the new investment policies and increased costs, started to face a situation of almost unstoppable job losses.[4] Since immigration was conceived as a 'tap' to turn on and off according to the labour market's needs,[5] the sudden changes in the labour market pushed the receiving countries to start convincing immigrants to return to their states of origin[6] and to limit the number of legal migrant workers who were granted access into the territory of the state.

[1] For the sake of completeness it is worth pointing out that, although in the previous chapter mainly labour immigration coming from the southern part of Europe was mentioned, the European post-Second World War period was characterised by huge immigration waves coming from ex-colonies. In particular, Algerians in France, West Indians in Great Britain and Indonesians in the Netherlands came over in large numbers in the fifties whereas Surinamese in the Netherlands and Pakistanis and Indians in the United Kingdom reached their peak in the sixties and seventies. Among the vast literature on this issue see in particular L Lucassen, D Feldman and J Oltmer, *Paths of Integration: Migrants in Western Europe (1880–2004)* (Amsterdam, Amsterdam University Press, 2006); U Bosma, J Lucassen and G Oostindie, *Postcolonial Migrants and Identity Politics: Europe, Russia, Japan and the United States in Comparison* vol 18 (New York, Berghan Books, 2012); Klaus Bade, *Migration in European History*, (Oxford, Blackwell Publishing, 2002); AM Messina, *The Logics and the Politics of Post-WWII Migration to Western Europe* (Cambridge, Cambridge University Press, 2007).

[2] J Handoll, *Free movement of persons in the EU* (New York, Wiley, 1995) 351.

[3] The price of a barrel of oil, which had remained at $2 or less for 15 years up to the end of 1971 and had only risen gradually for the next two years, quadrupled within the span of three months. The UK monthly average crude oil bill, which was £78m in 1973 rose to £308m in the second quarter of 1974, representing nearly one-quarter of the monthly import bill compared with less than one-tenth a year previously. For an economic explanation of the crisis see A Peacock, *The oil crisis and the professional economist*, Sir Ellis Hunter memorial lectures, lecture delivered at the University of York on 11 December 1974 (York, University of York publication, 1975) 2.

[4] M Martiniello, 'The new migratory Europe: towards a proactive immigration policy' in CA Parsons and TM Smeeding (eds), *Immigration and Transformation of Europe* (Cambridge, Cambridge University Press, 2006) 302–03.

[5] See R Hansen, 'Migration to Europe since 1945: its History its Lessons' (2003) 74 *The Political Quarterly* 25, 31.

[6] Martiniello, above n 4 at 303. France and Germany raised their ban on entry to non-EU workers in 1974 and 1973 respectively. In 1974 the Netherlands ceased its recruitment programmes. See in particular S Castles, 'The Guest-Worker in Western Europe—an Obituary' (1986) 20 *International Migration Review* 761, 761. In January 1973 the Immigration Act 1971 came into force in order to 'stop large-scale permanent migration', in particular from the Commonwealth. See J Solomos, 'Racism and Anti-Racism in Great Britain: Historical Trends and Contemporary Issues', in BP Bowser, *Racism and Anti-Racism in World Perspective* (Thousand Oaks, Sage Publications, 1995) 169.

Tight controls on immigration started to be accompanied by structural state actions to make sure only national workers supplied the demand for labour.[7] For instance, France responded to this economic downturn with policies both aimed at reducing the number of foreigners entering France and reducing the numbers of those foreigners already in the country. The first French policy was adopted in 1974 when the French government imposed a temporary stop on all immigration from outside the EU. The second French policy was adopted in 1977 and aimed to persuade some of the foreign workers living in France to leave by offering a free ticket home and a 10,000 franc bonus.[8] A similar approach was adopted also by Luxembourg[9] and Denmark.[10] In Belgium a recruitment ban came about abruptly and unexpectedly at the outbreak of the oil crisis. The country put a halt to all foreign manual immigration in 1974 and enhanced this new restrictive policy in 1985 with the Gol Law, which limited immigrants' access to welfare benefits and to family reunification.[11] Unlike France and Belgium, the Netherlands did not immediately put an official stop to foreign immigration. However, from the beginning of the seventies, the rules regarding the issuing of labour permits had been sharpened, making it more difficult for foreigners to qualify for a work permit. Eventually, in 1975 a law was proposed and finally agreed in 1979 in order to further restrict immigration from outside the EU.[12] Finally in Germany, when the oil crisis hit, the government also reacted by stopping foreign recruitment. The only channels that remained open were for EU nationals and for workers from selected high-income countries from which significant labour migration was not expected. This led, at the beginning of the eighties, to the promotion of voluntary return policies similar to those promoted by France.[13]

In spite of these restrictions, immigration did not end. Although a stop was put on economic immigration, foreigners that established themselves in the host country pursued other ways of gaining residence, such as asylum,[14] family

[7] Handoll, above n 2, at 351.

[8] On this point see J Rudolph, *Politics and Ethnicity: a Comparative Study* (New York, Palgrave Macmillan, 2006) 65.

[9] S Minter, *Irregular Immigration: An Economic Analysis of Policies in the EU* (Tübingen, Mohr Siebec, 2015) 46.

[10] A Triandafillydou and R Gropas, *European Immigration: A Source Book* (Oxford, Ashgate, 2014) 97.

[11] On Belgium see J Cesary, *The Oxford Handbook of European Islam* (Oxford, Oxford University Press, 2014) 224.

[12] On the Netherlands see S van Walsum, *The Family and The Nation: Dutch Family Migration Policies in the context of changing family norms* (Newcastle-upon-Tyne, Cambridge Scholars Publishing, 2008) 141.

[13] On Germany see OECD, *Recruiting Migrant Workers: Germany* (OECD Library, 2013) 62.

[14] Martiniello, above n 4 at 304. See also W De Lobkowicz, 'Intergovernmental Cooperation in the Field of Migration—From the Single European Act to Maastricht' in J Monar and R Morgan (eds), *The Third Pillar of the European Union, Cooperation in the fields of justice and home affairs*, Proceedings of an International Conference organised by the College of Europe, Bruges, the Institut für Europäische Politik, Bonn, and the European University Institute, Florence, Conférences de Bruges—Bruges Conferences—Volume 5 (Brussels, European University Press, 1994) 105.

reunification[15] and illegal immigration.[16] Rather than bringing immigration to a halt, the restrictions imposed by some European states on foreigners ended up favouring international immigration.[17] The economic emergency and the realisation by states of their inability to tackle the immigration problem triggered the stigmatisation of immigrants. In order to understand how the stigmatisation of aliens occurred at this particular moment in time it is worth looking at its origins. In Europe, the fear of aliens has very deep roots, dating back to the racist medieval concepts of physiognomy, down to the crystallisation of attitudes to Indians, Blacks, Jewish people and travellers in the early modern era.[18] In the twentieth century these racist and xenophobic attitudes eventually matured into the Nazi ideology before and during the Second World War. The post-war crusade against racism was not able to eradicate the deep historic roots of European racism.[19] The reasons are multiple. First of all, the post-war anti-racist discourse was counterintuitive as it denied differences (for example, between whites and blacks) that for the majority of people were objective.[20] Second, anti-racist education was not able to immediately uproot the racial stereotypes that over time became so common in European culture.[21] Finally, it is important to point out that Europe witnessed a striking continuity between pre-war and post-war elites, the majority of which were not purged after the final solution and carried with them racist ideologies.[22] Hence, what the outcome of the Second World War gained, rather than uprooting racism, was the switching of its target from the Jewish people to other minorities, especially the black minority.

In the context of the European post-Second World War labour immigration system this switch is particularly evident. As already seen, the years from 1945 to 1973 witnessed an unprecedented economic growth that could be sustained by workers moving from Southern Europe and from former European colonies such

[15] S Castles and G Kosack, *Immigrant Workers and Class Structure in Western Europe* (Oxford, Oxford University Press, 1973) 31: 'By restricting labour immigration, Western European governments inadvertently transformed a movement of workers, many of whom intended to stay temporarily, into a permanent immigration of families.'

[16] Bade, above n 1 at 250. The author underlines how one of the main consequences of illegal immigration and irregular employment was the expansion of *bidonvilles* at the outskirts of major cities in the sixties and seventies. In 1970, there were around 25,000 residing in *bidonvilles* in Marseilles and Paris.

[17] See Figure 1 in S de la Rica, A Glitz and F Ortega, 'Immigration in Europe: Trends, Policies and Empirical Evidence', discussion paper No 7778 IZA 2013, available at www.econ.upf.edu/~glitz/ImmigrationEurope2013.pdf.

[18] On this topic see in particular M Eliav-Feldon, B Isaac and J Ziegler, *The Origins of Racism in the West* (Cambridge, Cambridge University Press, 2013).

[19] N MacMaster, *Racism in Europe: 1870–2000* (New York, Palgrave, 2001) 170–72. Many are the examples of the fight against racism over those years. See eg the work of J Huxley, *We Europeans* (London, Penguin, 1935) and the 1949 UNESCO statement against racism.

[20] MacMaster, above n 19 at 170–72.

[21] ibid. The author points out how pre-war generations were brought up in a society imbued with racism and for them it was very difficult to discard old ways of seeing, thinking and acting.

[22] ibid. Apparently post-war Germany and France, discretely, reintegrated racists into the relevant structures of the state (eg ministers, academics, doctors, judges, police forces, etc).

as some north African and sub-Saharan states, the Caribbean, Pakistan, India, Turkey etc. As mentioned, the drive towards mass recruitment schemes was based on the initial recruiting states' conviction that they would be able to shut the doors to labour immigrants as soon as the need for foreign immigration ended. During this period, black communities never came to be a concern of political racism. Indeed, when they started to arrive in Europe, their presence was initially tolerated because it was believed that they would move back to their countries once their employment finished.[23] However, when the oil crisis broke out and Europe started to understand that things were turning out very differently from what had been originally planned, racism began to escalate. Political rhetoric increasingly started to link migration to social unrest and destabilisation of the public order.[24] The fear of the 'other' also took the form of populist alarmism, dramatisation and demonisation of immigrants at the level of media and political discourse[25] and led to the racialisation of immigration.[26] The new wave of immigrants caused the birth of a 'poor white' racism, when the lowest social classes started to blame the newcomers as the cause of their problems.[27] In Britain, for example, the local population, especially of lower socioeconomic status, interpreted the presence of the newcomers, particularly of black origin, 'as an invasion, a threat to British culture, a taking over of our jobs, our housing, our women'.[28] The popular move against immigrants also opened the way to extremist parties, which started to mobilise and found support.[29]

The stigmatisation of foreigners ended up morphing immigration into a security dilemma. According to Buzan, 'security is the move that takes politics beyond the established rules of the game and frames the issue either as a special kind of

[23] The initial tolerance towards coloured immigrants did not mean that their presence was welcomed. For example, as far as the UK is concerned, secret documents show that as early as 1950 both the Labour and Tory parties expressed a preference for white immigrants to be employed in their recruiting schemes rather than Caribbeans and Asians, who had full rights to enter anyway under the 1948 Nationality Act. Indeed, The Royal Commission Report of 1949 stated that migrants had to be 'of good stock and not prevented by their religion or race from intermarrying with the host population and becoming merged', ibid, 177.

[24] See J Huysmans, 'The European Union and the Securitization of Migration' (2003) 38 *Journal of Common Market Studies* 751, 753.

[25] Bade, above n 1 at 280. See also C Dauvergne, *Making People Illegal. What Globalization Means for Migration and Law* (Cambridge, Cambridge University Press, 2008). In this book the author underlines how globalisation had an impact on the concept of migration to the extent that if at the outset of the twentieth century migration was in the process of becoming legalised, with the development of a globalised world, the illegalisation of migration became the new trend.

[26] On racialisation of immigration see J Rath, 'The ideological representation of Migrant workers in Europe: a matter of racialization?' in J Solomos and J Wrech (eds), *Racism and Migration in Western Europe* (Oxford, Berghan Books, 1993); R Miles, 'The Articulation of Racism and Nationalism: Reflections on European History' in J Solomos and J Wrech (eds), *Racism and Migration in Western Europe* (Oxford, Berghan Books, 1993) 36–41.

[27] MacMaster, above n 19 at 175.

[28] ibid, 177.

[29] ibid. As a matter of fact, right-wing political parties began to move their political campaigns against the newly arrived migrants and found good public response. See the examples of Oswald Mosley's Union Movement in the UK, the Front National in France and the Republikaner in Germany.

politics or as above politics'.[30] When an issue is securitised it becomes presented as an existential threat that requires emergency measures and actions outside normal political procedures.[31] As noted before, the perception of immigrants as a challenge to the local culture and society contributed to the build-up of the insecurities of the locals. Locals' anxieties, rather than the actual challenges triggered by immigration itself, acted as the force that led towards the securitisation of immigration.[32] This dynamic ended up firmly entrenching immigration as a security issue initially within regional and national policies.[33] Immigration increasingly became the subject of political debates about the protection of public order and domestic stability;[34] eventually these issues began to form part of the broader EU policy debates.

3. THE CREATION AND DEVELOPMENT OF A FORTRESS EUROPE: HOW FOREIGNERS STARTED TO BE STIGMATISED BY THE EU

During the period spanning from the end of the Second World War to the oil crisis, migration policy was not an important issue for the EU.[35] Indeed, EU national migratory policies regarding third country nationals were still very much 'nationally oriented'.[36] However, when the oil crisis broke and European governments realised that foreign workers were there to stay, Member States started to look at each other and think of a European common response.

The idea of Fortress Europe seems to have its roots in the start of the oil crisis,[37] although it officially took shape in the context of the Paris summit in 1973. On this occasion it was confirmed that only EU workers could benefit from the special rights laid out by Regulation 1612/68/EEC and that the EU should formulate an independent common legislation for foreigners.[38] The broader EU context managed to give the word 'foreigner' a different nuance. Indeed the term 'foreigner', which previously referred to the nationals of any country other than the host one, began to be associated with the nationals of countries who were not part of the Union and who started to be called 'third country nationals'.[39]

[30] B Buzan, O Waver and J de Wilde, *Security: a New Framework for Analysis* (London, Lynne Rienner Publishers, 1998) 23.

[31] ibid.

[32] S Castles, H de Haas and MJ Miller, *The Age of Migration: International Population Movements in the Modern World* (New York, Palgrave Macmillan, 1993) 211.

[33] Messina, above n 1 at 48.

[34] Huysmans, above n 24 at 756.

[35] ibid, 754.

[36] Martiniello, above n 4 at 312–13.

[37] KF Zimmerman, 'Tackling the European Migration problem' (1995) 9 *The Journal of Economic Perspectives* 45, 45. The author clearly states that the Fortress Europe policy finds its roots in the 1973 economic recession.

[38] Huysmans, above n 24 at 755.

[39] The creation of a free movement space started to change the conception of 'foreigner': foreigners were no longer those who came from any other state apart from the host state but those who came from outside the European Union. For a deeper account of the issue of European borders see K Groenendijk,

Initially, the discussion about a common policy on immigrants was simply focused on illegal crimes somehow connected to illegal immigration. In 1975, on the occasion of the Rome Council, the heads of each Member State decided to proceed together with regard to terrorism, equipment, public order, training, drugs, serious crime and, later on, internal security implications,[40] by setting up a special working group called Trevi.[41]

However, a significant step towards the Europeanisation of immigration policies took off at the beginning of the eighties. During this period, a new and stronger wave of discriminatory and xenophobic phenomena began to predominate. The formation of racially mixed societies 'prompted many locals, encouraged by political agitation and support by the media, to set in motion processes of negative integration and defensive crowding together at the expense of strangers'.[42] In the light of these concerns, Member States decided for the first time to act together at EU level both on illegal and legal immigration.

With regard to illegal immigration in 1986[43] all the states that were already part of the EU at that time decided to create an Ad Hoc Group on Immigration. The Ad Hoc Group practically had to monitor, among other things, 'illegal immigration, drug trafficking and other crime'.[44] It is also interesting to note that asylum, which up until then was treated as different from immigration,[45] started to be explicitly

E Guild and P Minderhoud, *In Search of Europe's Borders* (Leiden, Martinus Nijhoff, 2002). It has been argued that these days we cannot now find a clear line between third country national and citizens in the EU. This is due to practices of semi-inclusion, and expression of security relationships between individuals, community and states. On this point see in particular E Guild, *Security and Migration in the 21st Century* (Cambridge, Polity Press, 2009) 190.

[40] A Geddes, *Immigration and European Integration: Towards a Fortress Europe?* (Manchester, Manchester University Press, 2000) 74–75. On the structure and development of Trevi see also V Mitsilegas, J Monar and W Rees, *The European Union and Internal Security: Guardian of the People?*, (Basingstoke, Palgrave Macmillan, 2006) 23–27. Initially Trevi consisted of only two working groups, comprising senior officials from national ministries, senior police officers and intelligence personnel. The first group was called TREVI I and dealt with international terrorism. The second group was called TREVI II and dealt with general public order issues and the organisation and training of police forces. In June 1985 the Trevi ministers of Justice and Home Affairs decided to establish a third working group, TREVI III, on drugs and organised crime. TREVI III focused on the methods of fighting all forms of international and organised crime, with particular emphasis on drugs and arms trafficking and links to international terrorism. The creation of TREVI III was a major step towards wider police co-operation between EC Member States. Its existence and work prepared the ground for the establishment of Europol in 1990.

[41] Trevi, whose name was taken from the famous fountain of Rome, operated within the European Policy Cooperation stream of action. It ceased to exist in 1992, when the Maastricht Treaty integrated it into the Justice and Home Affairs Pillar.

[42] Bade, above n 1 at 279.

[43] The Ad Hoc Group on Immigration was the fruit of the London meeting of 1986. It was an intergovernmental structure of a particular type because besides the 12 Member States, the Community institutions also belonged to it. For a more detailed description see De Lobkowicz, above n 14 at 107–08.

[44] E Guild and J Niessen, *The developing immigration and asylum policies of the European Union: adopted conventions, resolutions, recommendations, decisions and conclusions* (The Hague, Kluwer Law International, 1996) 32.

[45] In the mid 1980s asylum started to be confused with immigration. With the closing up of national borders asylum started to be considered as an alternative route to economic immigration. See Huysmans, above n 24 at 755.

connected to illegal immigration by the Ad Hoc Group through the reference to 'asylum abuse'. This move was confirmed later on by the 1990 Convention applying the Schengen Agreement of 14 June 1985, which covered asylum together with immigration, terrorism, transnational crime and border control.[46] Moreover, this move was also verbalised by Rudge, who denounced the alarming detachment of asylum from the 'traditional field of policy making' and … its increasing subjection to the 'fora dealing with terrorism, drug trafficking and policing on the one hand, and with economic streamlining on the other'.[47] The confusion between illegal immigration and asylum has endured up to the present day, as evidenced by the many references to asylum seekers as illegal immigrants in the recent stories of third country nationals escaping atrocities in their homelands and landing on southern European shores.[48] The explicit connection between asylum and illegal immigration shows how the politicisation process of immigration issues has affected the number of foreigners since the early days of the EU and has ended up broadening the category of unwelcome people in Europe.

In relation to legal immigration, on 14 June 1985, the first Schengen Agreement was signed by France, Germany and the three Benelux countries.[49] Its ultimate goal was to dismantle internal European border controls in order to open up internal borders without checks on the person being carried out. However, if on one hand these provisions were particularly favourable to EU workers or citizens wanting to cross internal borders, they were on the other hand imbued with a strong security rationale, of which third country nationals were the main targets. Indeed, the approach of the Schengen Legislator was dictated by the aim of securitising the internal market, based on the assumption that the downgrading of internal frontier controls necessitated the strengthening of external border controls.[50] For example, the Convention clarified that the right to freedom of movement within the Schengen area was only granted to some specific and limited categories of third country nationals such as those who held a uniform Schengen visa, those who were residents of third countries and not subject to a visa requirement and those who were holding valid residence permits issued by one of the contracting

[46] Convention implementing the Schengen Agreement of 14 June 1985 between the Governments of the States of the Benelux Economic Union, the Federal Republic of Germany and the French Republic on the gradual abolition of checks at their common borders OJ L 239/19 22/09/2000.

[47] See P Rudge, 'European Initiatives on Asylum' in D Joly and R Cohen (eds), *Reluctant Hosts: Europe and its Refugees* (Aldershot, Avebury, 1989) 212, 212.

[48] See, eg, A Thomas, 'Asylum seekers continue to be stigmatized by the British Press', 31 October 2012, available at www.theguardian.com/media/2012/oct/31/asylum-seekers-stigmatised-british-press.

[49] The Schengen acquis—Agreement between the Governments of the States of the Benelux Economic Union, the Federal Republic of Germany and the French Republic on the gradual abolition of checks at their common borders OJ L 239/13 22/09/2000. The Schengen Agreement was originally signed by six Member States in 1985. This agreement, however, was not crowned with immediate success. Schengen countries had to struggle for five years before they were able to agree on the Convention Implementing the Schengen Agreement (CISA), which was only signed on 19 June 1990. The Schengen Agreement was largely programmatic. CISA was instead drawn up for the practical functioning of Schengen.

[50] Huysmans, above n 24 at 758.

parties.[51] If they did not meet these requirements or if they were considered a threat to public order they had to be refused entry unless a state considered it necessary to derogate on humanitarian grounds.[52] The Schengen Convention also introduced the principle of removal of third country nationals not fulfilling the conditions for a short stay applicable within the Schengen territory[53] and, finally, it created the Schengen Information System (SIS), which included data related to aliens who were reported for having been refused entry.[54]

Member States' concerns over immigration reignited once again at the end of the eighties.[55] In 1989 Europe was struck by the fall of the Communist states. This gave rise to new and specific fears of mass immigration from Eastern Europe and the former Soviet Union.[56] Statistics mooted at the beginning of the nineties pictured a situation of nearly 20 million refugees fleeing from war and more than 100 million poor legal migrants trying to escape extreme poverty.[57] Having realised that an overall immigration strategy was lacking, with the introduction of Maastricht Treaty,[58] Member States started collaborating in a 'formal intergovernmentalism'.[59] Member States introduced for the first time immigration within its text as a European independent subject. Moreover, Maastricht did not just provide the legal grounds to develop the legislation connected to illegal immigration such as border control and unauthorised migration[60] but it also did so in the area of legal immigration.[61] The measures adopted in this area, despite being rather limited and not legally binding, had a strong restrictive character.[62] For example the Resolution adopted on family reunification of third country nationals used a restrictive definition of family, including just the spouse and children.[63] Moreover, one year later, the resolutions regarding the admission of employed

[51] Arts 19–24 of the Schengen Convention. G Papagianni, *Institutional and Policy Dynamics of EU Migration Law* (Leiden, Martinus Nijhoff Publishers, 2006) 113.

[52] Art 5(2).

[53] Art 23 of the Schengen Convention. See Papagianni, above n 51 at 117.

[54] From Art 92 onwards of the Schengen Convention. The SIS became fully operational in 1995. The system is composed of a central database, located in Strasbourg, to which all the other national SIS databases are linked. According to Art 96 of the Schengen Convention, the decision of SIS for issuing an alert against a third country national must find its grounds on either a threat of public policy or national security. In 2006 work started on the creation of the second generation of Schengen Information System (SIS II). This new system has been operational since April 2013.

[55] On the politicisation of immigration in this period see A Tsoukala, 'Looking at migrants as enemies' in D Bigo and E Guild (eds), *Controlling frontiers: free movement into and within Europe* (Aldershot, Ashgate Publishing, 2005).

[56] Handoll, above n 2 at 352.

[57] Mitsilegas, Monar and Rees above n 40 at 25–26.

[58] On the negotiations and drafting of the Maastricht Treaty see Guild and Niessen, above n 44.

[59] On formal intergovernmentalism see S Peers, 'EU Justice and Home Affairs Law (non-civil)' in P Craig and G de Burca (eds), *The Evolution of EU Law* (Oxford, Oxford University Press, 2011) 270.

[60] Mitzigelas, Monar and Rees, above n 40 at 32.

[61] Papagianni, above n 51 at 127.

[62] ibid.

[63] Resolution on the harmonisation of national policies on family reunification, Ad Hoc Group on Immigration Copenhagen 1 June 1993 SN 2828/1/93 REV 1 WG I 1497. According to Art 2 access was granted to: the resident's spouse, the children, other than the adopted children, of the resident and his or her spouse, the children adopted by both the resident and his or her spouse while they were resident

and self-employed workers once again set a series of strict limitations granting extremely limited leeway for admission.[64]

The last two decades have been characterised by the gradual communitarisation of the areas of immigration and asylum starting from the Amsterdam Treaty.[65] Also in this new phase the EU continued to apply a strong security rationale to immigration issues. Four days after the collapse of the Twin Towers in 2001 the European Commission, in a communication to the European Parliament, stressed the necessity of fighting terrorism by tackling irregular immigration and stated that 'criminal activities, which are regularly connected with irregular migration flows, are a major concern in all Member States'.[66] Hence, terrorism started to be perceived as a threat that had surely to be combated through tackling illegal immigration.[67] To this regard Member States, within the Council, worked hard to create Frontex, an EU agency designed to help Member States to manage external borders, and VIS, a database containing information for all visa applicants.[68] The concern over new immigrants also touched the field of asylum,

together in the third country. Text reproduced in Guild and Niessen, above n 44 at 251–73. See also Papagianni, above n 51 at 128.

[64] Council Resolution of 20 June 1994 on limitation on admission of third country nationals to the territory of the Member States for employment OJ C 274/3 19/9/1996 and Council Resolution of 30 November 1994 relating to the limitations on the admission of third country nationals to the territory of the Member States for the purpose of pursuing activities of self employed persons OJ C 274/7 19/9/1996. For instance, the Resolution of the 20 June 1994 stated at C(i): 'Member States will consider requests for admission … only where vacancies in a Member State cannot be filled by national and Community manpower or by non-Community manpower lawfully resident on a permanent basis in that Member State … Such an offer is to a named worker or a named employee … An employer offers named workers vacancies only where the competent authority consider, if appropriate, that the grounds adduced by the employer, including the nature of the qualifications required, are justified in view of a temporary manpower shortage on the national or Community labour market.' On this point see again Papagianni, above n 51 at 128.

[65] For an explanation of how Maastricht developed into the Amsterdam Treaty see Geddes, above n 40 at 113–15.

[66] European Commission, *On a Common Policy on Illegal Immigration* Communication from the Commission and the European Parliament COM(2001) 672 final 15/11/2001, 10. Soon after, at the Seville European Council, Member States called for urgent action by the whole international community. See European Council 2002, Conclusions of the Presidency, Seville 21–22 June, available at www.cvce.eu/en/obj/seville_european_council_presidency_conclusions_21_and_22_june_2002-en-f96751f6-9eed-4390-99a8-3174841a1b2d.html, 35.

[67] G Pinyol-Jimenez, 'The migration security nexus in short: instruments and actions in the European Union' (2012) 4 *Amsterdam Law Forum* 36, 41.

[68] Papagianni, above n 51 at 281. The European Agency for the management of operational cooperation at the external borders of the Member States of the European Union, better known as Frontex, started to operate in October 2005. It was established in Warsaw. Frontex's mission was to help EU Member States implement EU rules on external border controls and to co-ordinate operational co-operation between Member States in the field of external border management. While it remains the task of each Member State to control its own borders, the Agency ensures that they all do so with the same high standard of efficiency. The European Union Visa Information System is a database containing information, including biometrics, on visa applications by third country nationals requiring a visa to enter the Schengen group. These systems have been considered to promote coercive sanctions such as refusal to travel, refusal of visa and asylum applications, refusal of admission to a country at external borders, detention and extradition. For a deeper comment see B Hayes, 'From the Schengen Information System to SIS II and the Visa Information (VIS): the proposals explained' (2004) available at http://www.statewatch.org/news/2005/may/analysis-sisII.pdf.

on which the directives adopted (Directive on minimum standards for asylum seekers,[69] Directive on procedure for granting and withdrawing a refugee status,[70] Directive for the qualification of the status of refugee[71] and Directive for temporary protection to refugees in a crisis situation)[72] were strongly criticised for their low standards of protection.[73]

The suspicions around third country nationals did not leave legal migration untouched. The first period after Amsterdam was characterised by legislation that set relatively low standards of protection for third country nationals such as the Family Reunification Directive, which was the subject of a challenge by the European Parliament because its standards fell below the minimum level of human rights protection, and the Long-Term Resident Directive, which omitted refugees and persons with subsidiary protection from its scope.[74]

More recent years have also been characterised by a heated debate over immigration. The economic crisis of 2008 triggered the re-emergence, even more vehemently, of the protectionist talk and anti-migration rhetoric which characterised the years of the 2004 EU enlargement[75] in many of the Member States.[76] The exacerbation of the 2004 Member States' paranoia due to the outbreak of the economic crisis of 2008 has had a significant impact on the free movement debate[77] and on the third country national immigration legislation in particular. As far as illegal immigration is concerned, new stringent measures against third country national unlawful immigration were applied, such as Directive 2008/115/EC[78] on common standards and procedures in Member States for returning illegally staying third-country nationals, Directive 2009/52/EC[79] on providing for minimum standards on sanctions and measures against employers of illegally staying third-country nationals and Directive 2011/36/EU[80] on preventing and combating the trafficking of human beings. Moreover, also on the side of legal migration, the

[69] Directive 2003/9/EEC [2003] OJ L 31/18.
[70] Directive 2005/85/EEC [2005] OJ L 326/13.
[71] Directive 2004/83/EEC [2004] OJ L 304/12.
[72] Directive 2001/55/EEC [2001] OJ L 212/12.
[73] Peers, above n 59 at 284.
[74] Directive 2003/109/EC [2003] OJ L 16/44, ibid, 289. See in particular footnote 140.
[75] E Spaventa, 'The Free Movement of Workers in the Twenty-first Century' in D Chalmers and A Arnull (eds), The Oxford Handbook of European Union Law (Oxford, Oxford University Press, 2015) 459. During the 2004 enlargement Member States argued that the derogation from free movement of workers was justified by the need to avoid serious disturbances in their labour markets. See also J Shaw, 'Between Law and Political Truth? Member State Preferences, EU Free Movement Rules and National Immigration Law' (2015) 17 *Cambridge Yearbook of European Legal Studies* 247, 252.
[76] Shaw, above n 75 at 252. This occurred in particular in the UK where, eventually, the immigration rhetoric led towards the Brexit referendum.
[77] Although the free movement legislative provisions did not change much, what did change was the reception and application of these provisions at national level in making sure that they are not applied more generously than they should be. Spaventa, above n 75 at 459.
[78] Directive 2008/115/EEC [2008] OJ L 348/98.
[79] Directive 2009/52/EEC [2009] OJ L 168/24.
[80] Directive 2011/36/EEC [2011] OJ L 101/1.

approach towards third country nationals has been very cautious. With regard to Directive 2009/50/EC[81] on the conditions of entry and residence of third-country nationals for the purposes of highly qualified employment, the initial ambitious aim of the Commission to replace the national admissions schemes has been left unsatisfied by a weak directive in which Member States still enforce significant barriers to intra-mobility.[82] Finally, with regard to Directive 2011/98/EC[83] on a single application procedure for a single permit for third-country nationals to reside and work in the territory of a Member State it was pointed out that the very low harmonising effect still leaves the procedure related to immigration very much on the national level and at the discretion of the Member States.[84]

Lately, the debate over immigration has been focused on the refugee crisis. One of the most important measures designed by the Commission to address the crisis is the action plan on returns. In its communication[85] the Commission stressed the need for a stronger application of EU rules, which also implies the use of detention as a legitimate measure to allow Member States to 'meet their obligation to enforce return'. The Commission has also threatened the immediate initiation of infringement procedures for those Member States that do not fully comply with the provisions of the Return Directive, in particular the obligation to issue and enforce return decisions.[86] It can be easily noted that a context of humanitarian crisis is also characterised by an EU approach very much imprinted by security concerns.

In the light of this excursus it is apparent how Member States, particularly since the advent of the oil crisis, and the EU have been constantly concerned in protecting their borders from the threat of a third country national wave of immigrants. The examples reported above show that the process of border strengthening involve not just illegal immigration and asylum but also legal migration.

4. CONCLUSIONS

This chapter has focused on how the Member States' approach toward immigrants changed after the outbreak of the oil crisis and how this approach continues today.

[81] Directive 2009/50/EC [2009] OJ L 155/17.

[82] For a literature on this Directive see S Peers, 'EC Immigration and Asylum Law Attracting and Deterring Labour Migration: The Blue Card and Employer Sanctions Directives' (2009) 11 *European Journal of Migration and Law* 387; E Guild, 'EU Policy on Labour Migration: A First look at the Commission's Blue Card Initiative' CEPS Policy Brief 145/2007 available at papers.ssrn.com/sol3/papers.cfm?abstract_id=1334076; L Cerna, 'The EU Blue Card: preferences, policies and negotiations between Member States' (2013) 1 *Migration Studies* available at migration.oxfordjournals.org/content/early/2013/07/26/migration.mnt010.full; E Collett, 'The Proposed European Blue Card System: Arming for the Global War on Talent?' Migration Policy Institute 7/1/2008 available at www.migrationinformation.org/feature/display.cfm?ID=667.

[83] Directive 2011/98/EC [2011] OJ L 343/1.

[84] On this point see Y Pascouau and S McLoughlin, 'EU Single Permit Directive: a small step forward in EU migration policy', European Policy Centre Policy Brief 24/1/2012 available at www.epc.eu/pub_details.php?cat_id=3&pub_id=1398.

[85] EU Action Plan on Return COM(2015) 453 final.

[86] ibid, 5.

This brief analysis is fundamental to set the background for the following part of the book. Indeed, the developments of the phenomenon of family reunification between EU citizens and third country nationals is better understood if looked at in the light of border restrictions versus European integration. Evidence of this is the fact that the first cases concerning family residence rights of third country nationals started to appear after the introduction of a stricter approach towards immigration occurring with the clash of the economic crisis. As a matter of fact, before the outbreak of the crisis no applications concerning the issue of family reunification between EU citizens and third country nationals can be found. Since the end of the seventies, at the beginning of the height of the debate over securitisation of immigration, several cases concerning third country national family members were submitted to the Court.[87] The Court's activity has never stopped and reached its climax, not surprisingly, after 2000. Moreover, it is also remarkable that the nationalities of the majority of third country nationals involved in the Court's proceedings on third country nationals' residence rights, as will be seen in the next two chapters, are of countries belonging to the 'black list' of the Schengen agreement.[88] Indeed, Member States seem to raise their concerns to the CJEU mostly when third country nationals of certain nationalities are involved and this suggests their continuous hostility toward third country national immigration.

In the light of these considerations it seems evident that a better understanding of the development of the European immigration context that this chapter has conveyed is crucial to decipher the legislative and jurisprudential development of the phenomenon of family reunification between EU citizens and third country nationals. Chapters 3 and 4 will explain whether and to what extent Member States' immigration concerns influenced and shaped this phenomenon. For the purpose of clarity I will distinguish between family reunification scenarios concerning EU moving citizens and third country nationals—the first scenarios that the legislation and the CJEU's jurisprudence envisaged—in Chapter 3 and scenarios concerning EU static citizens and third country nationals in Chapter 4.[89]

[87] See eg Case C-175/78 *R v Saunders* EU:C:1979:88 Joined cases C-35 and C-36/82 *Morson and Jhanjan v The Netherlands* EU:C:1982:368.

[88] By black list we mean countries in need of a visa when entering the Schengen space. Regulation 539/2001 [2001] OJ L 81/1 on listing the third countries whose nationals must be in possession of visas when crossing the external borders and those whose nationals are exempt from that requirement made a list of countries that need to have a visa when entering in the Schengen area. The updated list can be found at www.schengenvisainfo.com/who-needs-schengen-visa.

[89] The free-moving EU citizens scenarios concern circumstances in which a cross-border movement can be individuated. The EU static citizens scenarios concern circumstances in which the free movement legislation cannot be applied because the sponsor did not exercise his right of free movement.

3

Family Reunification between EU Moving Citizens and Third Country National Family Members

1. INTRODUCTION

THIS CHAPTER ASSESSES whether and to what extent the change of approach towards immigration affected the phenomenon of family reunification between EU citizens and third country nationals, both from a legislative and jurisprudential point of view. Specifically, this chapter focuses on the development of the phenomenon of family reunification from the early legislation and subsequent case law to this current period in the light of the tension between promoting free movement of workers and taking into account Member States' sovereignty claims over immigration. In particular, the chapter deals with the issue of family reunification involving EU moving citizens and third country nationals that, chronologically, was the first scenario that the free movement legislation envisaged and that the CJEU was approached by. After this introduction Section 2 of the chapter will focus on the origins and on the jurisprudential development of the first provisions on family residence rights of third country national family members. Section 3 will focus on the origins and jurisprudential development of the other provisions inserted in the first free movement legislation regarding third country national EU family members rights. Specifically, it will look at the requirement, to be fulfilled by the EU worker, of having proper housing available for himself and his family, the consequences faced by EU workers and their family members if the former ceases to work because of physical incapacity, retirement age or death, the condition of dependency of the third country national upon the EU worker, the conditions under which EU workers and their family members can be expelled for breach of public policy, public security and public health and the working status, education rights and social and tax advantages of EU workers' family members. Section 4 will focus on the origins and jurisprudential development of provisions concerning third country national EU family member rights inserted in more recent legislation such as the condition on sickness insurance and sufficient economic resources that the EU worker has to fulfil in order to reunite in the host Member State with his family, provisions on the rights of family members in case of separation or divorce from the EU worker and the provision on the right of permanent residence of family members of EU workers. Finally, Section 5 will be dedicated to some conclusions in which it will be pointed out that the approach of the Legislator and of the CJEU has been particularly open towards third country national family members' residence rights although not completely free from the influence of Member States' immigration concerns which have, at times, determined the outcome of the cases.

2. THE RIGHT OF RESIDENCE OF THIRD COUNTRY NATIONAL EU FAMILY MEMBERS

2.1. The Original Legislation

As already mentioned, it is possible to find the original provisions on family reunification in Council Regulation 15/1961/EEC, the first secondary legislation dedicated to freedom of movement of salaried workers. Regulation 15/1961/EEC, as stated in its preamble, found its legal base in Articles 48 and 49 of the Treaty of Rome. Family provisions were encompassed in Title II, named 'Workers' Family'. Articles 11 to 15 of Regulation 1961/15 EEC were the first five Articles in European Community history that faced explicitly the issue of family reunification. Their content can be traced up to Directive 2004/38/EC on the rights of citizens of the Union and their family members to move and reside freely within the territory of the Member States, which will later be the object of discussion. The first legislation on freedom of movement was also completed by Directive 1968/360/EEC,[1] which laid down provisions on formal entry requirements for European workers and their family members, and by Regulation 1970/1251/EEC[2] concerning the rights to remain in the host Member State when the worker ceased to work there. The first directive did not add anything more to family reunification provisions but simply listed the requirements that the European worker and his family members had to fulfil in order to be admitted into the host Member State.[3] The second regulation did not add any new provision to the core rules on family reunification either but simply specified the meaning of the right of permanent residence of the EU family member in the host Member State in more detail.[4]

[1] Council Dir 1968/360/EEC [1968] OJ Sp Ed L 257/13.

[2] Council Reg 1251/1970/EEC [1970] OJ Sp Ed L 142/24.

[3] Dir 1968/360 EEC, at Art 2, stated that 'Member States shall grant nationals referred to at Art 1 (nationals of a Member State) the right to leave their territory in order to take up activities as employed persons and to pursue such activities as employed persons and to pursue such activities in the territory of another Member State such right shall be exercised only on a production of a valid identity card or passport. Members of the family shall enjoy the same right as the national on whom they are dependent'. Art 3(2) instead, stated that 'no entry visa or equivalent document may be demanded save from the fact that members of the family are not of a Member State. Member States will accord any facilitation to the third country national family member to obtain the visa'.

[4] Reg 1251/1970 EEC, at Art 3(1)(2), established that: 'Members of a worker's family referred to in Art 1 of this regulation who are residing with him in the territory of a Member State shall be entitled to remain there permanently if the worker has acquired the right to remain in the territory of that state in

It is also important to note that the basic distinction between EC national workers who exercised free movement rights, and therefore were entitled to reunite with their families under EC law provisions in another Member State, and those who did not exercise free movement rights, and therefore were not entitled to reunite with their family members, finds its roots in Council Regulation 15/1961/EEC. Article 11(1) stated that the spouse and descendants under the age of 21 years could rejoin their EC national worker relative who was regularly employed in another Member State. The same point was confirmed by other provisions in the same piece of legislation such as Article 12 on the right of family members to take up a job position in the host Member State, and Article 14 on the right of third country national family members to work in the family business of their EC sponsor in the host Member State. The same criterion was used to define the sponsor in Council Regulation 38/1964/EEC, at Articles 17, 18 and 20, and in Council Regulation 1612/1968 EEC, at Articles 10 and 11. Also with regard to freedom of establishment and freedom to provide services, in Directive 1973/148/EEC the abolition of the restriction to the right to reunite with their European workers was granted to families when the sponsor is a national of a Member State who is established or who wishes to establish in another Member State in order to pursue activities as a self-employed person, who wishes to provide services in that State or who is a national of a Member State wishing to go to another Member State as a recipient of services.[5] In summary, European workers—self-employed or salaried—and providers of services in another Member State could rejoin with those belonging by law to the category of family members.

As far as the definition of those belonging to the category of family members is concerned, in one of her most famous books Professor Guild highlighted that secondary legislation on freedom of movement of workers contained generously fashioned provisions.[6] Originally, Article 11 of Regulation 15/1961 EEC stated that the spouse and descendants under the age of 21 years of a national worker of a Member State that is regularly employed in another Member State were allowed to establish themselves within the territory of the second Member State. The Committee for Social Affairs at the European Parliament in one if its reports[7] raised some issues on the content of this article. Indeed, it complained about the narrowness

accordance with Art 2, and to do so even after his death. If however the worker dies during his working life and before having acquired the right to remain in the territory of the state concerned, members of his family shall be entitled to remain there permanently on a condition that: the worker on the date of decease, has resided continuously in the territory of that Member State for at least two years; his death resulted from an accident at work or an occupational decease; or the surviving spouse is a national of the state of residence or lost the nationality of that state by marriage to that worker'.

[5] See Art 1 Dir 1973/148/EEC OJ 1973 L 172/14.

[6] E Guild, *The legal elements of European identity: EU citizenship and migration law* (Leiden, Kluwer Law International, 2004) 97.

[7] Assemblea Parlamentare Europea, Documenti di seduta 1960–1961, Relazione presentata a nome della Commissione degli Affari Sociali con riferimento alla consultazione richiesta dal Consiglio della C.E.E. all'Assemblea Parlamentare Europea 5 October 1960, Doc No 67.

of the notion of family household, arguing that special protection should have been given also to dependants older than 21 for study and health reasons.[8] The point raised by the Committee was adopted in the next piece of legislation. Council Regulation 38/1964 EEC, at Article 17(1), widened the category of family members allowed to join the European worker. These members were no longer just the spouse and children under 21 but also any ascendant or descendant of the worker or of the spouse who were their dependants, regardless of age. Article 11(2) stated also that every host Member State had to 'facilitate' the entry of 'other' family members who do not belong to the core family household but, nevertheless, were totally or partially dependent on the worker and lived under the same roof in the Member State of origin. This provision was equally maintained in Regulation 38/1964/EEC at Article 17(2) and was consolidated in Council Regulation 1618/1962/EEC at Article 10(1)(2).[9] The current version of Directive 2004/38/EC, which repealed the previous free movement of workers secondary legislation and amended Regulation 1618/1962/EEC, has maintained this definition and broadened it by including not just the spouse but also the civil partner officially recognised by the jurisdiction of the Member State in which the partnership was registered.[10]

Also, as mentioned in Chapter 1, since Regulation 38/1964/EEC it is possible to notice an expressed openness towards third country national family members. In Regulation 15/1961/EEC third country nationals were not mentioned at all. Article 12 on the right of the spouse and dependants of a Member State national worker regularly employed in another Member State to take up a job position in the host Member State at the same conditions applicable to their sponsor, generally used the words 'spouse' and 'sons' without referring to their geographical provenance. It is with Regulation 38/1964/EEC, at Article 17, that the Legislator specified that the spouse, dependants under 21 years old and ascendants or descendants who are dependants either of the European worker or his spouse were admitted to the host Member State regardless of their nationality. The same approach was kept in Regulation 1612/1968/EEC at Article 10, in Directive 1968/360/EEC at Article 3(2)[11] and in Regulation 1251/1970/EEC.[12] Also with regard to freedom of establishment and free movement of services, Directive 1973/148/EEC kept the same openness in Article 1(1)(c)(d).[13] Directive 2004/38/EC expressly mentions

[8] ibid, 16.

[9] The same happened as far as freedom of establishment and free movement of services is concerned. See Dir 73/148/EEC at Art 1(1).

[10] Art 2(2)(b) Dir 2004/38/EC [2004] OJ L 158/77.

[11] Dir 1968/360/EEC laid down provisions on formal entry requirements of European worker and his family members.

[12] Reg 1251/1970 EEC laid down provisions on the right of workers to remain in the territory of a Member State after having been employed in that state. Also in this piece of legislation family members are entitled to stay in the territory of the host Member State regardless of their nationality (see Art 1, which refers to Reg 1612/1968/EEC).

[13] According to this piece of legislation Member States shall abolish restrictions on movement and residence of nationals who want to move to another Member State as self-employed persons or service providers and recipient of services. Restrictions on movement have to be abolished also with regards to family members irrespective of their nationality.

third country nationals too. As seen in Chapter 1, most likely, the open approach adopted towards third country nationals can be explained by the fact that the Member States, at the beginning of the Common Market experience, did not perceive them as a threat but potentially as a resource for the internal economy.

2.2. The Application of the Original Provisions on Residence Rights of Third Country National EU Family Members

2.2.1. The Origins of the Deterrence Test

It has been said before that the basic distinction between workers that were allowed to enjoy EU family reunification rights and workers that could not avail themselves of the same advantage lies in the fact of having or not having exercised free movement rights. This distinction was explicitly made by the first legislation on free movement of workers and confirmed by the CJEU in the case of *Morson and Jhanjan*.[14] In this case the Court clearly spelled out the basic rule for the application of family residence rights contained in the free movement legislation. The CJEU stated that EU free movement law and family residence rights were applicable only in the circumstance in which a national of a Member State moved from his state of origin.[15]

Challenges to the original reading of these provisions started to arise at the level of the Court's jurisprudence when Member States began to deny family residence rights to third country national family members, despite the fact that the right of free movement had been exercised. The case that opened the door to a long list of Member States' challenges on the right of EU workers to remain with their third country national family members is *Singh*.[16] Surinder Singh, an Indian national, married Rashpal Purewal, a British national, in the UK in 1982. They then decided to move to Germany and work. In 1985 the couple returned to the UK to set up a business. Mr Singh was initially admitted to the UK for one year as the husband of a UK national. When the marriage broke down and the husband was refused indefinite leave and became an overstayer, the Secretary of State initiated deportation proceedings, against which Mr Singh appealed. He argued that the Home Office had been wrong in admitting him only for a year under the British Immigration Rules. Since his wife was an EU worker she was entitled to have her husband granted a long-term residence permit. Precisely, the question submitted for the preliminary ruling by the national Court concerned whether Article 52 of

[14] Joined cases C-35 and C-36/82 *Morson and Jhanjan v The Netherlands* EU:C:1982:368.

[15] The Court applied the purely internal rule established in the *Saunders* case (Case C-175/78 *R v Saunders* EU:C:1979:88). For a comment see A Tryfonidou, 'Family reunification rights of (migrant) union citizens: towards a more liberal approach' (2009) 15 *European Law Journal* 635, 636. For a comment on this case see also G Barret, 'Family matters: European Community Law and third country national family members' (2003) 40 *Common Market Law Review* 369, 377–78.

[16] Case C-370/90 *R v IAT and Singh ex parte Secretary of State* EU:C:1992:296.

the Treaty (right to establishment) and Directive 73/148/EEC required that 'the Member State should accept within its territory the third country national spouse of one of its nationals when, after having moved to another Member State to take up a job position, he decides to return to his Member State of origin to establish himself'.[17]

The CJEU held that a national of a Member State might be discouraged from leaving his country of origin if on returning his conditions (in this case the right of residence of the spouse) were not at least equivalent to those which he would enjoy under EU law in the territory of any other Member State.[18] The Court applied this rule to the situation at stake and concretely held that the right of Mrs Singh of moving back to the UK would have been obstructed if, when she decided to return, Mr Singh was not granted the same residence rights as those accorded to him in Germany. In other words the Court translated the market access language[19] to family reunification between EU workers and third country national family members by introducing the idea that family residence rights find protection under EU law when their denial would obstruct the primary right of free movement.

In the light of the Court's decision scholars proposed two readings of the case, according to which the decision can be perceived as either bad or good.[20] The sustainers of the idea that the Court struck an unfair balance between the state and the Union interests believe that a person in Mrs Singh's position could see her right of leaving her Member State of origin obstructed only 1) if upon her return her position would be worse off than if she had remained; or 2) if she would be prevented from enjoying any goods or qualification obtained during her stay in another Member State.[21] Neither of these two options happened in *Singh* and, for this reason, Mrs Singh should not have been deterred from moving from the UK to Germany since she knew that her spouse had a limited right to stay in the UK in the first place. On the other hand the decision of the Court could be seen as a good decision if instead of considering the right of free movement obstructed from the moment of the departure from the state of origin one considered the right of free movement to be obstructed at the moment of departing the host Member State towards the state of origin (this is the approach that the Court seems to have endorsed). As a matter of fact, it is plausible that the individual could be deterred

[17] *Singh* judgment, para 11.

[18] *Singh* judgment, para 23.

[19] The market access approach started to develop in the middle of the seventies in free movement of goods cases. According to this approach, national rules that pose obstacles to the market are always unlawful, irrespective of whether they discriminate or not against foreign goods or migrants. In the case of *Singh*, since Mrs Singh's free movement right would have been obstructed had long-term residence been denied to her husband, the Court decided to grant him the right to stay under EU law. See C Barnard, *The Substantive Law of the EU: the Four Freedoms* (Oxford, Oxford University Press, 2010) 256.

[20] Tryfonidou, above n 15 at 639–40.

[21] M Poiares Maduro, 'The scope of European Remedies: The Case of Purely Internal Situations and Reverse Discrimination' in C Kilpatrick, T Novitz and P Skidmore (eds), *The future of remedies in Europe* (Oxford, Hart Publishing, 2000) 124.

from going back to the state of origin once he had experienced better treatment in the host Member State. Avoiding the possibility of enjoying the same rights once back in the country of origin 'would arguably damage the notion of Common Market involving free movement of workers and self employed persons'.[22]

Without speculating on which option is the best one, this academic debate shows how the Court, decided to justify Mr Singh's right to reside in the UK by relying on the idea of deterrence. The choice of the Court of relying on deterrence could be explained by trying to acknowledge the UK's concerns over third country national immigration. The argument submitted by the UK government to the CJEU shows indeed the level of concern regarding the entry of third country nationals and their willingness to maintain immigration under the umbrella of their sovereignty. First, the UK relied on a very legalistic division of competences argument in order to justify in this case the application of a *Morson and Jianhan* purely internal situation, despite the evident fact that free movement in *Singh* clearly occurred, by stating that EU law was not applicable here since an EU returnee worker (Mrs Singh) re-entered the state of origin by virtue of national law. Hence, national immigration laws should be applied also to the third country national family member.[23] Second, the UK made its immigration concerns even more evident by arguing that allowing the third country national spouse to enter by virtue of EU law would increase the possibility of fraud and sham marriages.[24] The Court, by relying on deterrence using the 'obstacles to free movement' language implicitly admitted that the assessment of the right of entry of a third country national family member technically still remains within the Member State's competence if a denial of this right does not have any effect over the exercise of the primary right of free movement. This reading allows Member States to still claim sovereignty over immigration of third country nationals in cases in which the exercise of the EU citizen's right of free movement is not affected at all by the denial of family reunification rights, something that a literal application of the legislation would not have allowed.

In conclusion, it is undeniable that in *Singh* the Court upheld a position that prioritised the right of free movement and family rights. However, the fact that the Court referred to the idea that residence family rights should only be granted when their potential denial would hinder the right of free movement of the sponsor suggests a Court's attempt to acknowledge the Member States' concerns over immigration of third country nationals.

[22] Barret, above n 15 at 379.
[23] *Singh* judgment, para 14.
[24] ibid.

2.2.2. *The Development of the Post-*Singh *Case Law up until* MRAX: *The Dilution of the Concept of Deterrence*

After a relative period of silence, at the beginning of 2000 the Court was faced again with the question of whether to allow third country national family members to remain within the territory of the host Member State. Mrs Carpenter[25] was a national of the Philippines who had married a UK national while being present in the UK in breach of immigration legislation. Her application for a residence permit as the spouse of a UK national was refused and an order removing her to the Philippines was issued. Mrs Carpenter appealed against that deportation order, claiming that she was entitled to a right to remain in the UK under EU law. She essentially argued that Mr Carpenter was exercising a Treaty freedom since a substantial part of his business entailed providing services in other Member States. Her deportation would have been an obstacle to his right of providing services, since her taking care of his children facilitated Mr Carpenter's travelling in other Member States.

AG Stix Hackl found no difficulty in finding a link between the circumstances at stake and EU law. After having stated that third country national family members' right of residence in a Member State depended 'on the position of the citizen of the Union',[26] she found that the right being exercised by Mr Carpenter was the freedom to provide services.[27] Once the link with EU law was established, in order to verify whether Mr Carpenter's right to provide services would have been obstructed by the potential denial of Mrs Carpenter's residence rights in the UK, she compared the situation to *Singh*.[28] In her view the two cases were comparable, despite the different circumstances. First of all, they both dealt with the exercise of a Treaty freedom. Second, the Court in *Singh* did not treat the situation at stake as a returnee case to the Member State of origin but saw the situation as 'Mrs Singh moving to another Member State (from Member State of origin) to exercise her EU rights there'[29] and, for this reason, the *Singh* test was applicable to *Carpenter* too. Having found these similarities between the two cases, she concluded that the situation was not wholly internal and hence it could be solved through the utilisation of EU law. The outcome was that a right of residence was granted to Mrs Carpenter[30] relying on Directive 73/148/EEC.[31] Unlike the advocate general,

[25] Case C-60/00 *Mary Carpenter v Secretary of State for the Home Department* EU:C:2002:434.

[26] *Carpenter* opinion, para 42.

[27] ibid, para 59.

[28] ibid, paras 59 *et seq.*

[29] ibid, paras 65–66. As explained above with regard to the *Singh* case, the Court applied the concept of deterrence to the movement that occurred from the state of origin and not to the movement that occurred from the host Member State back to the state of origin. Indeed, the Court in *Singh* focused on the discouragement effect that the denial of family reunification provisions would have had on Mrs Singh's decision of leaving her Member State of origin and not on the deterrent effect that these norms would have had on her returning back home from the host Member State.

[30] ibid, para 73.

[31] AG Stix Hackl did not try to factually justify the principle of deterrence and found of no relevance the circumstance that Mrs Carpenter cared for Mr Carpenter's children in order to evaluate whether or

the Court ruled out the possibility of applying Directive 73/148/EEC on the grounds that both its wording and objective implied that it did not govern the right of residence of a service provider's spouse in his Member State of origin.[32] Indeed, the Court found that the link with EU law, and hence Mr Carpenter's rights, could directly be derived from Article 49 EC on the right to freely provide services.[33] However, like the advocate general, the Court argued that the deportation of Mrs Carpenter would have been detrimental to Mr Carpenter's family life because it would have been an obstacle to a condition under which he exercised his freedom of providing services.[34]

Despite the differences in the factual circumstances, the reasoning and the outcome proposed by the Court in *Carpenter* is very similar to that proposed in *Singh* and shows as well the same free movement rationale and willingness to promote it among workers. However, it is also worth noting that the reference to deterrence in *Carpenter* once again resembles the path the Court adopted in order to take into account the UK's stance over immigration. Indeed, this judgment shows that the UK government relied again upon a legalistic reading of EU competences pointing out that the right of providing services abroad and its derivative right of residence of family members could not be claimed, given that there was no link with EU law because Mr Carpenter did not exercise his right of movement and residence in another Member State[35] and hence the situation had to be considered purely internal. The Court in reply found that a link with EU law existed and consisted in Mr Carpenter's exercise of the right to provide services. Applying deterrence, it concluded that Mrs Carpenter had to be granted the right of residence in order not to hinder the former's exercise of a fundamental freedom. Using this approach, the Court was able to protect the third country national right of residence in a concrete fashion but, at the same time, not to extend this protection to all the cases in which a third country national is related to a EU worker who has exercised a fundamental freedom. In this way the Court preserved national sovereignty confirming once again that when a relation of deterrence with EU law does not exist it is up to the national Member State to assess whether a third country national is entitled to reside within its territory.

not the latter had exercised his rights in such a way as to grant his spouse the right of residence under EU law. See para 103.

[32] *Carpenter* judgment, paras 32 *et seq*.

[33] ibid, paras 30 and 37.

[34] ibid, para 39. The *Carpenter* judgment raised a lot of criticism. Among the critical literature see P Oliver and W Henning Roth, 'The Internal Market and the Four Freedoms' (2004) 41 *Common Market Law Review* 407; G Davies, 'Freedoms unlimited? Reflections on Mary Carpenter v Secretary of State' (2003) 40 *Common Market Law Review* 537; A Tryfonidou, '*Mary Carpenter v Secretary of State for the Home Department*: The Beginning of a New Era in the European Union?' (2003) 14 *King's College Law Journal* 81; and L Jadoul and F Vanneste, 'Casenote under case C-60/00. Mary Carpenter v Secretary of State for the Home Department (ECJ July 11, 2002) (2003) 9 *The Columbia Journal of European Law* 447.

[35] *Carpenter* judgment, paras 22–27.

Despite the similarities with *Singh* it is noteworthy that the Court since *Carpenter* began a process of slow dilution of the application of the concept of deterrence in cases involving free moving workers and third country national family members. Indeed, in *Carpenter* it is evident how the application of the deterrence test is purely theoretical and does not need to be supported by factual evidence. For example, the Court failed to show why the deportation of Mr Carpenter could be detrimental to his family life as the deterrence argument providing the necessary link with EU law was dealt with in the single paragraph 39 of the judgment and the obstacle raised, the disturbance of family life,[36] was only described in vague terms without really engaging with the importance of the child care provided by Mrs Carpenter for the success of her husband's business. In this way, the CJEU 'seemingly bypassed any need for the obstacle to be direct and substantial'.[37] Moreover, some commentators also pointed out that the deportation in *Carpenter* was not a measure that could hinder the freedom to provide services to another Member State because the same detrimental effect would have happened even if the business of Mr Carpenter was just confined within the UK borders.[38]

The willingness of the Court to depart from a rigid application of the deterrence became clearly evident in *MRAX*.[39] In this case the CJEU was involved in a challenge, raised by an interest group, on the Belgian application of the EU legislation with regard to visa requirements. Among the questions asked of the Court, the most relevant to this analysis[40] was whether 'Art 3 of Directive 68/360/EC and Art 3 of Directive 73/148/EC could be read as meaning that the Member States

[36] It seems that the Court was also particularly concerned with the protection of Mr Carpenter's right to family life under Art 8 ECHR. Indeed, the Court scrutinised the deportation order in terms of its compliance with the right to family life as enshrined in Art 8 ECHR and protected by EU law by virtue of Art 6(2) EU and found that Mrs Carpenter's deportation would have been disproportionate (see judgment, paras 41 et seq). On this point see E Spaventa, 'From Gebhard to Carpenter: Towards A (Non-) Economic European Constitution' (2004) 41 *Common Market Law Review* 743, 767. The author underlined that the Court failed to indicate how the deportation order could have been a barrier to one's ability to provide services abroad. See also S Acierno, 'The *Carpenter* judgment: fundamental rights on the limits of the Community legal order' (2003) 28 *European Law Review* 398, 405.

[37] On this point see H Toner, 'Comments on Mary Carpenter v Secretary of State, 11 July 2002 (Case C-60/00)' (2003) 5 *European Journal of Migration and Law* 163, 169.

[38] See in particular Davies, above 34 at 541; S Harbacevica and N Reich, 'Citizenship and family on trial: a fairly optimistic overview of recent court practice with regard to free movement of persons' (2003) 40 *Common Market Law Review* 615, 628.

[39] Case C-459/99 *Mouvement contre le racisme, l'antisémitisme et la xénophobie ASBL (MRAX) v Belgian State* EU:C:2002:461.

[40] Apart from this question the others were: should Member States refuse to issue a residence permit to the spouse of a EU national who has entered their territory unlawfully and issue an expulsion order against him; should Member States neither withhold a residence permit nor expel a foreign spouse of a EU national who has entered national territory lawfully but whose visa has expired when application is made for the issue of that permit; should foreign spouses of EU nationals who are not in possession of identity documents or a visa or whose visa has expired have the right to refer the matter to the competent authority when applying for the issue of a first residence permit or when they have an expulsion order made against them? To the first question the Court answered that Member States are not allowed to refuse to issue a residence permit or to issue an expulsion order to the spouse of a EU national who can prove his/her identity and the relationship with the EU relative. On the second question the Court answered that the Member State may neither refuse to issue a residence permit to a third country

may, at the border, send back foreign nationals subject to a visa requirement and married to an EU national who attempt to enter the territory of a Member State without being in possession of an identity document or visa'.[41] Unlike the previous *Singh* and *Carpenter* cases, the reasoning of the Court[42] this time did not seem to contemplate any possible hypothesis in which a Member State could be allowed to refuse the entry of a third country national EU family member. As a matter of fact, the Court did not make any reference to the idea of deterrence and to the fact that the right of entry should be granted to the third country national family member in order not to discourage the primary right of free movement of the EU worker. The Court simply stated that family residence rights had to be granted to third country nationals because they derive from the family ties alone.[43]

The reasoning proposed by the Court in *MRAX* is surprisingly bold and consistent with the literal meaning of the family reunification provisions contained since the first free movement legislation. Indeed the Court preferred to rely on the literal reading of the legislation rather than referring to the deterrence discourse. This was done despite the immigration concerns of the Belgian government, which in its submissions pointed out how 'the obligation to apply for a visa before entering the territory of a Member State provides the Member States with means of checking both whether a third country national who wishes to enter their territory as the spouse of a Member State national fulfils the requisite conditions and whether he does not fall within the category of persons liable to be refused entry on grounds of public policy, public security or public health'.[44]

The decision to adopt a literal interpretation of the legislation may have been eased by the peculiarity of the question in this case. Indeed, the preliminary ruling

national married to a EU national and entered the territory of that Member State lawfully, nor issue an order expelling him from the territory, on the sole ground that his visa expired before he applied for a residence permit. Finally, on the last question, the Court answered that a foreign national married to a national of a Member State has the right to refer to the competent authority a decision refusing to issue a first residence permit or ordering his expulsion before the issue of the permit, including where he is not in possession of an identity document, or has entered the territory of the Member State without a visa or his visa has expired.

[41] *MRAX* judgment, para 37.

[42] AG Stix Hackl reached the same conclusions as the Court but with a different reasoning. Indeed, she referred to the human rights discourse in order to justify the presence of third country national family members by stating that the refusal of entry to a third country national family member must be presumed as an interference with the right to respect for family life, unless the measure satisfies the requirement of Art 8(2) ECHR (paras 65–66). She concluded that Member States can refuse entry to a third country national family member who is not in possession of a visa only if that measure is compatible with the right to respect family life and, in particular, with the principle of proportionality (para 72).

[43] *MRAX* judgment, para 59. Some criticism has been raised on this point. In particular, see A Tryfonidou, 'Jia or Carpenter II: the edge of reason' (2007) 32 *European Law Review* 908, 911. The author defines *MRAX* as a generous interpretation of family rights because, once the family link is established, EC law applies an automatic right to accompany the EU sponsor into the host Member State despite showing the link to the exercise of one of the fundamental freedoms.

[44] *MRAX* judgment, para 44.

was issued by the Belgian national court to the CJEU due to a challenge raised by *MRAX* on the legality of the national application of Article 3 of Directives 68/360/EC and 73/148/EC, despite the fact that no individuals had actually been involved yet in the alleged misapplication of EU law. As a matter of fact, the lack of a factual issue directly affecting an applicant would have rendered the deterrence justification a completely fictitious one. Moreover, the fact of not having an immediate concrete request from any applicant may have triggered the bolder approach of the Court, as this was simply a decision on principle and not on the circumstances of the case. The cases following *MRAX* did not explicitly embrace such a bold literal approach. However, this judgment has to be given credit since it managed not just to dilute the application of the concept of deterrence but also to unveil clearly that the predominant interest of the Court in this stream of cases has always been the promotion of free movement.

2.2.3. A Sudden Strict Application of the Deterrence Test

In 2003 the case of *Akrich*[45] was decided. Mr Akrich was a Moroccan national who was deported from the UK and prohibited from re-entry and residence owing to having been convicted of criminal offences. Despite the prohibition, he returned to the UK and, while being present there unlawfully, he married a UK national. His subsequent application for a residence permit as the spouse of a British citizen was refused and again he was deported to Ireland, where his spouse had meanwhile taken up residence rights. After having worked in Ireland for a few months, the couple claimed a EU law right of residence for Mr Akrich in the UK, relying on the CJEU's ruling in *Singh*.

It is interesting to look first at the opinion of AG Geelhoed, since his view shaped the final judgment of the Court. According to him this particular case posed a dilemma in terms of the approach that the Court had to take with regard to family reunification between EU citizens and third country nationals. In his view, following the *Singh* reasoning would have meant that any time a third country national was married to a Member State national, regardless of being legally or illegally present within the territory of the Union, the national migration rules could have been overcome.[46] In other words, according to AG Geelhoed, granting the right of family reunification to a European worker willing to rejoin with a third country national relative without the previous assessment of the host Member State constituted a legal anomaly[47] which the Court needed to deal with.[48] After having argued how the Court, in previous freedom of movement cases, applied a 'friendly'

[45] Case 109/01 *Secretary of State for the Home Department v Akrich* EU:C:2003:491.

[46] *Akrich* opinion, para 10.

[47] ibid, para 62. The advocate general underlined the difference with third country nationals that reunify with a national of a Member State that has never exercised his right to move and that, therefore, have to comply with the national more stringent immigration rules.

[48] ibid, para 125.

interpretation of family reunification,[49] AG Geelhoed posed the crucial question of whether the national immigration legislation must always remain inapplicable where EU third country national family members are involved but are not lawfully on the territory of the EU.[50] In his view, *Singh* created both a right to move and reside in another Member State with the third country national relative, and a right to be accompanied and reside in the Member State of the EU national on the way back. In this second hypothesis, the third country national relative should not be subject to any previous individual assessment by the Member State of origin.[51] However, according to his reading of the case, *Singh* did not create a right in favour of the third country national to enter the territory of the European Union.[52] Consequently 'the right conferred on the spouse of the migrant worker under Article 10 of Regulation No 1612/68/EEC may be limited[53] in a case involving a spouse who is a national of a non-Member State and has not been granted entry to the European Union in conformity with immigration law'.[54]

The Court, following the opinion of the advocate general pointed to the fact that Regulation 1612/68/EEC only covered freedom of movement within EU law and was silent regarding the right of first entry.[55] It concluded that a third country national, in order to be able to exercise the rights stemming from Regulation 1612/68/EEC and enjoy the favourable family residence rights provided by it, had to be lawfully present in a Member State first.[56] In order to justify this assertion the Court referred again to the concept of deterrence but proposed a new and stricter interpretation of the test. According to the Court, if the third country national relative is not legally resident within the territory of the Union the denial of granting family reunification between the latter and the EU worker is not considered a dissuasive factor that could hinder the decision of the worker to install himself in another Member State.[57]

From this reading it is evident how this judgment does not sit well with the previous ones and, in particular, with *MRAX*. For this reason, *Akrich* has been classified as a 'surprising judgment that created uncertainty as the position of family members from third countries'.[58] First of all, the Court refused to apply the literal

[49] ibid, paras 65–108 (summary from paras 109–12).

[50] ibid, para 108.

[51] ibid, para 133.

[52] ibid, para 134.

[53] It has been argued that the opinion of the advocate general lacked persuasiveness because it failed to explain how a non-limited right could be limited. See on this point E Spaventa, 'Case C-109/01, *Secretary of State for the Home Department v H Akrich*, judgment of the Full Court of 23 September 2003' [2003] ECR I-9607' (2005) 42 *Common Market Law Review* 225, 230 et seq.

[54] *Akrich* opinion, para 136.

[55] *Akrich* judgment, para 49.

[56] ibid, para 50.

[57] ibid, para 54.

[58] S Currie, 'Accelerated justice or a step too far? Residence rights of non EU family members and the court's ruling in Metock' (2009) 34 *European Law Review* 310, 321. However, some found this judgment convincing. For example see Tryfonidou, above n 15 at 637–38. Tryfonidou praised the approach of the Court by defining *Akrich* as a 'rationalizing judgment'. According to her, the introduction of the requirement of the previous lawful residence complies with the deterrence factor: if no right of

approach to family reunification provisions suggested by *MRAX* and referred again to the concept of deterrence. Moreover, rather than applying deterrence as suggested in the previous *Singh* and *Carpenter* cases, the Court decided to treat the situation at stake as a matter of national competence by stating that the third country national family member right of first entry should be assessed by national authorities.[59] Consequently, the Court ended up making up the condition of previous lawful residence, which was not contemplated in the previous case law—in *Carpenter* Mrs Carpenter was illegally resident and in *MRAX* the Court did not make any distinction between lawfully and unlawfully resident family members as the right to entry of the third country national derived from the family ties alone—and a literal interpretation of the provision was excluded anyway.[60] Moreover, the Court linked the made-up condition of the previous lawful residence to a stricter interpretation of the ancillary relationship between residence rights of third country nationals and free movement rights. This meant that, whereas the Court in *Carpenter* held that also the denial of granting residence rights to an illegal third country national family member could have hindered the rights of the EU relative to provide services abroad, in *Akrich* the illegal residence of the third country national family member within the territory of the Union did not count as being a hindering factor on the decision of the sponsor to move to another Member State.

The strict interpretation of the ancillary relationship between free movement and family reunification provisions seems to suggest how the reasoning of the Court may have been driven by the sense of protecting Member States' sovereignty on immigration. The claim of the UK government, as summarised by AG Geelhoed in his opinion, fundamentally expressed the fear that, were the Court to decide that

previous lawful residence is enjoyed by the third country national family member in the territory of the State from which he moved with his European sponsor it seems that 'the refusal of a right of residence for family members in the receiving State would not have any impact on the exercise of the freedom to move and, thus, would not have a sufficient link with the economic aims of the market freedoms'. Nevertheless, overall this judgment was heavily criticised. See in particular S Peers, 'Free Movement, immigration control and constitutional conflict' (2009) 5 *European Constitutional Law Review* 173, 181. He considered the deterrence argument profoundly unconvincing given that the whole point of moving to Ireland was to avoid the more restrictive national law on family reunion. If the same advantage was not granted on the way back to the UK this would be a great deterrent for the EU citizen to move back.

[59] It seems that the distinction of competences established by the deterrence principle was blurred by a statement made by the Court. In its view Member States, when making the first assessment on whether or not family reunification rights should be granted by national law, should have regard to the need to respect family rights (*Akrich* judgment, para 58). On this point see C Schiltz, 'Akrich: A Clear Delimitation without Limits' (2005) 12 *Maastricht Journal of European and Comparative Law* 241, 250–51. On the same point see also N Nic Shuibhne, 'Margins of Appreciation: national values, fundamental rights and EC free movement law' (2009) 34 *European Law Review* 230, 235.

[60] Peers, above n 58, 181. On the literal interpretation he stated that while Reg 1612/68/EEC set out a condition relating to accommodation of family members, it made no reference to any condition relating to their prior residence in another Member State. For this reason, the requirement of the previous lawful residence of the third country national was completely made up, in contrast with the legislation and the previous line of law cases.

Mr Akrich had a right under EU law to remain in the UK, that would have made it possible for all spouses from non-Member States to evade national law with impunity and marginalise Member States' right to adopt measures to combat abuse.[61] The Court endorsed this claim by basically filling the silence of the legislation with the specific requirement of previous lawful residence and by supporting it with a stricter explanation of the ancillary relationship between free movement and family residence rights.[62] The decision of the Court to endorse this approach was probably bolstered by the concrete circumstances of the case. It is important to remember that, unlike *Carpenter* for example,[63] Mr Akrich was not simply an overstayer but a criminal, according to the UK authorities. As a matter of fact, Mr Akrich did not just become illegal after having overstayed in the UK but rather managed to elude UK immigration laws several times and, furthermore, was also found guilty of committing some crimes.[64] One should also remember that *Akrich* was decided 'when the 2004 enlargement and the connected sensitivities around free movement were particularly prevalent in discussion and discourse at Union and Member State level'.[65] As seen before, the EU enlargement provoked serious fears towards immigration of third country nationals,[66] which were exorcised by the continuous strengthening of the external borders through stricter measures on illegal and legal immigration. It is likely that the several attempts of Mr Akrich to of enter the UK illegally and the increasing states' concerns over third country nationals pushed the Court to completely accommodate its decision to the Member States' sovereignty claims.[67]

2.2.4. *The Road to* Metock*: Overcoming the Deterrence Test*

The preference of the Court for recurring to a more friendly application of the deterrence test was made evident in *Eind*.[68] Mr Eind, a Dutch national, moved

[61] *Akrich* opinion, para 114.

[62] C Costello, 'Metock: free movement and normal family life in the Union' (2009) 46 *Common Market Law Review* 587, 593. In regard to this point Professor Peers argued that since Art 10 Reg 1612/68/EEC did not mention the requirement of previous lawful residence, it was not the task of the Court to introduce it. See Peers, above n 58 at 181. See also Spaventa, above n 53 at 232.

[63] As a matter of fact, in this case, the marriage between Mr and Mrs Carpenter practically rectified an illegal status by avoiding immigration deportation. On this point see M Elsmore and P Starup, 'Case C-1/05, Yunying Jia v Migrationsverket' (2007) 44 *Common Market Law Review* 787, 796.

[64] Mr Akrich was deported to Algiers after having been convicted for attempted theft and possession of a stolen identity in 1991. The year after, he re-entered the UK illegally and was re-arrested and deported again.

[65] Currie, above n 58 at 321, footnote 56.

[66] On this point see J Wieclawski, 'The Eastern Enlargement of the European Union: Fears, Challenges and Reality' (2010) *Globality Studies Journal* available at https://gsj.stonybrook.edu/wp-content/uploads/2010/03/0015Wieclawski.pdf.

[67] On this point see CJ Carrubba and M Gabel, 'Do Governments Sway European Court of Justice Decision-making?: Evidence from Government Court Briefs' (2005) 6 IFIR Working Paper Series, available at www.ifigr.org/workshop/fall05/gabel-workshop.pdf. In this paper the authors elaborated an empirical test of Member State influence on CJEU decisions over the time span of three years and demonstrated that the Court really takes into account the concerns and the views of Member States in order to ponder its decisions.

[68] Case C-291/05 *Minister voor Vreemdelingenzaken en Integratie v Eind* EU:C:2007:771. Before *Eind*, case C-1/05 *Jia v Migrationsverket* EU:C:2007:1 was decided. In this case the Court did not refer to

to the UK in order to work. His Surinamese daughter, coming directly from her home country, later joined him there. Ms Eind enjoyed a right of residence in the UK under Article 10 of Regulation 1612/68/EEC. However, when Mr Eind and his daughter decided to go back to the Netherlands she was refused a residence permit. The case was referred to the CJEU.

The Court, in a departure from the advocate general's opinion,[69] did not consider the option of encompassing the circumstances of the case under Article 10 Regulation 1612/68/EEC, but it referred to the idea of European citizenship.[70] It pointed out that the right of Mr Eind to return to his state of origin could not be made conditional to the fact of being engaged in an economic activity: being a Dutch citizen was enough to allow him to re-enter the Netherlands although he was not actively working any more.[71] After having confirmed the right of Mr Eind to return to his country, the Court answered the contention raised by the Netherlands and Denmark on the relationship of deterrence between free movement and family reunification rights.[72] The Court, following the *Singh* approach,[73] stated that barriers on family reunification were liable 'to undermine the right to free movement which the nationals of the Member States have under Community law'.[74] In particular, the national of a Member State could be deterred from leaving his home country in order to take up an economic activity 'if he does not have the

the concept of deterrence at all but simply ruled out the application of *Akrich* to the circumstances of the case based on factual differences. On this point see A Tryfonidou, 'Jia or Carpenter II: the edge of reason' (2007) 32 *European Law Review* 908, 910. This case can be considered an anomaly because it did not just curtail *Akrich* but distanced itself also from *MRAX* because it implicitly accepted that in case of unlawful presence within the Member State by the third country national family member the *Akrich* logic could still be applied.

[69] In his opinion AG Mengozzi concluded that the right to return to the national Member State should not be made 'conditional upon the performance, upon his return, of an economic activity' (para 97). The status of a migrant worker in fact also includes the right to re-enter the Member State of which he is a national after employment in the host Member State has come to an end (para 99) because, if this were not the case, the useful effect of the provisions guaranteeing free movement of workers would not be ensured (para 101). After having established that the return of an EU worker, although no longer engaged in a working activity, was granted by Art 39 TEC and Art 1 Reg 1612/68/EEC (para 102), and therefore that the situation fell under EU law, the advocate general focused on the right of residence of Ms Eind. He held that Mr Eind could enjoy the family rights in accordance with Art 10 of the same regulation because 'the Community right of the worker to return to his state of origin would not be effective if he could be dissuaded from exercising it by obstacles raised in that state to the residence of his closest family members' (para 103).

[70] The topic of citizenship will be analysed in Chapter 4.

[71] *Eind* judgment, paras 28 et seq.

[72] ibid., para 33. The Dutch government, in particular, claimed that 'Mr Eind could not have been deterred from exercising that freedom, through moving to the United Kingdom, by the fact that it would be impossible for his daughter to reside with him once he returned to his Member State of origin, given that at the time of the initial move Miss Eind did not have a right to reside in the Netherlands'.

[73] This was seen as repeating the *Singh* doctrine. JB Bierbach, 'European Citizens' Third-Country Family Members and Community Law' (2008) 4 *European Constitutional Law Review* 344, 353.

[74] *Eind* judgment, para 37.

certainty to be able to return to his Member State of origin'.[75] This certainty can be given by the faculty of continuing to live with his closest relatives in that same state.[76] For this reason, the Court denied that the fact that Ms Eind did not previously enjoy residence in the Netherlands could have a negative effect on granting the same right now, first of all because such a requirement was not provided in any provision of EU law[77] and, second, because 'such a requirement would run counter to the objectives of the EU legislature, which has recognized the importance of ensuring protection for the family life of nationals of the Member States in order to eliminate obstacles to the exercise of the fundamental freedoms guaranteed by the Treaty'.[78]

It is interesting to note that, despite the reference to the concept of deterrence, the way in which the Court applied the *Singh* logic to the *Eind*'s facts ended up reaching broader consequences as far as protection of free movement is concerned,[79] to the detriment of Member States' concerns over immigration. Indeed, the Dutch, German and Danish governments tried to raise some issues in order to prevent granting Ms Eind the right to reside back in the Netherlands with her father. In particular, they submitted that deterrence to move to the UK could not apply to Mr Eind in this case—and therefore Ms Eind should have been denied residence in the Netherlands—because he knew that she did not have a right to reside in the Netherlands anyway, even before moving to the UK. However, in replying to these submissions, the Court denied the governments' assertion by stating that deterrence operated since the original decision of the EU worker to move from the Member State of origin. In other words, since *Eind* the Court has started to state that the denial of family reunification can determine an obstructive role on the decision of the sponsor of moving from the state of origin even when the family member, at the time of the initial move of the former, did not have a permit to reside there.[80] Hence it is evident the Court in *Eind* was not keen to take into account the Member States' stances but rather it seemed interested in guaranteeing free movement by asserting that the right to family reunification should be always granted, no matter how, when and where the family member appears.

This reading was finally made official by *Metock*.[81] It is worth looking at this case in detail as it is considered to be the judgment that finally put an end to a

[75] ibid, para 35.
[76] ibid, para 36.
[77] ibid, para 43.
[78] ibid, para 44.
[79] Peers, above n 58 at 184.
[80] See *Eind* judgment paras 33–37. This understanding of deterrence also attracted a lot of criticism. Tryfonidou pointed out that in reality, the right of family reunification was granted on the grounds of a non-existent link with EU law. Ms Eind did not enjoy a right of residence in the Netherlands before Mr Eind exercised his freedom of movement to the UK and, therefore, it was perfectly right that, on Mr Eind's return to the Netherlands, the Dutch authorities applying Dutch law did not grant her a right of residence. See Tryfonidou, above n 15 at 645.
[81] Case C-127/08 *Blaise Baheten Metock and Others v Minister for Justice, Equality and Law Reform* [2008] EU:C:2008:449.

controversial jurisprudential decade. The case was brought before the CJEU by a reference from the Irish High Court, which had to deal with four third country national applicants challenging Irish national law implementing Directive 2004/38/EC. The third country nationals had entered Ireland coming directly from outside the EU and subsequently married migrant Union citizens residing there. Their applications for residency cards were refused on the grounds that they did not meet the requirements laid down in the Irish implementing law, namely prior lawful residence in another Member State and having obtained the status of family members before entering the host Member State of the Union citizen. The four applicants applied for judicial review before the Irish High Court. The latter sent a preliminary ruling to the CJEU asking whether Directive 2004/38/EC precluded the legislation of a Member State from requiring the previous lawful residence in another Member State and whether the third country national spouse could benefit from the Directive irrespective of when and where the marriage took place and of the circumstances in which he entered into the host Member State.

AG Maduro started his opinion by focusing on a crucial question: 'Does Directive 2004/38 guarantee for non-EU nationals who are family members of a Union citizen only freedom of movement within the territory of the Union or also, in certain cases, access for them to the territory of the Union?'[82] In order to answer this question, since this piece of legislation was silent on the point, he looked at the general scope of Directive 2004/38/EC, which is the 'primary and individual right to move and reside freely within the territory of the Member States' conferred on Union citizens directly by Article 18 EC.[83] Having regard not just to the right of free movement but also to the right of residence of the European citizen, AG Maduro reassessed the interpretation of the ancillary relationship between free movement and family residence rights. He pointed out that applying the *Akrich* logic[84]—the requirement of previous lawful residence—also to Directive 2004/38/EC would end up infringing 'the right of the Union citizen to lead a normal family life and, therefore, his right to reside in the host Member State'.[85] Indeed, not allowing the applicants the right to be rejoined by their third country national family members coming directly from outside the EU would obstruct the applicants' free choice of living in the host Member State and would, consequently, push them to move to another state in which family reunification is guaranteed.[86] For all these reasons he concluded that 'the effectiveness of the right of a Union citizen to reside in a Member State other than his State of origin requires that the consequential right of residence conferred on non-EU national members of his family by Directive 2004/38/EC must be construed as entailing the right to join him, including directly from outside the Union'.[87] Finally, using the same

[82] *Metock* opinion, para 4.
[83] ibid, para 5.
[84] ibid, paras 11–13.
[85] ibid, para 9.
[86] ibid.
[87] ibid.

functional interpretation AG Maduro added that, since Directive 2004/38/EC was meant to protect not just the right of free movement but also the right of residence of the Union citizen, not allowing him to reunite with his third country national family member would hinder his right of residence regardless of when the third country national became a member of his family. This includes, like in this case, cases in which the third country national entered the host Member State before the marriage with the EU citizen took place.[88]

The CJEU's approach was very similar to that endorsed by AG Maduro, although more explicit.[89] For instance, with regard to the first question the CJEU, like AG Maduro, argued that no provisions in Directive 2004/38/EC made its application conditional on prior lawful residence in another Member State[90] and this was supported by previous case law.[91] However, in this respect, the Court did something that AG Maduro failed to do explicitly. Indeed the Court, very boldly, stated that the decision in *Akrich* had to be reconsidered on the grounds that 'if Union citizens were not allowed to lead normal family life in the host Member State the exercise of the freedoms they are guaranteed by the Treaty would be seriously obstructed'.[92] By doing this, the Court asserted that *MRAX*, and not *Akrich*, was the right approach adopted by the Court. Indeed, the Court singled out *Akrich* as the odd case and stated that, since the right to reside was granted to third country nationals despite their lawful residence through Regulation 1612/68/EEC,[93] 'the same interpretation must be adopted a *fortiori* with respect to Directive 2004/38 EC … as Union citizens cannot derive less rights from that directive than from the instruments of secondary legislation which it amends or repeals'.[94]

Interestingly, the Court referred again to the idea of deterrence by stating that 'the refusal of the host Member State to grant rights of entry and residence to the family members of a Union citizen is such as to discourage that citizen from moving to or residing in that Member State'.[95] However, it is worth noting that unlike the previous cases that referred to deterrence such as *Singh*, *Carpenter* and *Eind*, the Court made a step forward in *Metock* and interpreted the role of family reunification provisions as functional not just to the primary right of movement but also to the right of residence of the EU sponsor in the host Member State.

[88] *Metock* opinion, paras 16 et seq.

[89] This fact should not come as a surprise because the judgment was approved on an accelerated hearing. Art 23a of the statute of the CJEU states that the Court will rule after hearing the advocate general anyway. This probably explains why the content of the judgment is in accordance with the advocate general although not as accurate. For a detailed explanation of the accelerated procedure adopted in Metock see Currie, above n 58 at 317–18.

[90] *Metock* judgment, paras 49 et seq.

[91] ibid., see para 56. Apart from *Carpenter*, *MRAX* and *Eind*, the Court quoted also Case C-157/03 *Commission v Spain* EU:C:2005:225, para 26; Case C-503/03 *Commission v Spain* EU:C:2006:74, para 41; Case C-441/02 *Commission v Germany* EU:C:2006:253, para 109.

[92] *Metock* judgment, para 58.

[93] ibid, paras 56–57.

[94] ibid, para 59.

[95] ibid, para 64.

The extension of the interpretation of the *Singh* test also to the right to reside is potentially inclusive of an indefinite number of circumstances because, no matter when and how the relationship began, it is always possible to argue that the denial to grant family residence rights would interfere with the right to reside of the sponsor in the host Member State.[96] Hence, the extension of the 'obstacle to free movement' approach also to the right of residence of the EU worker, together with the reconsideration of the *Akrich* case with the repealing of the requirement of previous lawful residence of the third country national family member within the territory of the EU, seems to have finally triggered the application of family reunification provisions as automatic ancillary rights attached to the primary right of the EU worker and hence brought the Court in line with the original rationale of the free movement legislation. As a consequence of this reasoning, on the second question the Court felt free to state that a national of a non-member country can accompany or join the Union citizen in the host Member State irrespective of when their marriage took place and of how the national of a non-member country entered the host Member State.[97]

Metock was a very much praised judgment by academics and practitioners because it clarified the ambiguities introduced by *Akrich* by clearly setting the limits between state and EU competences:[98] the CJEU concluded in fact that the EU is in charge of regulating the entry and the residence in the Member States of third country national EU family members and that Member States therefore cannot impose any condition of prior lawful residence.[99] The success of this judgment was also proved by the fact that it was subsequently followed by such cases such as *Sahin*,[100] in which the Court confirmed that family residence rights should be granted to family members who arrived in the Member State independently from the EU sponsor and despite the fact that they arrived as asylum seekers.

[96] Bierbach above n 73 at 360. 'But the reasoning behind the "dissuasive effect" remains extremely conjectural, and could creatively be extended to cover almost any situation.'

[97] *Metock* judgment, paras 64–65.

[98] N Cambien, 'Case C-127/08, Blaise Baheten Metock and Others v Minister for Justice, Equality and Law Reform' (2008) 15 *Columbia Journal of European Law* 321, 332–33.

[99] *Metock* was also very much criticised too. Among the numerous critiques, some argued that the Court was too liberal. For instance, Professor Dashwood denounced the detachment of the right of residence to the right of entry and movement. In his view the right of movement should be asserted before the right of residence can arise in order to avoid the 'perverse consequence of enabling third country nationals to circumvent Member States' immigration rules'. Alan Dashwood, 'Judicial Activism and Conferred Powers—Is the CJEU Falling into Bad Habits?' paper presented at 10th IEL (Institute of European Law) Annual Lecture, Birmingham University, 27 June 2012. *Metock* was also perceived as part of a cumulative build-up of judgments on free movement and this triggered, as Currie underlined, serious dissatisfaction in the Member States (see Currie, above n 58 at 326). Some others instead underlined that the approach of the Court was too narrow. It was pointed out that the Court was guilty of 'fundamental rights reticence' as the only fundamental right referred to the judgment was the 'right of residence of Union citizens in a Member State other than that of which they are national' (*Metock* judgment, para 89) and the final reference to fundamental rights at paragraph 79 'serves simply to remind the Member States of their duties when they act purely in internal situations'. On this point see Costello, above n 62 at 611.

[100] Case C-551/07 *Sahin v Bundesminister für Inneres* EU:C:2008:755.

It can also be noted that in this judgment Member States' concerns over immigration were raised. The Irish Minister for Justice plus several other governments[101] submitted that, in a contest characterised by strong pressure over migration, it is fundamental for the Member States to be able to require prior lawful residence in another Member State in order not to undermine their capacity to control migration at their external borders.[102] However, the Court decided to prioritise free movement over immigration concerns. The fact that the new broad application of the *Singh* test applied not just to the right of movement but also to the right to reside, together with the fact that finally the Court dismissed openly the requirement of third country national family members' previous lawful residence, shows how the Court is aiming to protect the right of residence of EU third country national family members at all times a cross-border movement can be identified, as was originally envisaged by the EU Legislator of the sixties. The *Metock* approach has made crystal clear how the priority of the Court, up until 2008 at least, was clearly the removal of all possible obstacles to family reunification in order not to jeopardise the right of free movement. Overall, since *MRAX* up until *Metock*, with the brief exception of *Akrich*, the Court seems to have managed to dilute the application of the deterrence test completely and, hence, developed a way of not easily giving in to Member States' concerns about their shrinking competence over immigration in order to promote free movement.

2.2.5. *A Recent Revival of Deterrence: The* O and B *and* S and G *Cases*[103]

In 2014 a sudden revival of a strict application of the concept of deterrence occurred in the cases of *O and B* and *S and G*. The *O and B* case concerned the question of whether Directive 2004/38/EC and Article 21 TFEU had to be interpreted as precluding a Member State from refusing a right of residence to a third country national who is a family member of a Union citizen holding the Member State's nationality, following the return of that citizen after having resided with the family member in another Member State solely by virtue of being an EU citizen and not a worker. On the facts O, a third country national, applied for a document showing lawful residence in the Netherlands with his Dutch partner after having resided in Spain for three years during which every weekend his Dutch partner would travel there to visit and enjoy services. B instead applied for a document showing his lawful residence in the Netherlands after having lived some time in Belgium where his Dutch wife, who worked in the Netherlands, would visit him every weekend. Both applications were rejected.

The Court relied on Article 21(1) TFEU by referring to the concept of deterrence. However, rather than applying the test in the light of *Metock*, it specified that

[101] Czech, Danish, German, Greek, Cypriot, Maltese, Dutch, Austrian, Finnish and the UK governments made submissions.

[102] *Metock* judgment, para 71.

[103] Case C-456/12 *Minister voor Immigratie, Integratie en Asiel v O* [2012] EU:C:2014:135 and Case C-457/12 *Minister voor Immigratie, Integratie en Asiel v S* [2012] EU:C:2014:136.

deterrence applies just under certain conditions. In particular, the Court stated that an obstacle to free movement and residence arises only when the residence of the Union citizen in the host Member State is 'sufficiently genuine'. According to the Court, if someone moves to another Member State pursuant to Article 6(1) Directive 2004/38/EC, residence cannot be considered sufficiently genuine because the Union citizen does not intend to settle there.[104] Consequently, in such circumstance denying the third country national family member right of residence in the Member State of origin of his partner does not deter the latter from exercising his right of free movement. However, if the Union citizen intends to exercise his right to reside for more than three months in another Member State pursuant to Article 7(1) and (2) of Directive 2004/38/EC, the potential denial of the right of residence to the third country national family member once back in the state of origin is likely to deter the citizen from leaving in the first place. According to the Court, having moved relying on Article 7(1) presupposes the fact that residence is sufficiently genuine because family life is created and strengthened in the host Member State.[105] For this reason, the Union citizen has to be able to keep on enjoying the same conditions of family life once he returns to his Member State. Interestingly, the Court concluded that it was up to the referring court to determine whether sponsor O and B settled and genuinely resided in the host Member State.

In the *S and G* case, the main question referred was whether Article 45 TFEU (the basic rule on free movement of workers)[106] had to be interpreted as precluding a refusal by a Member State to grant family residence rights to a third country national family member where the EU sponsor is a national of the Member State and resides regularly in that Member State but regularly travels to another Member State in the course of his professional activities. On the facts Mr S and Mr G, both Dutch citizens, travelled to another Member State for work (Mr S once a week and Mr G every day) and claimed family rights. In particular, Mr G claimed family rights of residence for his Peruvian wife in the Netherlands and Mr S claimed residence family rights for his Ukrainian mother-in-law, who looked after his child in the Netherlands.

Following *Carpenter* and the application of deterrence introduced by *Metock*, the answer that should have been given was supposed to be positive and straightforward. However, the Court concluded that it was up to the national court to determine whether, in the circumstances at stake, the grant of a derived right of residence to the third country national family member was necessary to guarantee the EU citizen's effective exercise of the fundamental freedom guaranteed by Article 45 TFEU. In the case of S the Court also added that the mere fact that it

[104] Art 6 concerns just the right of the EU citizen to stay in another Member State for three months. See *O and B* judgment, para 52.

[105] ibid, paras 53–54.

[106] *S and G* judgment, para 32. The application of Dir 2004/38/EC and Art 20 and Art 21 TFEU was dismissed at the start.

might appear desirable that the child is taken care of by the Union citizen's ascendant was not sufficient in itself to constitute a deterrent effect to the right to move of the EU citizen.[107]

These judgments have been deeply criticised.[108] In particular, Spaventa pointed out the aleatory nature of the Court's interpretation[109] of deterrence. Indeed, after the certainty achieved with the ruling of *Metock* with the idea that deterrence acts not just on movement but on the right of residence too, these two judgments have managed to muddy the waters again by failing to mention this important point and suggesting that there are still situations in which the refusal of a right to reside for a family member may not deter Union citizens from exercising their right to move alone. One of the factors that might have played in favour of this sudden revival of a stringent application of the deterrence test could be related to the fact that Member States such as the Netherlands, Belgium, the Czech Republic, Denmark, Estonia, Poland and the UK[110] submitted observations to the Court. Moreover, the fact that, at the time the judgment was released, the nationalities of the third country nationals involved were encompassed in the list of Schengen countries needing a visa before entering Europe even for short stays[111] may have played a role in the complaints raised to the Court too. Overall, despite the *communautaire* trend of promoting free movement as evidenced in many cases up until *Metock*, it seems that recently the Court has decided to go back on its steps of building up the sufficiently genuine residence test and curtailing the *Carpenter* reasoning in order to be more receptive to some Member States' immigration concerns.

3. OTHER CONDITIONS INSERTED IN THE EARLY FREE MOVEMENT LEGISLATION TO BE FULFILLED BY THE EU WORKER

At the origins of the Common Market experience, workers of a Member State employed in another Member State had to fulfil very few conditions in order to be

[107] For a further comment on this case see E Spaventa, 'Striving for Equality: Who "Deserves" to Be a Union Citizen?' paper, 2014, available at http://ssrn.com/abstract =2518955, 7.

[108] See in particular S Bartolini and A Biondi, 'Life as Human Rights Court: Challenges and Developments in the EU Courts Activity in 2014' (2016) 22 *European Public Law* 22 3, 22–23; J Shaw, 'Between Law and Political Truth? Member State preferences, EU Free Movement Rules and National Immigration Law' (2015) 17 *Cambridge Yearbook of European Legal Studies* 247, 269; F Ippolito and S Sanchez, *Protecting Vulnerable Groups: The European Human Rights Framework*, (Oxford, Hart Publishing, 2015) 26.

[109] E Spaventa, 'The Free Movement of Workers in the 21st Century' in A Arnull and D Chalmers (eds), *The Oxford Handbook of European Union Law* (Oxford, Oxford University Press, 2015) 465.

[110] As far as the UK is concerned, the government even decided not to comply with the judgment by amending Reg 9 of the 2006 EEA Regulations. The new regulation implements a 'centre of life' test, which is excluded by the Court in the judgment. See Shaw, above n 108 at 270.

[111] Nigeria (Nigerians entering the EU also need an airport transit visa), Morocco, Ukraine and Peru. As far as Peru is concerned, the situation changed in 2016 with the Elimination Visa Agreement signed on 15 March 2016.

able to reunite with their family members. First of all the EU worker had to have accommodation suitable for the family. Regulation 15/1961/EEC, at Article 11(3), stated that 'for the purposes of paragraphs 1 and 2, the worker must have available for his family housing considered as normal for national workers in the region where he is employed; this provision, however, must not give rise to discrimination between national workers and workers from the other Member States'.[112] The Court intervened to dilute the strictness of this requirement in the case of *Commission v Germany*, when it ruled that this condition could only be applied to the initial admission of the family and not when the family expanded later.[113] The requirement of normal housing was finally dropped by Regulation 492/2011/EC, which finally took up the Committee for Social Affairs at the European Parliament's view in its report on Regulation 15/1961 of 5 October 1960.[114] This report shows how even in these early days both the Commission and the Committee itself considered that leaving the requirement of normal housing aside would have been a remarkable step towards facilitating the reunification of the family. In their view it was the worker, not the authorities, that was most competent in assessing whether or not the housing was suitable to the needs of his family.[115] The fact that the strict housing requirement was inserted, despite the early friendly provisions on family reunification, seems to find its explanation in the problem of the housing crisis which affected some of the northern European states after the Second World War.[116] The scarcity of available houses could explain why the EU Legislator decided to allow family reunification only in cases in which a 'normal' house was available to the family.

The early legislation on free movement of workers also inserted an interesting condition that allowed the EU worker to keep his family members in the host Member State if he ceased to work because of physical incapacity, if he reached retirement age or if he died in the host Member State. This requirement was inserted for the first time in Regulation 1251/1970/EEC,[117] which stated that once members of the worker's family were admitted to the host Member State, they were 'entitled to remain there permanently' if the European worker had acquired the right to remain in the territory of that state after having been employed there for a sufficient period of time, in accordance with the provisions stated in Article 2[118]

[112] The requirement of suitable accommodation for the family was not encompassed in Dir 1973/148/EEC on freedom of movement of self-employed and service providers.

[113] Case C-249/86 *Commission v Germany* [1989] EU:C:1989:204.

[114] See above n 7 at 16.

[115] ibid, 36.

[116] ibid, 27. See also 'Relazione presentata a nome della Commissione Sociale sulle proposte della Commissione della CCE al Consiglio circa un Regolamento e una Direttiva relativi alla libera circolazione dei lavoratori all'interno della Comunita', 25 March 1963, Doc no 7, 9.

[117] This was the first regulation in which this requirement was inserted. The main idea was to contribute to the settling of the European worker after he finished his working activity in the hosting state. See Opinion European Parliament on Regulation 1251/1970 EEC OJ C65/16 at point 4.

[118] These were the conditions stated in Art 2(1): a) a worker who, at the time of termination of his activity, has reached the age laid down by the law of that Member State for entitlement to an old-age pension and who has been employed in that State for at least the last twelve months and has resided

and, in case of death, under the provisions stated in Article 3(2).[119] The same requirement was inserted in Directive 1975/34/EEC with regard to workers pursuing an activity in a self-employment capacity in another Member State.[120] These provisions have been preserved until now by Directive 2004/38/EC at Article 17.

The original Commission proposal for Regulation 1251/1970/EEC shows how this piece of legislation was thought out and prepared in order to remove any sort of obstacle to free movement. Indeed, the preamble of the Commission proposal highlights how, in order not to hinder the mobility of European manpower, the exercise of the right to remain by the EU worker had to imply that the same right was extended to all the members of his family and that, in the case of the worker's death, it had to be retained.[121] However, it is interesting to recall the jurisprudential reading offered to these early provisions by the Court several years after their introduction. In 2000, the Court came out with the *Givane* judgment.[122] In this case the Court had to rule on the interpretation of Article 3(2) of Regulation 1251/70/EEC, which, inter alia, provided that if a worker died during his working life, his family members were entitled to remain permanently in the host Member State on the condition that the worker, at the date of his death, had resided there continuously for at least two years. Mr Givane was a Portuguese national who had worked in the UK for three years before moving to India for 10 months. In February 1996, he returned to the UK with his Indian wife and children to work there again. However, Mr Givane died in November 1997, whereupon his family members applied for permanent leave to remain in the UK under Article 3(2). The Secretary of State refused the application on the ground that the two-year period of residence in the host Member State had to immediately precede the worker's death, a condition which was not fulfilled by Mr Givane. The main question referred to the CJEU thus was whether the Secretary of State's interpretation of Article 3(2) was correct or whether it was sufficient that the worker had completed the two-year period of residence at some time in the more remote past

there continuously for more than three years; b) a worker who, having resided continuously in the territory of that State for more than two years, ceases to work there as an employed person as a result of permanent incapacity to work. If such incapacity is the result of an accident at work or an occupational disease entitling him to a pension for which an institution of that State is entirely or partially responsible, no condition shall be imposed as to length of residence; c) a worker who, after three years' continuous employment and residence in the territory of that State, works as an employed person in the territory of another Member State, while retaining his residence in the territory of the first State, to which he returns, as a rule, each day or at least once a week.

[119] Art 3(2) stated: 'If, however, the worker dies during his working life and before having acquired the right to remain in the territory of the State concerned, members of his family shall be entitled to remain there permanently on condition that: the worker, on the date of his decease, had resided continuously in the territory of that Member State for at least two years; or his death resulted from an accident at work or an occupational disease; or the surviving spouse is a national of the State of residence or lost the nationality of that State by marriage to that worker.'

[120] See Arts 2 and 3.

[121] COM (1969) 1203 final at 2.

[122] Case C-257/00 *Givane and Others v Secretary of State for the Home Department* EU:C:2003:8.

(in Mr Givane's case the three-year period of residence in the UK before his move to India). Mrs Givane and her children referred to the objective of Article 48 EC (now Article 54 TFEU) and Regulation 1251/70/EEC and in this context raised a deterrence argument. They submitted that 'had Mr Givane considered, when he finally left India, that he might die of natural causes within the next two years and that an interpretation of the type adopted by the Secretary of State would be applied, he would have been discouraged from exercising his right to freedom of movement because of the unfavourable consequences for the welfare of his family members'.[123] Despite the reliance of the applicants on deterrence to free movement the Court did not mention it at all and simply underlined that being entitled to reside in the territory of the host Member States by the third country national family members of a EU citizen, should the latter die prematurely, is a right subject to the conditions laid down in Article 3(2).[124] It then affirmed the argument raised by the UK and German governments, pointing out that the condition of a two-year period of residence was intended to establish a significant link between the host Member State and the worker and his family, and to ensure a certain level of integration into the society of that Member State, which was why it had to immediately precede the worker's death.[125]

The Court's line of argument seems to be very technical, leaving little space for a flexible open approach towards residence rights for third country national family members as one perhaps would have expected considering that the intention of the Legislator when the Directive was drafted was not to take away the residence right of family members that established themselves with the EU worker in the host Member State at the time he was still economically active.[126] This technically stringent approach might have arisen mainly due to third country nationals' immigration concerns. This reason may not be so unfounded if we consider that not just the directly interested respondent state—the UK—submitted observations to the Court but also Germany, which in the nineties was very busy trying to strengthen measures that would reduce the numbers of immigrants.[127]

Another condition that the early legislation on free movement introduced was the condition of dependence with regard to certain family members. As seen before, the category of dependants was not immediately introduced by Regulation 15/1961/EEC. However, owing to the Committee for Social Affairs at the European Parliament, which complained about the narrowness of the notion of family household,[128] arguing that special protection should also have been given to dependants older than 21, the Legislator at Article 17(1) of Regulation 38/1964/

[123] ibid, para 20.
[124] ibid, para 34.
[125] ibid, paras 46 et seq.
[126] See above n 121 at 4.
[127] See A Ette, 'Germany's Immigration Policy, 2000–2002. Understanding Policy Change with a Political Process Approach' (Bremen: COMCAD, 2003) available at www.uni-bielefeld.de/tdrc/ag_comcad/downloads/workingpaper_3.pdf, 28.
[128] See above n 7 at 16.

EEC widened the category of family members allowed to join the European worker also to any ascendant or descendant of the worker or of the spouse who were their dependants, regardless of their age. The fact that Italy was at the time the only country that still had 'at its disposal sufficient reserve of labour force not only to avoid the danger of internal penury but also enough to satisfy the demand of other states'[129] is a relevant consideration that may have pushed the Legislator to take up the suggestion of the Committee for the sake of the development of free movement of workers among the Member States.

The concept of dependency has been the object of an intense debate by the Court. The definition of dependence was first examined in the case of *Lebon*,[130] a case involving an EU family member wanting to live in the host Member State with her EU father. In this case the Court for the first time held that dependence is a factual concept, which applies whenever the sponsor assists the person in question despite whether there is a legal obligation to assist the dependant and despite the fact that the dependant claims social benefits. The application of this principle was applied and further extended by the Court in cases involving EU workers and third country national family members. In the second part of its judgment in *Jia*, to the national court which referred a question on the real meaning of dependence (Mrs Jia claimed the right to stay as a dependent ascending relative of an EU citizen) the CJEU answered that there was no need to determine the reason for the recourse of the EU relatives' support and that the material support should exist either in the state of origin or in the state in which the family members file the application.[131] Such interpretation of the concept of dependence should be applied by the Member State in order to 'ensure both the basic freedoms guaranteed by the EC Treaty and the effectiveness of … directive containing measures to abolish obstacles to free movement'.[132] The same attention to the enhancement of free movement has been confirmed more recently, when the Court further clarified the circumstances under which a family member of an EU citizen who moves to another Member State can be considered a dependant within the meaning of the Directive 2004/38/EC. In *Flora May Reyes v Migrationsverket*[133] the Court stated that once a situation of dependence is found either in the state of origin or in the state the applicant is applying for residency, there is no need to determine the reasons behind it. In the situation at stake, the fact that a Union citizen paid a regular sum of money to the applicant was enough to show that the latter was in a situation of dependence and, therefore, there was no need to show unsuccessful attempts to find a job or the potential economic support from the authorities in the country of origin.[134] Indeed, the potential requirement of proving the attempts to find a job or social assistance would make it excessively difficult for the

[129] ibid, at 5.
[130] Case C-316/85 *Centre public d'aide sociale de Courcelles v Marie-Christine Lebon* EU:C:1987:302.
[131] *Jia* judgment, paras 36–37.
[132] ibid, para 40.
[133] Case C-423/12 *Flora May Reyes v Migrationsverket* EU:C:2014:16.
[134] ibid, see paras 23–24.

descendant to obtain the right of residence.[135] It is possible to note that in this judgment the Court's interpretative approach of the legislation has been particularly generous. Once again this seems to find its roots in the willingness of the Court to give priority to the enhancement of the right of free movement and residence around the EU despite the concerns raised by some Member States.[136] Indeed, the Court in *Reyes* explicitly stated that free movement rules, like those included in Directive 2004/38/EC, have to be interpreted broadly.[137]

The generous approach of the Court has also developed in cases involving primary carers. The right of residence has been granted to third country national family members as primary carers in order to support the dependant EU citizen and allow him to reside within the EU. In *Baumbast*[138] one of the questions referred to the CJEU consisted in assessing whether the fact that EU children were attending education courses in a host Member State under Article 12 Regulation 1612/68/EEC could grant their third country national relatives the right of residence. The Court stated that residence to third country national primary carers should be granted because, if it were refused, that 'might deprive those children of a right [the right of education] which is granted to them by the Community legislature'.[139] The same approach was repeated in the *Ibrahim* and *Teixeira*[140] cases and extended in the more recent *Alarape* case,[141] in which the Court stated that even reaching the age of adulthood does not have a direct effect on the rights of residence of the third country national family member carer of the EU citizen if the latter is still in need of financial and emotional support.[142] However, primary carers have also been granted the right to stay despite the link with education but simply to allow the right of free movement and residence of the EU sponsor in the host Member State. A clear example can be found in the *Chen* case.[143] Pursuant to the peculiarities of Irish citizenship law at the relevant time, the daughter of a

[135] ibid, para 25.

[136] The Swedish, Czech, Dutch and UK governments submitted observations. In particular, the UK government went as far as defending 'the idea that only persons who, due to their state of health, disability or age, require real support on the part of the Union citizen concerned can be regarded as dependants'. In addition, the Swedish government argued that, in certain circumstances, a 'Member State may require anyone claiming the status of dependent family member for the purpose of Article 2(2)(c) of Directive 2004/38 to show that he has tried without success to find employment or to obtain help with supporting himself from the authorities of the country of origin and/or otherwise attempted to support himself'. See *Reyes* opinion, para 47.

[137] *Reyes* judgment, para 23.

[138] Case C-413/99 *Baumbast and R v Secretary of State for the Home Department* EU:C:2002:493.

[139] ibid, para 71.

[140] Case C-310/08 *London Borough of Harrow v Nimco Hassan Ibrahim and Secretary of State for the Home Department* EU:C:2010:80; Case C-480/08 *Maria Teixeira v London Borough of Lambeth and Secretary of State for the Home Department* EU:C:2010:83. Please note that the *Teixeira* case, despite being very helpful in terms of reasoning, does not involve third country national family members.

[141] Case C-529/11 *Alarape and Tijani v Secretary of State for the Home Department* EU:C:2013:290.

[142] ibid, paras 24–30.

[143] Case C-200/02 *Zhu and Chen v Secretary of State for the Home Department* EU:C:2004:639.

Chinese couple who was born in Belfast, UK territory, acquired Irish nationality and was thus a Union citizen. After some months, the mother and the young daughter decided to move to Cardiff and the former applied for a long-term residence permit as the mother of a EU citizen residing in another Member State. The national court asked whether the young daughter could derive the right to reside in the UK by reason of her Irish nationality and, in the case of a positive answer, whether the right to reside of the mother could derive from it as well. With regard to the question of the daughter's residence, as suggested by Tizzano, the now Article 21 TFEU and Directive 90/364/EEC conferred the little girl the right to reside for an indefinite period in the UK.[144] With regard to the right of residence of Mrs Chen, the Court also derived her right to reside from the right of her daughter by stating that 'a refusal to allow the parent, whether a national of a Member State or a national of a non-member country, who is the carer of a child to whom Article 18 EC (now Article 21 TFEU) and Directive 90/364/EEC grant a right of residence, to reside with that child in the host Member State would deprive the child's right of residence of any useful effect.'[145]

It is evident that the Court was more interested in experimenting to what extent the idea of free movement could be stretched by using as a link with EU law a fictitious idea of movement (the little girl never really moved outside the UK) rather than paying attention to Member States' concerns over immigration. The Court in fact ignored the UK's statement, which strongly emphasised the need of 'taking measures to prevent individuals from improperly taking advantage of provisions of Community law or from attempting, under cover of the rights created by the Treaty, illegally to circumvent national legislation'.[146] The view of the UK was clearly shared also by Ireland which, straight after the ruling, rushed to amend the *ius soli* rule contained in the Constitution to restrict the constitutional right to citizenship by birth to those who are born on the island of Ireland to at least one parent who is (or is someone entitled to be) an Irish citizen.[147]

The concept of dependency was also explored with regard to extended family members. Article 11(2) Regulation 15/1961/EEC stated that the Member State should facilitate the right entry and residence of 'any other family member, irrespective of their nationality, … who are dependants or members of the household

[144] ibid, paras 24 et seq.

[145] *Chen* judgment, para 45. Chen was the object of an intense debate among scholars. On the one hand it was highly praised for recognising children as full legal personalities and for the refusal to rely on a definition of citizenship that would entail economic aspects. On this point see C Sawyer, 'Civis Europeanus sum: the citizenship rights of the children of foreign parents' (2005) *Public Law* 475. On the other hand it was also underlined how the *Chen* judgment was 'family reunification friendly' simply because there was no risk that the parties could become a burden on the social welfare state, given that Catherine's health expenses were covered by health insurance and her parents were able to look after her economically. On this point see JY Carlier, 'Case C-200/02, Kunqian Catherine Zhu, Man Lavette Chen v Secretary of State for the Home Department' (2005) 42 *Common Market Law Review* 1121, 1131.

[146] *Chen* judgment, para 34.

[147] Art 9 of the Irish Constitution was amended by the Irish Nationality and Citizenship Act 2004, signed into law on 15 December 2004, which entered into effect on 1 January 2005.

of the Union citizen having the primary right of residence, or where serious health grounds strictly require the personal care of the family member by a Union citizen'. Once again, the fact that at the time of the introduction of this provision Italy had a surplus of labour and northern European states had a deficiency may have pushed the Legislator to promote free movement also by making it easier for EU workers to reunite with third country national relatives not strictly belonging to the core household.

The Court found itself dealing with the current version of this provision—Article 3(2)(a) Directive 2004/38/EC—in the *Rahman* case.[148] In this case the brother, half-brother and nephew of a third country national spouse of an Irish citizen living in the UK applied for EEA family permits in order to obtain the right to reside in the UK as his and the EU citizen's dependants. The Court pointed out that it is up to the competent national authority to take into account the various factors that may be relevant in order to identify whether the appellants can be allowed entry and residence within the EU such as to 'the extent of economic or physical dependence'.[149] Despite the effort to describe what the term 'facilitate' means,[150] the Court in the end decided to grant Member States wide discretion in assessing the dependency of extended family members. Despite the openness of the Legislator towards extended family members the approach of the Court in these cases is arguably more stringent than the one accorded to core family members. This is not surprising since the Legislator itself made a difference between core and extended family members by using the verb 'facilitate'. The preference of the Court to stick to a more stringent interpretation of the legislation is probably triggered by the fact that in circumstances in which it would be harder to argue that the presence of the third country national relative is crucial for the protection of the EU sponsor's free movement rights, the Court considers it fair to leave the assessment of this issue to the Member States.

The early legislation on free movement of workers also introduced the requirement of public policy, public security and public health. Directive 64/221/EEC[151] on the co-ordination of special measures concerning the movement and residence of foreign nationals (covering employed, the self-employed and recipients of services), which are justified on grounds of public policy, public security or public health, stated that its provisions did not have to apply simply to 'any national of a Member State who resides in or travels to another Member State of the Community, either in order to pursue an activity as an employed or self-employed person, or as a recipient of services' but also to 'the spouse and to members of the family' who come within the 'provisions of the regulations and directives adopted

[148] Case C-83/11 *Secretary of State for the Home Department v Muhammad Sazzadur Rahman and Others* EU:C:2012:519.

[149] ibid, para 23.

[150] ibid, para 22: Member States should 'make it possible for persons envisaged in the first subparagraph of Article 3(2) to obtain a decision on their application that is founded on an extensive examination of their personal circumstances and, in the event of refusal, is justified by reasons'.

[151] Dir 1964/221/EEC [1964] OJ L 850/64.

in this field in pursuance of the Treaty'.[152] In other words, this requirement became applicable also to family members, regardless of their nationality. These provisions were later on extended to people that exercise their right to remain and their family members according to Directive 70/1251/EEC by Directive 72/194/EEC,[153] and can be traced up until Directive 2004/38/EC at Articles 27, 28 and 29.

From the opinion of the Social and Economic Committee[154] it is evident how the original purpose of these requirements was to be applied as restrictively as possible both to EU citizens and their family members, including third country nationals. Indeed, the Committee stressed the fact that the removal on grounds of public policy, health and security had to be relied upon just in exceptional cases (at Article 6) and that the requirement of 'particularly serious gravity' had to be read in the light of international conventions (at Article 6). The original intention of the Legislator has been upheld by Directive 2004/38/EC, which sets out three strong levels of protection against expulsion: 1) general level of protection for all individuals covered by EU law, 2) an enhanced level of protection for individuals who have already gained the right of permanent residence in the territory of the Member State, and 3) a super-enhanced level of protection for minors or for those who have resided for 10 years in a host state.[155] These provisions, as explicitly stated by the Directive itself, are available both for EU citizens and their family members, regardless of their nationality. The fact that these provisions were planned to set a very high threshold to be fulfilled can be read once again not just as way to respond to the humanitarian need of preserving family units but also as a way to allow the right of free movement and residence of EU workers to be protected and not threatened by the potential departure of family members, including those from third countries.

The Court has often been faced with cases involving deportations and often came out with rulings that boldly interpreted the relevant provisions against expulsion by protecting the right to stay of EU citizens and EU family members.[156] As far as third country national family members are concerned, the Court dealt for the first time with this specific matter in the case of CS.[157] This is a case that

[152] See Art 1(1)(2).

[153] Council Directive 1972/194/EEC [1972] OJ L 121/32.

[154] OJ C 56/856, 4/4/64 Art 2.

[155] P Craig and G De Burca, *EU Law: Text, Cases and Materials* (Oxford, Oxford University Press, 2011) 786.

[156] Among the many examples see Case C-131/79 *Santillo v Secretary of State for Home Affairs* EU:C:1980:131; Case C-30/77 *R v Pierre Bouchereau* [1977] EU:C:1977:172; Case C-441/02 *Commission v Germany* [2006] EU:C:2006:253; Case C-67/74 *Bonsignore v Stadt Koeln* EU:C:1975:34; Cases C-115/81 and C-116/81 *Adoui and Cornuaille v Belgian State and City of Liège* EU:C:1982:183; Case C-340/97 *Nazli and others v Stadt Nürnberg* EU:C:2000:77; Cases C-482/01 and C-493/01 *Orfanopoulos and Oliveri v Land Baden-Württemberg* EU:C:2004:262; Case C-383/03 *Ergül Dogan v Sicherheitsdirektion für das Bundesland Vorarlberg* EU:C:2005:436; Case C-503/03 *Commission v Spain* EU:C:2006:74; Case C-348/96 *Calfa v Arios Pagos* EU:C:1999:6; Case C-41/74 *Yvonne van Duyn v Home Office* EU:C:1974:133.

[157] Case C-304/14 *Secretary of State for the Home Department v CS* EU:C:2016:674. This case touches upon the issue of expelling a third country national family member who is the parent and primary

concerns Mrs CS (a Moroccan national with a minor son of UK nationality), residing in the UK, who was issued with an expulsion order because of her criminal convictions. Also in these circumstances the Court held that the expulsion measure should be applied restrictively. This means that expulsion should occur only in cases in which the personal conduct of the third country national constitutes a genuine, present and sufficiently serious threat adversely affecting one of the fundamental interests of the society of the Member State involved. This decision should be left in the hands of the national court, which should base its assessment on the various interests involved, in particular the protection of the right to family life and the best interests of the child.[158] The Court decided to embrace a favourable approach also in a case concerning the expulsion of third country national family members, despite the submission of the UK government underlying how a Member State should be entitled to derogate from the third country national family member derived right of residence flowing from Article 20 TFEU and to proceed with an expulsion order if a criminal offence of a certain gravity has been committed within its borders. As will be pointed out in more detail in the next chapter, the fact that the right of free movement and the substance of citizenship rights of the EU sponsor—a child—were in jeopardy in this case, may have pushed the Court to strike a balance towards the protection of EU citizenship and the enhancement of the Common Market rather than upholding the Member States' immigration concerns.

In the first piece of secondary legislation it is also possible to find provisions concerning the status of family members. The first condition has to do with the working status of family members. Article 12 of Regulation 15/1961/EEC stated that the spouse and the children of a worker who is regularly employed in another Member State are authorised to take up a salaried job position at the same conditions granted to the sponsor. Moreover, Article 14 stated that the spouse and the children of a worker who runs a family business in another Member State can work in the same activity without the need to ask for an authorisation. Regulation 38/1964/EEC remained pretty much unchanged although an important specification was introduced. At Article 18(1), in which the content of the previous Article 12 Regulation 15/1961/EEC was transposed, the Legislator specified that any spouse and children can take up a salaried job position regardless of their nationality. This reconstruction was definitely accepted with regards to the spouse, children under 21 and dependants by Regulation 1612/1968/EEC which stated, in Article 11, that 'where a national of a Member State is pursuing an activity as an employed or self-employed person in the territory of another Member State, his spouse and those of the children who are under the age of 21 years or dependent

carer of a child who is a citizen of the EU. The reasoning of this case is very much focused on the concept of EU citizenship and to the extent to which this concept should protect family rights. For this reason the case will be discussed in more detail in Chapter 4, where we will deal with the concept of EU citizenship.

[158] *CS* judgment, paras 40–49.

on him shall have the right to take up any activity as an employed person throughout the territory of that same State, even if they are not nationals of any Member State'. This provision survived up until Directive 2004/38/EC,[159] which broadened it and now states at Article 23 that, irrespective of nationality, all the family members of a Union citizen 'who have the right of residence or the right of permanent residence in a Member State shall be entitled to take up employment or self-employment there'.

Once again the openness of the Legislator towards the possibility of third country national family members to take up a job activity in the host Member State to which their EU sponsor moved is evident. The Economic Committee for Social Affairs pointed out that the Legislator, in allowing access to work by family members, tried to take into account the needs and exigencies of the entire family.[160] In particular, as the Court pointed out in 1986 in the case of *Commission v Germany*,[161] the Legislator took seriously into account the importance of integrating the worker and his family 'into the host Member State without any difference in treatment in relation to nationals of that state'.[162] From the words of the Committee and the Court it is not clear whether this choice was dictated by just the motivation of achieving a common market of workers or also by humanitarian reasons. However, considering the limited scope of the Regulation and the fact that, overall, the original legislation was drafted in order to enhance the movement of economically active EU workers, it seems that the openness towards the possibility of allowing third country national family members to work in the host Member State was mainly motivated by free movement concerns.

The Court, over the years, has not frequently been faced with issues concerning the right of third country family members to take up a job activity.[163] However, in the case of *Mattern*[164] on the interpretation of Article 11 of Regulation 1612/68/EEC, the Court showed a strict application of the provisions by deciding to restrict the right of the third country national family member to take up a job activity only to the country in which the EU citizen resides since 'the right conferred by Article 11 of the Regulation on family members of migrant workers to pursue employed activity is not a direct right to free movement'[165] but an ancillary right. This interpretation seems to accommodate situations that fall within the classic family vision but does not seem to take into account circumstances in which the

[159] The same provision was also kept in the Residency Directives. Before the entry into force of Directive 2004/38/EC the Court held that the right to take up employment applied also to family members of self-employed people according to Case C-337/97 *Meeusen v Hoofddirectie van de Informatie Beheer Groep* EU:C:1999:284.

[160] See above n 7 at 16.

[161] Case C-249/86 *Commission v Germany* EU:C:1989:204.

[162] ibid, para 11.

[163] The seminal case in this area is Case C-131/85 *Gul v Regierungspräsident Düsseldorf* EU:C:1986:200.

[164] Case C-10/05 *Mattern and Cikotic v Ministre du Travail et de l'Emploi* EU:C:2006:220.

[165] ibid, para 25

family may be living close to the border of two Member States and the family member decides to take up a job in the bordering state but not in the host state or situations in which the family may be still be together but decide, for any reason, to live separately and take up job positions in two different states.[166] This view on where third country national family members can be employed seems to be connected to a strict application of the idea that the right to work of the third country national family member is not independent but ancillary to the primary right of free movement and, for this reason, the right of the family member cannot be geographically detached from the primary one of their sponsor. The Court has not been engaged recently on the interpretation of the new Article 23 of Directive 2004/38/EC. It will be interesting to see, when this does happen, whether a new more flexible approach will be adopted. For the moment the *Mattern* case shows clearly the attention of the Court of not overstepping Member States' sovereignty in assessing who can grant the right to work to a third country national family member.

The second condition on the status of family members deals with education. Article 15 Regulation 15/1961/EEC stated that the children of a national of a Member State who is or has been employed in the territory of another Member State shall be admitted to that State's general educational, apprenticeship and vocational training courses under the same conditions as the nationals of that State, if such children are residing in its territory. The same phraseology was maintained in Regulation 34/1963/EEC, 1612/1968/EEC and in the recent Article 10(1) Regulation 492/2011/EC.[167] The already quite generous approach adopted by the Legislator was enhanced by the Court over the years. In *Casagrande*[168] Article 10 was applied not just to cover admission to courses but also educational grants. In *Gaal*[169] the Court ruled that educational rights could also be conferred to those above 21 and non-dependent. Also, in *Echternach and Moritz*,[170] the CJEU ruled that Article 10 covers the child's right to educational assistance even when the parents have returned to their state of nationality.

As far as third country national family members are concerned it was the Court that eventually ended up filling the gap left by the Legislator by stating, in the case of *Baumbast*, that the fact that the children are third country nationals is irrelevant to the enjoyment of the rights under Article 10. According to the Court,

[166] *Mattern* opinion, para 38.

[167] There is no mention in the EU treaties or secondary legislation of a right to education for family members rather than children. However, the Court extended these provisions to spouses in Case C-152/82 *Forcheri v Belgium* EU:C:1983:205, in which it decided that it represents forbidden discrimination to demand the spouse of a EU citizen fees for professional education if they are not expected from national students.

[168] Case C-9/74 *Casagrande v Landeshauptstadt München* EU:C:1974:74.

[169] Case C-7/94 *Landesamt für Ausbildungsförderung Nordrhein-Westfalen v Lubor Gaal* EU:C:1995:118.

[170] Joined Cases C-389/87 and C-390/87 *Echternach and Moritz v Minister for Education and Science* EU:C:1989:130.

since the third country national children of the EU worker have the right to install themselves with him (or her)[171] in the host Member State they should also have the right to pursue their education there.[172] The openness of the Court towards granting the right to education to children of EU citizens, including third country national children, can be explained in the light of the fundamental need of integration of the migrant worker and his family in the host Member State 'in order to attain the objective of Regulation No 1612/68, namely freedom of movement for workers, in compliance with the principles of liberty and dignity'.[173]

Finally, Article 7(2) Regulation 492/11/EC contains a condition on tax advantages and social benefits. The original provision inserted in the first piece of secondary legislation did not envisage any right to family members but just to EU migrant workers who were entitled to 'the same social and tax advantages as national workers'. In *Even*,[174] however, the Court gave a broad reading of this provision stating that 'the social advantages encompassed by Article 7(2) are "all advantages which whether or not linked to a contract of employment, are generally granted to national workers primarily because of their objective status as workers or by virtue of the mere fact of their residence on the national territory and the extension of which to workers who are nationals of other Member States therefore seems suitable to facilitate their mobility within the community"'.[175]

The words of the Court make it clear that this formula was introduced in order to enhance free movement of EU workers by removing obstacles that could hinder their presence in the host Member State such as not receiving a benefit for one of their family members. The *Even* formula was successful and broadly applied by the Court, both in cases involving EU and third country national family members without making any distinction.[176]

4. OTHER CONDITIONS INSERTED IN THE MORE RECENT LEGISLATION

At the beginning of the nineties the Residency Directives were introduced.[177] These pieces of legislation introduced the requirement, for the sponsor and the

[171] *Baumbast* judgment, paras 56–57.

[172] ibid, para 58.

[173] ibid, para 59.

[174] Case C-207/78 *Criminal Proceedings v Even* EU:C:1979:144.

[175] ibid, para 22.

[176] Case C-94/84 *ONEM v Deak* EU:C:1985:264. In this case it was held that although Mr Deak, a Hungarian national living with his Italian mother in Belgium, could not claim unemployment benefit under Reg 1408/71/EEC, the principle of Art 7(2) of Reg 492/11/EC could apply as it was designed to prevent discrimination against descendants of a worker who were dependent on him, regardless of their nationality. It is also possible to find cases in which benefits to third country national family members were denied. However, the reason for the denial does not seem to be related to nationality issues. See eg Case C-243/91 *Belgian State v Taghavi* ECLI:EU:C:1992:306.

[177] In 1989 the Commission withdrew its proposal of a Directive on the right of residence of all nationals of a Member State on the territory of another Member State and proposed instead three 'Residency Directives' that opened the right of movement and residence also to students, retired persons

family members, of having health insurance and the requirement of having sufficient resources to avoid becoming a burden on the social assistance system of the host Member State.[178] The proposal of the Commission[179] shows how the reason lying behind this choice was connected to the idea of promoting a homogeneous free movement of workers with the aim of avoiding migration flows of EU citizens that would move only because social security and social assistance systems were not harmonised.

The proposal of the Commission clearly pointed out the importance of the right of residence to be granted to family members, including third country nationals.[180] This is because the real exercise of the right of free movement becomes a real possibility only if it is also granted to the members of the family.[181] Article 7(1)(b) and (c) of Directive 2004/38/EC essentially incorporated these main conditions from the previous Residency Directives: citizens must have sufficient resources for themselves and their family members not to become a burden on the social assistance system of the host Member State during the period of residence and must have comprehensive health insurance cover in the host state. The Directive also added that family members that retain their right of residence on a personal basis despite the link with the EU sponsor[182] should show that they are workers or self-employed or have sufficient resources to avoid becoming a burden on the host state and have comprehensive health insurance cover in the host state in order to qualify for the right of permanent residence. The Directive also specifies the meaning of 'sufficient resources', stating that no fixed amount should be set by Member States and that the personal situation of the applicant should be taken into account.[183]

These provisions seem to suggest that the Legislator tried somehow to put some boundaries to entry of immigrant workers by setting out these requirements. However, from the reading of the first Commission report on the Directive, it is evident how the Legislator never intended to raise strict boundaries by introducing insurmountable obstacles to immigration. Proof of this is the fact that the necessary resources to look after the sponsor and his family in order not to be a burden on the Member State can come from a third person.[184] The Court also upheld this view and confirmed that spouses and dependent children's incomes should be considered when assessing whether the sponsor can meet the sufficient

and more generally to all the economically inactive persons. The Residency Directives extended the scope of residence rights to non-economically active migrants and their third country national family members, provided they were covered by sickness insurance and had sufficient resources not to become a burden on the host Member State's welfare system.

178 Art 1 Directive 90/364/EEC; Art 1 Directive 90/365/EEC; Art 1 Directive 93/96/EEC.

179 COM (1989) 275 final at 5.

180 Reference was made to Art 10 Reg 1612/68/EEC.

181 See above n 179.

182 These are cases of death, divorce or annulment, which will be covered later in this section.

183 Art 8(3)(4).

184 COM (2003) 101 final at 11.

resources test. In the already-mentioned *Chen* case, the Court found the argument of the Irish and UK governments unfounded as to where they pointed out how the availability of sufficient resources means that the EU citizen must possess those resources personally and may not use for that purpose those of an accompanying family member. Indeed, the Court argued that such a requirement would not just be contrasting the broad interpretation that should be given to free movement legislation[185] but also, following *Baumbast*, adding a requirement as to the origin of the resources would constitute a disproportionate interference with the exercise of the fundamental right of freedom of movement and of residence.[186] More recently the Court in the cases of *Alopka*[187] and *Singh and others*[188] confirmed the same principle by stating respectively that it was for the referring court to ascertain whether the EU children had, on their own or through their third country national mother, sufficient resources and comprehensive sickness insurance cover[189] and that a Union citizen had sufficient resources for himself and his family members not to become a burden on the social assistance system of the host Member State during his period of residence where those resources derived in part from those of the spouse who was a third-country national.[190] Once again, in the same line of *Baumbast*, the Court underlined the priority of free movement by stating that the 'interpretation of the condition concerning the sufficiency of resources as meaning that the person concerned must have such resources himself' would constitute a disproportionate interference with 'the exercise of the fundamental right of freedom of movement and residence'.[191]

Another new condition concerns the status of divorced family members. This condition was introduced by Directive 2004/38/EC. Article 13(1) now provides that the residence of family members, including third country nationals, is not affected in cases following a divorce, annulment of marriage or termination of a registered partnership as long as the marriage or registered partnership has lasted at least three years including one year in the host Member State, or where the spouse who is not a EU national retains custody of the EU citizen's children; or where it is warranted by particularly difficult circumstances such as the applicant having been victim of domestic violence during the marriage partnership or where the non-EU national spouse or partner has the right of access to a minor child and where the court has ruled that such access must be in the host Member State for as long as required.

With this provision the Legislator ended up clarifying some issues regarding the status of third country national spouses under Regulation 1612/68/EEC, which had arisen first in the *Diatta* case.[192] This case concerned a Senegalese national,

185 *Chen* judgment, para 31.
186 ibid, para 33. On the same line see also Case C-408/03 *Commission v Belgium* EU:C:2006:192.
187 Case C-86/12 *Alokpa v Ministre du Travail, de l'Emploi et de l'Immigration* EU:C:2013:645.
188 Case C-218/14 *Singh and others v Minister for Justice and Equality* EU:C:2015:476.
189 *Alokpa* judgment, para 30.
190 *Singh and others* judgment, paras 70–77.
191 ibid, para 75.
192 Case C-267/83 *Diatta v Land Berlin* EU:C:1985:67.

Mrs Diatta, who married a French national living and working in Berlin. After separating from him and having moved to different accommodation, she applied for an extension of her residence permit, which was refused by the German authorities on the basis that she was no longer a member of the family of an EU worker moving and working in another Member State. The Court, after having pointed out that free movement legislation and Article 10 Regulation 1612/68/EEC could not be interpreted strictly,[193] highlighted that the content of this provision simply implied that the accommodation that the worker had to provide as available had to be 'normal' and not also that the family had to live under the same roof permanently.[194] The same principle was also upheld in the following cases of *Singh* and *Baumbast*, already mentioned, and more recently extended in the case of *Ogieriakhi*.[195] This case concerned a Nigerian national, Mr Ogieriakhi, who married a French national living in Ireland, Ms George. In August 2011 Ms George moved out and began to reside with another man. Soon afterwards Mr Ogieriakhi started to reside with Ms Madden, an Irish citizen with whom, after a while, he had a child. The main question referred to the Court consisted in whether Article 16(2) of Directive 2004/38/EC had to be interpreted as meaning that a third country national who, during a continuous period of five years before the transposition date for the Directive, resided in a Member State as the spouse of a Union citizen working in that Member State, must be regarded as having acquired a right of permanent residence even though, during that period, the EU spouse decided to reside with another person and no longer provided the home in which the third country national lived. The Court based its reasoning on the *Diatta* and *Iida*[196] cases, stating that what matters for the counting of the years of residence is the marital relationship, even if the spouses are separated and do not live under the same roof.[197]

These cases above show how the Court has, since the early eighties, preferred to take a very friendly approach towards third country national family members, despite the fact that the relationship with the EU sponsor was no longer ongoing. From the words of the Court it seems that this approach was taken in order to promote the free movement of workers.[198] Indeed, according to the reasoning followed since *Diatta* it is evident that the Court's aim is to avoid interpreting free movement legislation strictly by requiring the third country national family member to live permanently with his EU sponsor because that requirement would hinder the right of the latter to move to another Member State.[199] Despite the immigration concerns of Member States, which have

[193] ibid, para 17.
[194] ibid, para 18.
[195] Case C-244/13 *Ogieriakhi v Minister for Justice and Equality* EU:C:2014:2068.
[196] To be discussed later on.
[197] *Ogieriakhi* judgment, para 37.
[198] *Diatta* judgment, para 18 and *Ogieriakhi* judgment, para 44.
[199] *Diatta* judgment, paras 15–18.

continuously arisen in these kinds of cases,[200] the Court decided not to take them into account.

Finally, another important condition introduced by Directive 2004/38/EC was the right of permanent residence for EU citizens and their families, including third country national family members, who have resided lawfully for a continuous period of five years in the host state.[201] Article 16 and Article 18[202] define the right of permanent residence in general terms, indicating the length of residence time required to obtain such a status and the necessary conditions to be fulfilled. Article 16 now states that Union citizens who have resided in the host Member State for a period of five years can be entitled to the right of permanent residence and that this right cannot be jeopardised by temporary absences. Article 18 specifies that the right of permanent residence should be extended to EU nationals' family members who are not nationals of a Member State and who have resided legally for a period of five years in the host Member State.[203]

It is noteworthy that, despite the fact that the initial Commission proposal for the Directive indicated four years as the necessary length of time required by EU citizens and their family members to be entitled to the right of permanent residence,[204] the Council decided to raise the length of residence to five years.[205] The change introduced by the Council suggests that Member States were not keen on granting the right of permanent residence and all the advantages that it entails in terms of equality of treatment between EU workers and their families and national workers[206] lightly. This arguably still shows the reluctance of Member States to give in their sovereignty over immigration, both on EU workers and third country nationals.

Interestingly the Court has also shown its strictness in granting the right of permanent residence in circumstances in which the applicant was convicted and spent time in prison. This is evident as far as EU citizens are concerned[207] and

[200] For instance in *Diatta* the UK government and the Dutch government submitted that Art 10 and Art 11 of Reg 1612/68/EEC were deeply connected as, together, they allowed the integration of the family within the host Member State. This common purpose could not be advanced if the legislation allowed to look at these rights distinctively and allowed the third country national family member to live and work somewhere other than where the EU sponsor lives. See *Diatta* judgment, para 12.

[201] Before Dir 2004/38/EC some other legislation referred to this concept, although in a limited way. See Art 4(1) Dir 1973/148/EEC and Art 2 Dir 1975/34/EEC Directive 1975/34/EEC OJ L 14/10 concerning the right of nationals of a Member State to remain in the territory of another Member State after having pursued therein an activity in a self-employed capacity.

[202] Art 17 basically takes up the conditions referred to by Dir 1975/34 EEC, at Art 2.

[203] This is without prejudice of the right of third country nationals to obtain the right of permanent residence after one year of lawful residence preceding the death of the EU citizen (Art 12(2)) and in case of divorce, annulment of marriage or termination of the registered partnership (Art 13(2)).

[204] COM (2001) 257 final point 1.4 at 2.

[205] 2001/0111 (COD) SEC (2003) 1293 final at 3.

[206] These advantages amount to full material equality and equal access to social benefits alongside nationals of the host state and not being the object of an expulsion order except on serious grounds of public policy or public security.

[207] In Case C-400/12 *Secretary of State for the Home Department v MG* EU:C:2014:9 paras 28 and 38 the Court found that the EU applicant, in order to be entitled to enhanced protection from expulsion, has to have resided continuously in the host Member State for 10 years and that, potentially, the

equally true when third country national family members are involved. In the case of *Onuekwere*,[208] the CJEU ruled that periods of imprisonment in the host Member State could not be taken into consideration in the context of the acquisition of the right of permanent residence after five years by a third country national family member of an EU citizen. The Court first pointed out that the acquisition of the right of permanent residence for third country nationals not only depends on the fact that the Union citizen himself satisfies the conditions of Article 16(1) of Directive 2004/38/EC but also that the family member himself has resided legally and continuously with the EU citizen for the required period.[209] The Court continued by recalling the Directive's preamble and stated that, since the right of permanent residence is meant to promote social cohesion, social integration becomes a key factor for obtaining that right.[210] The imposition of a prison sentence by a national court clearly shows the lack of integration of the person concerned with the values expressed by the host society.[211]

Unlike what happens normally to non-nationals in a host Member State where time alone seems to be the only criterion that creates the link between the former and the latter, when the Court deals with prisoner immigrants it seems to suggest that integration is not based on temporal factors but on their conduct within the society.[212] When it comes to breaching rules of conduct, the Court is indeed more likely to adopt a strict interpretation of free movement rules. This approach highlights the influence that immigration concerns can have on the reasoning of the Court which, when it comes to criminal convictions and time of imprisonment, prefers to prioritise Member States' sovereignty claims on immigration over free movement.

5. CONCLUSIONS

Chapter 1 looked at the origins of the concept of family reunification. It has been seen that the right to family reunification was inserted from the first bilateral agreements and those provisions were characterised by openness towards family members, of all nationalities, for the sake of enhancing the movement of workers, mainly Italians, to the northern host countries in need of labour. It has been seen that this approach was also translated into the early EU legislation on free movement. Chapter 2 focused instead on the oil crisis and how this event, among the many other consequences that it triggered, also marked a new stringent and

period of imprisonment is capable both of interrupting the continuity of the period of residence and of affecting the decision regarding the grant of the enhanced protection.

[208] Case C-378/12 *Onuekwere v Secretary of State for the Home Department* EU:C:2014:13.

[209] *Onuekwere* judgment, para 23.

[210] *Onuekwere* judgment, para 24.

[211] *Onuekwere* judgment, para 26.

[212] Spaventa, above n 107 at 8.

suspicious attitude towards immigrants, particularly those coming from third countries, on the part of European national states. It has also been seen that the suspicious attitude of Member States towards immigrants has been a constant to this day.

This chapter has tried to assess to what extent the clash between the objective of free movement and Member States' immigration concerns have shaped the legislation and case law on family reunification between EU citizens and third country nationals. The analysis shows, overall, that as far as the legislation is concerned, the new immigration concerns seem not to have overly affected the provisions' content. As a matter of fact, as noted above, the original free movement legislation contained generously fashioned provisions on family members and, if anything, time just helped to improve this openness. Moreover, since the early days the Legislator was open to extend these rights to all family members, regardless of their nationality, and the same approach has been endorsed by Directive 2004/38/EC, despite the heated immigration debates of the last decade. For instance, Regulation 1612/68/EEC contained broad provisions concerning the category of family members allowed to join the European worker and this category was even more expanded by Directive 2004/38/EC, which now also includes civil partners regardless of their nationality. The same can be said with regard to the right of family members to take up job positions, which was broadened by Directive 2004/38/EC to all the family members who have permanent residence and also to those family members wishing to engage in self-employed activities, regardless of their nationality. The strict housing requirement, rather than being maintained, was repealed in 2011, despite the fact that the immigration debate had been reignited in that year by population movements resulting from the Arab spring and by the beginning of the Syrian crisis. Moreover, despite the numerous immigration debates of the last decade and a half, the recent legislation on free movement contains additional friendly provisions regarding family members, such as the right of permanent residence, which was introduced officially by Directive 2004/38/EC and also covers third country national family members. The early legislation also contained provisions on the right of family members to remain in the host Member State despite the fact that the EU worker ceased to work due to physical incapacity, retirement age or death, and they have been preserved up until now with Directive 2004/38/EC. The same can be said with regard to the condition of dependence. Indeed, the category of family members was expanded by Regulation 38/1964/EEC to include dependants older than 21 years and this has been preserved by the current legislation. As far as the requirement of public policy, public security and public health is concerned the idea of applying them as restrictively as possible was upheld by Directive 2004/38/EC, to which goes the merit of setting up strong levels of protection against expulsion. Finally, as far as divorced family members are concerned, Directive 2004/38/EC confirmed and clarified the friendly jurisprudential approach towards third country nationals, rather than reducing its impact.

The fact that the Legislator's approach has largely not been affected by the Member States' change of attitude towards immigration can easily be explained by the constant EU interest in pursuing the right of free movement of workers, which finds its expression in the way the legislation is drafted despite the changes in the political discourse about immigration. Geddes underlines that free movement of workers and tighter immigration controls are two trends inextricably linked. According to him, 'freer movement for EU citizens has brought with it tighter controls on movement by non-EU citizens'.[213] The fact that friendly provisions concerning third country nationals have been allowed does not mean that third country national immigration is not a source of preoccupation for Member States and EU institutions or that immigration restrictions do not exist[214] but simply that the Legislator has preferred to put them aside when third country nationals are effectively linked to EU citizens exercising their right of free movement. Whilst the numbers of EU workers and now citizens taking advantage of free movement has always been quite small,[215] free movement has always been of crucial importance being one of the four corners of the EU integration process. Since the ambitions of Europe in establishing free movement rights have been and still are great, focusing not just on the elimination of labour restrictions within the Member States but also in making sure that Member States cannot adopt protectionist policies and that EU workers can react easily to a change of economic conditions and move accordingly,[216] the prioritisation of the Legislator of these rights over immigration concerns is then not surprising.

Having said this, it is true that the Legislator has not been completely unaffected by the Member States' immigration concerns, which began after the oil crisis. Hints of this fact can be found in the preparatory works of Directive 2004/38/ EC, where the Council managed to change the original proposal of the Commission by extending from four to five the years necessary to claim permanent residence in the host Member State by EU citizens and their third country national family members. Interestingly this change seems to suggest the Council's reluctance to entrust both EU[217] and third country national immigration fully, although the Council tried to justify this choice for consistency with Directive 2003/109/EC, which grants permanent residence to third country nationals after five years.[218]

However, despite this exception, the overall approach of the EU Legislator towards third country national family members can be considered friendly and

[213] A Geddes, *Immigration and European Integration: Towards a Fortress Europe?* (Manchester, Manchester University Press, 2000) 32.

[214] See the European Agenda on Migration—Legislative Documents, available at ec.europa.eu/dgs/home-affairs/what-we-do/policies/european-agenda-migration/proposal-implementation-package/index_en.htm.

[215] Shaw, above n 108 at 250–51.

[216] Spaventa, above n 109 at 458.

[217] Concerns about EU immigration increased particularly owing to the 2004 enlargement. Interestingly, the 2004/38/EC Directive, which included the provision of permanent residency, was passed precisely in those years.

[218] E Guild, S Peers and J Tomkin, *The EU Citizenship Directive* (Oxford, Oxford University Press, 2014) 178–82. In reality, this consistency argument does not really work because Art 6 Decision 1/80 of the EC–Turkey Association Agreement grants the same advantage of permanent residency after four years to Turkish workers.

aimed at the fulfilment of free movement of workers. This does not mean that all Member States necessarily agreed with this friendly arrangement but rather that, perhaps, the voting system prevented the dissenting voices from being heard.[219] For this reason it is not surprising that some Member States have started to raise their voice by acting outside the EU legislative framework, particularly by not complying with the EU legislation.[220]

In a similar manner to the Legislator, overall the approach of the Court seems to have been characterised more by the concern of promoting free movement rather than preoccupations on third country national immigration. However, unlike what happened with the legislation, in which immigration concerns can rarely be spotted in the wording, from the judgments of the Court the tension between free movement and Member States' anti-immigration feelings transpires more easily. For instance, as far as the issue of granting family residence rights to third country national family members is concerned, it was shown above that in cases such as *Singh*, *Carpenter*, *MRAX*, *Eind* and *Metock* the Court adopted a friendly approach to third country nationals' residence rights by granting them the right to stay in the host country with their EU sponsor for the sake of enhancing free movement and residence rights of the latter. However, the Court, rather adopting the literal reading endorsed by the Legislator as to the right of family members to join their EU sponsor who moved in another Member State (approach that just occurred in the *MRAX* case), preferred to introduce the concept of deterrence to the relationship between free movement rights of EU citizens and the right of residence of family members, most likely in order to take into account Member States' concerns over immigration. As a matter of fact in *Singh*, the Court decided to interpret family residence rights as functional to the exercise of the primary right of free movement by using the 'obstacles to free movement' language to allow Member States to still claim sovereignty over immigration of third country nationals in cases in which the exercise of the EU citizen's right of free movement was not affected at all by the denial of family reunification rights. The same approach was adopted in *Carpenter* and extended to the Treaty right of free movement of services and reapplied in *Eind* and *Metock*, although in a diluted form, as mentioned above. However, the choice of the Court to rely on deterrence was not free of consequences. First of all it created the legal anomaly of *Akrich*, which required the Court to admit that a mistake was made in that case. Moreover, more recently, the use of

[219] States such as the UK, Germany, Austria, the Netherlands and Belgium are often challenging free movement. However, governments of Central and Eastern Europe and the Nordic states plus Italy and France are often defending free movement because of their low birth rate, debt crisis and higher unemployment. See Shaw, above n 107 at 251–52.

[220] Famous are the guidelines issued by the Commission in 2009 on the application of Directive 2004/38/EC in which the Commission complained about the lack of proper transposition by pretty much all the Member States COM(2008) 840 final, point 3 at 3: 'The overall transposition of Directive 2004/38/EC is rather disappointing. Not one Member State has transposed the Directive effectively and correctly in its entirety. Not one Article of the Directive has been transposed effectively and correctly by all Member States.'

deterrence has been reutilised and reread in a strict key in the judgments of *O and B* and *S and G*, as explained above.

It is noteworthy that there are also some areas in which the Court not only acknowledged Member States' fears about immigration in the reasoning but also allowed these fears to determine the outcome of the judgment. For instance, in cases concerning the right of EU workers to keep their family members in the host Member State in cases where he or she ceased to work because of physical incapacity, retirement age or death in the Member State, the Court came out with the *Givane* case in which arguably its strict interpretation of Article 3(2) Regulation 1251/70/EEC was dictated by states' concerns on securitising their borders, in particular of the UK and Germany. Likewise, in cases concerning the right of permanent residence, the Member States' securitisation priorities and fears over the capacity of foreigners to integrate in the host country have been upheld by the Court. As mentioned above, in *Onuekwere* the time spent in prison by the third country national family member of a EU citizen was considered not accruing to the counting of the five years necessary to acquire the right of permanent residence. Finally, also in cases concerning the working status of family members the Court ruled that the third country national family member can be allowed to work just within the Member State in which the EU sponsor resides.

In synthesis, if we had to describe in a few words the approach of the Court over family reunification rights of third country national family members of EU moving citizens we could conclude that, in line with the Legislator, its overall approach definitely bounces more in favour of the promotion of free movement although, more than in the legislation, there is clear evidence of Member States' concerns having shaped the reasoning and, at times, even the outcome of the Court's decisions. It is worth pondering the reasons behind the Court's attitude. Indeed, it may look strange that despite the fact that the fears about third country nationals are shared by many Member States and there is constant concern about their shrinking competence over immigration, the Court decided to run against them and promote openness towards families composed of EU workers and third country national family members. One important factor that may have influenced openness shown towards this kind of family was, as for the Legislator, the continuous promotion at the level of EU institutions of the freedom of movement of workers. Historically, in view of the lack of improvement in European free movement that began to characterise the years following the oil crisis, the EU began to refer to free movement of workers not as a macroeconomic need but more as an individualistic right or, as Lionello Levi Sandri did more boldly, as an embryonic form of European citizenship.[221] The clear disclosure by the EU of its vision of what free movement should have been and yet was not, might indeed have encouraged the Court to prioritise this EU aim in its jurisprudence, above any other competing interests. This was initially evident from the early case law that nothing had

[221] Bulletin of the European Communities vol 1(11) 1968, 6.

to do with family reunification but in which the Court immediately started to turn the EU vision on free movement into reality by interpreting free movement provisions broadly in order to promote mobility.[222] These cases confirmed the crucial role of the Court's jurisprudence for the development of free movement of workers and citizens in Europe over the years. Indeed, in the field of free movement of workers a 'quiet revolution of the Court' occurred not just 'in imposing a compliance regime'[223] with the relevant free movement norms but also interpreting them to turn the EU free movement of persons vision into a reality sooner rather than later, sometimes anticipating the Legislator.[224] As Beck points out in his book 'The Legal Reasoning of the European Court of Justice', this approach is familiar to the Court because its interpretative take over EU law matters has an intrinsic '*communautaire* tendency', due to the *communautaire* flavour[225] and integrationalist scope[226] of the EU legislation that it has to interpret, of which EU

[222] Originally, this move consisted in extending the conditions of free movement outside the original category of workers and providing total equality among European nationals coming from different Member States. The Court particularly focused on the definition of the term 'worker' and insisted that this was a matter for EU law and not national law because if the definition was a matter relegated to national law competence 'it would therefore be possible for each Member State to modify the meaning of the concept of migrant worker and to eliminate at will the protection afforded by the Treaty to certain categories of persons' (Case C-75/63 *Hoeckstra v Bestuur der Bedrijfsvereninging voor Detailhandel en Ambachten* EU:C:1964:19). The Court then continued by extending free movement benefits to other categories that were not originally included in the free movement legislation (Case C-53/81 *Levin v Staatssecretaris van Justitie* EU:C:1982:105; Case C-344/87 *Bettray v Staatssecretaris van Justitie* EU:C:1989:226; Case C-197/86 *Brown v Secretary of State for Scotland* EU:C:1988:323; Case C-139/85 *Kempf v Staatssecretaris van Justitie* EU:C:1986:223; Case C-66/85 *Lawrie-Blum v Land Baden-Württemberg* EU:C:1986:284; Case C-196/87 *Steymann v Staatssecretaris van Justitie* EU:C:1988:475; Case C-48/75 *Procureur du Roi v Royer* EU:C:1976:57; Case C-292/89 *R v Immigration Appeal Tribunal, ex p Antonissen* EU:C:1991:80) and extending Art 7(2) to be read to include social and tax advantages to be applied not just to workers but also to surviving family members of a deceased worker or to any family member that provides an indirect advantage to the worker (Case C-32/75 *Cristini v SNCF* EU:C:1975:120; Case C-63/76 *Inzirillo v Caisse d'Allocations Familiales de l'Arrondissement de Lyon* EU:C:1976:192; Case C-94/84 *ONE v Deak* EU:C:1985:264; Case C-152/82 *Forcheri v Belgium* EU:C:1983:205; Case C-65/81 *Reina v Landeskreditbank Baden-Württemberg* EU:C:1982:6). Moreover, the further legislative steps of the EU Legislator also introduced free movement to categories not directly connected to workers such as students, retired persons and economically inactive persons via the three 'Residency Directives' and, shortly afterwards, inserted the concept of EU citizenship into the Maastricht Treaty. The Court developed a long list of case law that developed the rights of EU citizens living in another Member State, despite the fact of being involved in a job activity (see Case C-85/96 *Maria Martinez Sala v Freistaat Bayern* EU:C:1998:217; Case C-184/99 *Grzelczyk v Centre Public d'Aide Sociale d'Ottignies—Louvain la Neuve* EU:C:2001:458).

[223] JHH Weiler, 'A Quiet Revolution The European Court of Justice and its Interlocutors' (1994) 26 *Comparative Political Studies* 510, 534.

[224] For instance see *MRAX*, owing to which Art 5 Directive 2004/38/EC was inserted, and the actual concept of EU citizenship, which found its roots in some cases of the Court. In particular on the development of the concept of EU citizenship see J Shaw, Citizenship: Contrasting Dynamics at the Interface of Integration and Constitutionalism' in G de Burca and P Craig (eds), *The Evolution of EU Law* (Oxford, Oxford University Press, 2011) 575, 584.

[225] G Beck, *The Legal Reasoning of the European Court of Justice* (Oxford, Hart Publishing, 2013) 318.

[226] On the attempt to achieve integration by the Court see W Mattli and A Slaughter, 'Revisiting the European Court of Justice' (1998) 52 *International Organization* 177.

free movement law is no exception. For this reason, one should not be surprised if the free movement rationale and its openness towards family rights did supersede the numerous immigration concerns of the Member States even in family reunification cases involving EU workers or citizens and third country nationals. Finally, it should also be noted that the Court's decision to give priority to free movement to the detriment of states' interests is no accident because intentionally the Court, over the years, has often willingly managed to escape Member States' control[227] when it thinks that it is fair to do so.

However, as mentioned before, the approach of the Court, more evidently than that adopted by the Legislator, has shown also a tentative attention towards Member States' concerns which, more frequently, has presented itself as a peculiar way to shape the Court's reasoning and, at times, has also shaped the final outcome of the case. It is again Gunnar Beck who suggests that despite the preference of adopting the communitarian approach that gives priority to EU aims such as free movement, the Court is often also very careful not to challenge Member States too much on issues that are particularly sensitive such as immigration,[228] especially when security concerns are at stake. For example, when the number of State interventions in a specific case is high, the Court prefers to stand by the requests of the governments and offer a narrow construction of the relevant provisions.[229] As a matter of fact, several cases on family reunification in which the Court decided to rule strictly have witnessed a high number of Member States that intervened in order to protect their sovereignty like, for example, in *Onuekwere* and the *O and B* and *S and G* cases where, respectively, the UK, Czech, German, Irish, Italian and Polish governments and the Dutch, Belgian, Czech, Danish, German, Estonian, Polish and UK governments submitted observations. Sometimes instead the level of sensitivity of the issue is not triggered by the number of intervening states but simply by the general political debates characterising the time in which the Court is called upon to decide. This may explain why, in the cases of *Givane* and *Akrich*, decided when the fear of immigrants coming from East Europe after the EU enlargement was high, the Court adopted a strict approach.[230]

Overall, it can be concluded that the approach of the Legislator and the CJEU on family reunification cases between EU moving workers or citizens and third country national family members has been particularly open with respect to third country national rights. However, it is evident that immigration concerns towards third country nationals, developed since the oil crisis, have, at times, played their part and influenced in particular the action of the Court. The next chapter will try to assess whether the same level of influence can be found in cases concerning EU static citizens and third country nationals.

[227] KJ Alter, 'Who are the 'Masters of the Treaty'?: European Governments and the European Court of Justice' (1998) 52 *International Organization* 121, 122.

[228] Beck, above n 226 at 351–52.

[229] ibid.

[230] See above the comment on *Akrich*.

4

EU Static Citizens Law Cases

1. INTRODUCTION

THIS CHAPTER FOCUSES on the concept of EU citizenship and on how and to what extent the Court managed to develop it in order to grant family rights notwithstanding Member States' concerns over immigration. The idea of EU citizenship, which at the beginning was considered an empty concept by many scholars, soon after its introduction in the Maastricht Treaty revealed itself to be much more than a simple academic exercise owing to the activity of the Court. Indeed, as far as family rights are concerned, the Court began to use the concept of EU citizenship in order to grant protection to family members of EU citizens that never crossed their state of origin's borders, as will soon be seen. However, the introduction of the concept of EU citizenship and its expansive interpretation adopted by the Court occurred at a time when Member States' concerns over immigration were growing.[1] The aim of this chapter's analysis, like that of the previous chapter, is to look at family reunification cases concerning EU static citizens and third country nationals to try to assess whether the general hostility towards third country national immigration shaped the reasoning of the Court and its application of the concept of EU citizenship.[2] It will be shown that the reasoning of the Court's most recent cases can be better understood if looked at in terms of the interplay between Member States' fears over immigration, driven by increased levels of xenophobia and security concerns as explained in Chapter 2, and the idea of enhancing the EU citizenship status. However, as opposed to what occurred in cases involving EU moving citizens in this strand of case law, overall, the Court has let the aim of enhancing the concept of EU citizenship to be overtaken by Member States' concerns over losing their control on assessing the right of residence of third country national family members of EU static citizens.

This chapter will be divided into seven sections. After this brief introduction, Section 2 will put the concept of EU citizenship and its development into context. Sections 3, 4, 5 and 6 will be dedicated respectively to the *Zambrano* case, to the

[1] The year in which a seminal case on EU citizenship such as *Chen* came out was characterised by the fear of the EU enlargement.

[2] This chapter will focus necessarily just on the case law of the Court because the provisions concerning third country national rights are contained in the secondary free movement legislation and have already been analysed in Chapter 3.

McCarthy case—the first curtailment of *Zambrano*, to the *Dereci* case—the second curtailment of *Zambrano*, and to the post-*Zambrano* cases of *O and S* and *Ymeraga*, *Iida* and *Alokpa*. In this analysis the chapter will explore how much and to what extent Member States' concerns over immigration influenced the outcome of the Court. Finally, Section 7 will be dedicated to some conclusions. It will be shown that, overall, the Court preferred to endorse a strict approach that consisted in prioritising Member States' immigration concerns over the enhancement of the concept of EU citizenship as a source of independent family residence rights, and the reasons why this approach has been endorsed will be suggested.

2. THE DEVELOPMENT OF THE CONCEPT OF EU CITIZENSHIP

The development of the concept of EU citizenship started in 1967 when Walter Hallstein, the first president of the European Commission, in his speech for the 10th anniversary of the signature of the Treaty of Rome, stressed how the achievement of the free movement of workers was a step to be taken in order to allow the blossoming of European integration.[3] The issue of European integration was raised seriously in the debate during the Paris Summit of October 1972.[4] The spirit of the summit was in fact moved not just by the aim of creating an Economic and Monetary Union but also by finding solutions for improving the integration and the social and political face of Europe. This is evidenced by the summit declaration: 'the Member States reaffirm their resolve to base their community development on democracy, freedom of opinion, free movement of men and ideas and participation by the people through their freely elected representatives' and in the opening speech of the President of the French Republic Georges Pompidou: 'Europe, the community of prosperity, must not become a community of inflation. But Europe must not become a community of tradesmen. Europe must be designed and constructed in the service of mankind.'[5]

The willingness to promote integration in Europe also characterised the Paris Summit of December 1974. The task of this second summit was to overcome all the difficulties deriving from a profound recession generated by the oil crisis by giving a new momentum to the process of European unification.[6] Practically, Heads of Government were instructed with the task of verifying 'the possibility of establishing a passport union'[7] and to give to the citizens of the Member States

[3] W Hallstein, 'Halfway to Europe Unity', EU speech held on the occasion of the 10th anniversary of the signature of the Rome Treaty, published in *Die Zeit*, 17 and 24 March 1967, available at the Archive of European Integration University of Pittsburgh aei.pitt.edu/13606/01/S22.pdf.

[4] The Paris Summit of 1972 was called mainly to establish a Monetary Union by 1980. However, the outcome of this summit went far beyond what was originally thought and ended up discussing many other issues such as co-operation and integration.

[5] Bulletin of the European Communities (1972) 5 (11) at 14.

[6] Bulletin of the European Communities (1974) 7(12) at 6, para 1102.

[7] ibid, at 8, para 10.

'special rights as members of the community'.[8] Although there was no definition of these special rights it was argued that 'the linking of the concept of citizens and special rights might even suggest that the will existed to confirm the civil and political character of these special rights'.[9]

It was 1976 when finally Leo Tindemans, the Belgian prime minister at the time, was asked to prepare a report on the overall concept of European Union.[10] Among the various policies he developed, he dedicated the whole of paragraph IV of his report to the 'Citizen's Europe'.[11] Although he did not mention expressly the word European citizenship, he referred to 'Europeans' as people of a unique country. Tindemans believed in fact that, in order for Europe to be close to its citizens, it was necessary 'to adopt a further protection of the rights of the Europeans' and to pursue 'a concrete manifestation of European solidarity by means of external signs discernible in everyday life'.[12]

The Tindemans Report did not have immediate direct consequences on the development of the concept of European citizenship.[13] In the middle of the eighties, the debate on European citizenship restarted under the more committed and more driven motivation of giving to the citizens of Europe a deeper identity and image, within Europe and towards external countries.[14] This trend was made apparent in the Fountainbleau European Council of 1984.[15] On this occasion an Ad Hoc Committee was set up to promote the identity and the image of the Union. The results of this summit were two reports from the Ad Hoc Committee on a People's Europe that took its name from their chairman, Mr Adonnino. The first of these reports was specifically focused on certain matters such as freedom of movement and wider opportunity for workers relating to employment and residence.[16] The second report instead gave a concrete shape to the concept of

[8] ibid, at 8, para 11.

[9] G Van de Berghe, *Political Rights for European Citizens* (Aldershot, Gower Publishing Company Limited, 1982) 32.

[10] Bulletin of the European Communities, Supplement 1/76.

[11] ibid, 11.

[12] ibid, 26.

[13] Although no concrete action was taken immediately after the Tindemans report, the idea of citizenship was still present. In October 1978, in Florence, the Round Table Conference on 'Special Rights and a European Community Civil Rights Charter' organised by the European Parliament with the participation of representatives of the Community Institutions, members of the national parliaments and experts in general, took place. At that time 'nobody wanted a super constitution' but simply a 'transformation from a Community of states to a community of people' (see proceedings of the round table on special rights and a charter of the rights of citizens of the European community and related documents, Florence, 26–28 October 1978, Luxembourg, European Parliament, September 1979) and EU citizenship was considered the adequate instrument to get to that stage.

[14] Mehan argued that the strengthening of the European Union as a political unified entity allowed a 'resuscitation of the idea of citizen as human being'. E Mehan, *Citizenship and the European Community* (London: Sage Publications, 1993) 147.

[15] Bulletin of the European Communities (1984) 6. The Fountainbleau European Council was held on 25–26 June 1984. The conclusions of this Council put a particular emphasis on the necessity to strengthen and promote the identity and the image of the European Community among its citizens and in the world.

[16] Bulletin of the European Communities, Supplement 7/85, at 12–14.

special rights to be associated with the idea of European citizenship (such as the participation of citizens in the political process of the Member States or the need of assistance in case of travelling outside the community).[17]

Simultaneously, some lawyers started to talk about an 'incipient form of European citizenship' looking at the case law of the CJEU. The Court, in fact, in some of its cases, began to interpret the Treaty rights of free movement and non-discrimination with the willingness of extending them also to people that did not belong to the traditional group of economically active persons protected by the EEC Treaty (workers, self-employed and service providers).[18] In *Gravier*,[19] for example, a French national who was studying for a course in strip-cartoon design in Belgium was granted the right not to pay an additional fee for non-Belgians under the now Article 18 TFEU (the right of not being discriminated on the grounds of nationality), although she was not involved in a job activity. Similarly in *Cowan*[20] a British tourist in France was granted compensation for being the victim of a violent crime through the application of Article 18 TFEU despite not being a worker but a recipient of services. Following the CJEU approach, in the nineties secondary legislation regulating the right of residence of the economically inactive was introduced too.[21]

With the fall of the Berlin Wall the development of European citizenship was finally advanced. In the changed geopolitical context, one of the main key concerns of the Dublin Summit of April 1990 was to shape the future political Union by introducing European citizens' rights. One of the questions that the states submitted to the Council was: 'how will the Union include and extend the notion of Community citizenship carrying with it specific rights (human, political, social, the right of complete free movement and residence etc.) for the citizens of Member States by virtue of these states belonging to the Union?'[22] In this backdrop, it was the Spanish Prime Minister Felipe Gonzales that urged the official inclusion of the concept of European citizenship in the European Community Treaty.[23] By the time the Heads of Government reconvened in Dublin, they agreed to call for another Intergovernmental Conference (henceforth IGC) on political union

[17] ibid, 28.

[18] J Shaw, 'Citizenship: Contrasting Dynamics at the Interface of Integration and Constitutionalism' in G de Burca and P Craig (eds), *The Evolution of EU Law* (Oxford, Oxford University Press, 2011) 584.

[19] Case C-293/83 *Gravier v City of Liège* EU:C:1985:69.

[20] Case C-186/87 *Cowan v Le Trésor public* EU:C:1989:47. In this case the Court referred to *Luisi and Carbone* (Cases C-286/82 and C-26/83 *Luisi and Carbone v Ministero del Tesoro* EU:C:1984:35) in which the Court, for the first time, confirmed that the Treaty covers the situation of recipients as well as providers of services.

[21] Council Dir 90/366/EEC on the right of residence of students [1990] OJ L 180/30, replaced by Council Dir 93/96/EEC [1993] OJ L317/59; Council Dir 90/365/EEC on the right of residence for employees and self-employed persons who have ceased their occupational activity [1990] OJ L180/28, and Council Dir 90/364/EEC on a general right of residence [1990] OJ L180/26.

[22] Bulletin of the European Communities 6/90, I Annex I.

[23] M Lister and E Pia, *Citizenship in Contemporary Europe* (Edinburgh, Edinburgh University Press, 2008) 164.

parallel with the one on the EMU.[24] In preparation for the IGC, Spain tried to define the concept of European citizenship in a memorandum called 'Towards a European Citizenship'.[25] The content of this memorandum was based on the idea that the European citizen was not just a privileged foreigner but also a fundamental actor in the life of the European institutions. It underlined how the European citizen had to be conceived as a subject with duties and rights stemming not just from the Member States but also from the Community.[26]

The following European Council held in Rome in October 1990 unfolded this statement by listing a number of defined rights: right to participate in the election of the European Parliament and local elections, freedom of movement irrespective of economic activity, protection of citizens outside the EU border and right to petition the Ombudsman.[27] The result of the European Council of Rome was adopted by the Treaty of Maastricht for the first time.[28] Part II of the Maastricht Treaty was completely dedicated to the citizenship of the Union. Article 8(1) stated that 'every person holding the nationality of a Member State shall be a citizen of the Union. Citizenship of the Union shall complement and not replace national citizenship', and Article 8(2) that 'Citizens of the Union shall enjoy the rights conferred by this Treaty and shall be subject to the duties imposed thereby'. The other paragraphs of Article 8 were related to the right to freedom of movement of European citizens (art 8a), who have the right to move and reside freely within the territory of the Member States, the right to vote in municipal elections and in the elections of the European Parliament (art 8b), protection of the diplomatic and consular authorities of any other Member State in any territory of third countries (art 8c), and the right to petition the European Parliament and the Ombudsman (art 8d). Nothing more was added in the Amsterdam Treaty whereas the Charter of Fundamental Rights of the European Union, proclaimed at Nice in 2000, included a full chapter (Chapter V) totally dedicated to citizens' rights. This chapter, however, just added the rights of good administration and the right of access to documents (arts 41 and 42) and basically ended up replicating the provisions already mentioned in the previous Treaties. Finally, in December 2009, the Lisbon Treaty entered into force. Although the main structure of the Articles dedicated to European citizenship remained more or less the same, two interesting modifications are noteworthy. First of all, the idea that EU citizenship should complement

[24] ibid.

[25] Towards a European Citizenship, Europe Documents No 1653 October 1990. For a detailed explanation of the content of the memo see J Handoll, *Free Movement of Persons in the EU* (New York, Wiley, 1995) 175–276.

[26] ibid.

[27] Rome European Council, 27–28 October 1990. The Rome Council, however, failed to identify duties of European citizens properly. This is a deficit that can still be noticed today in the provisions dedicated to EU citizenship.

[28] The Maastricht Treaty is the first treaty that mentioned explicitly the concept of EU citizenship. The Single European Act, in 1986, very timidly addressed in its preamble the issue of political rights of nationals of Member States, without, however, expressly referring to European citizenship.

national citizenship was modified with Lisbon. Article 20(1) TFEU in fact states that 'Citizenship of the Union shall be additional to and not replace national citizenship'. Finally, the Lisbon Treaty makes clear that the rights listed in the Treaty are not an exhaustive group, but are rights 'inter alia'.[29]

The content of Maastricht on citizenship testified how the Union's aim was to move beyond its economic and market oriented views towards a deeper idea of integration. This point was highlighted as well in the Report from the Commission on citizenship of the Union, which stressed how 'the introduction of these new provisions underscores the fact that the Treaty of Rome is not concerned solely with economic matters, as is also plainly demonstrated by the change of name of the EEC to the EC'.[30] By introducing the concept of EU citizenship the Legislator therefore 'created a direct political link between the citizens of the Member States and the European Union … with the aim of fostering a sense of identity with the Union'.[31]

The concept of EU citizenship, far from being an empty shell as some scholars suggested, was immediately the object of further interpretation by the CJEU. The Court interpreted the new concept of EU citizenship according to what is called new constitutionalism, a theory that engages with the question of what it means to be a European citizen regardless of the classic EU rules of supremacy, direct effect, transnationalism and freedom of movement.[32] Indeed, if in free movement cases the Court still paired the concept of EU citizenship to free movement, in cases concerning static citizens the Court stressed the intrinsic value of the concept of EU citizenship as a source of self-standing rights, regardless of the exercise of the right of free movement.

The initial challenges for the Court in these directions concerned the issue of wholly internal situations and raising the problem of reverse discrimination, according to which a static home national may be treated less favourably than someone from another Member State who could invoke EU law in similar factual circumstances. The CJEU initially ruled[33] that the concept of EU citizenship was not intended to extend the scope *ratione materiae* of the Treaty provisions also to internal situations that had no link with community law. Hence, situations of discrimination towards nationals of the Member State had to be dealt with necessarily by the national legislation.[34] Already from this early stage, however, not everybody shared the views of the Court. In his opinion in the *Shingara* case,[35] AG Ruiz-Jarabo

[29] Art 20(2) TFEU.

[30] COM (93) 702 final.

[31] ibid.

[32] Above n 18 at 585.

[33] Case C-299/95 *Kremzov v Austrian State* EU:C:1997:254 and Joined Cases C-64/96 and C-65/96 *Uecker and Jacquet v Land Nordrhein-Westfalen* EU:C:1997:285.

[34] P Craig and G de Burca, *EU Law: Text, Cases and Materials* (Oxford, Oxford University Press, 2011) 829. See also A Tryfonidou, *Reverse Discrimination in EU Law* (The Hague, Kluwer Law International, 2009) 142.

[35] Joined Cases C-65/95 and C-111/95 *The Queen v Secretary of State for the Home Department ex parte Shingara and Radiom* EU:C:1997:300.

Colomer seemed to suggest that the drafters of the Maastricht Treaty were seriously trying to create a meaningful citizenship status.[36] He stated in fact that 'the creation of Citizenship of the Union, with the corollary … of freedom of movement for citizens throughout the territory of the Member States, represents a considerable qualitative step forward that … separates that freedom (freedom of movement) from its functional or instrumental elements (the link with an economic activity or attainment of the internal market) and raises it to the level of a genuinely independent right inherent in the political status of the citizens of the Union'.[37]

The bold approach of AG Colomer was initially isolated.[38] Nevertheless, some years later, the Court seemed to be more willing to rule favourably even in cases in which applicants did not exercise their free movement rights. In *Garcia Avello*[39] and *Chen*,[40] for example, 'the treaty provisions on citizenship conferred rights on the applicants in a situation where they had never left the territory of the Member State other than that of the host state'.[41] The *Garcia Avello* case concerned a dispute between Mr Avello and the Belgian state regarding the refusal of the latter to grant his children, of Belgian and Spanish nationality, the double surname as in the Spanish tradition. The Court held that, in principle, this was a matter that fell within the competence of the Member States. However, the simple fact that the children had dual nationality and were residing in Belgium enabled them, without necessarily having to physically move to another Member State, to be granted protection under Article 18 TFEU on non-discrimination. The *Chen* case, already mentioned in the previous chapter, found its roots in *Garcia Avello*. Also in this case the Court, in answering the objection raised by the English and Irish governments, which upheld how the facts of the case could be described as purely internal for the simple reason that the young daughter never physically moved from one state to the other, stated that the link with EU law could be established even when a person having nationality of a Member State resided in another Member State without having necessarily exercised his right to free of movement.[42]

In both cases the Court decided that, in order to be able to be granted the more favourable protection under the EU citizenship status, it was not necessary to have exercised the right to move to another Member State but the simple fictional movement through mismatching of nationalities was enough to make the situation fall under EU competence. In more recent years, however, the Court pushed itself forward considerably and began to offer protection through the use of

[36] Tryfonidou, above n 34 at 143.

[37] Opinion in Joined Cases C-65/95 and C-111/95 *Shingara and Radiom* EU:C:1997:300, para 34.

[38] Tryfonidou, above n 34 at 143–44.

[39] Case C-148/02 *Garcia Avello v Belgian State* EU:C:2003:539. Before this case the *Micheletti* case was also decided (Case C-369/90 *Mario Vicente Micheletti a.o. v Delegación del gobierno en Cantabria* EU:C:1992:295). Also in this case the Court granted an Italo-Argentinian the right to reside in Spain owing to his Italian citizenship without having ever resided in Italy.

[40] Case C-200/02 *Zhu and Chen v Secretary of State for the Home Department* EU:C:2004:639.

[41] Craig and de Burca, above n 34 at 830.

[42] *Chen* judgment, para 19 (taken directly from the *Garcia Avello* judgment).

Article 20 TFEU even despite the presence of the element of fictional movement. The *Rottman* case[43] found its grounds in an application made by a German national against the German administrative authorities which deprived him of his German nationality because they found out that the German citizenship had been acquired in a procedure vitiated by fraud. The decision of the German authorities to withdraw his German nationality, given that he had already lost his Austrian nationality of origin once he became a German citizen, would have had rendered him stateless and deprived him of his status as a Union citizen and of the rights attached to that status. While AG Maduro tried to encompass the situation within the boundaries of EU competences using the logic of freedom of movement,[44] the Court simply stated that the situation of an EU citizen who is faced with a decision withdrawing his naturalisation and with the possibility of losing the status conferred by Article 20 TFEU and attached rights 'falls, by reason of its nature and its consequences, within the ambit of European Union law'.[45]

In conclusion, on top of the cases involving moving EU citizens, the Court's activity also focused on developing the concept of EU citizenship regardless of its connection with the right of free movement. Through this process a new conception of EU citizenship as a source of self-stemming rights began to develop. In the next sections it will be seen whether this new concept of citizenship managed to grant protection to third country national family members.

3. THE FINAL DETACHMENT OF THE CONCEPT OF EU CITIZENSHIP FROM THE RIGHT OF FREE MOVEMENT: *ZAMBRANO*[46]

As seen in the previous chapter, the outcome of *Metock* was welcomed by many,[47] quoted in later cases[48] and will hopefully develop even further in the

[43] Case C-135/08 *Janko Rottmann v Freistaat Bayern* EU:C:2010:104.

[44] In the view of AG Maduro the applicant was born Austrian and had only acquired German nationality as a result of availing of his free movement rights and settling in that Member State. In other words a border had been crossed and movement had occurred, albeit in the past. See para 13: 'The fact nevertheless remains that the exercise by Mr Rottmann of his right, as a citizen of the Union, to move and reside in another Member State had an impact on the change in his civil status: it was because he transferred his residence to Germany that he had been able to satisfy the conditions for acquiring German nationality, namely, lawful habitual residence within that country's territory. The existence of such a link is sufficient for acceptance of a link with Community law'.

[45] *Rottman* judgment, para 42.

[46] Case C-34/09 *Gerardo Ruiz Zambrano v Office national de l'emploi* (ONEm) EU:C:2011:124.

[47] The approach of the Court in *Metock* was highly praised within the academic community. Professor Peers considered *Metock* as a highly welcomed judgment since it was able to restore clarity after the uncertainties introduced by *Akrich* and for its practical implications on national legislation and proceedings. On this point see S Peers, 'Free movement, Immigration Control and Constitutional Conflict' (2009) 5 *European Constitutional Law Review* 173, 191–96. See also N Cambien, 'Case C-127/08, Blaise Baheten Metock and Others v Minister for Justice, Equality and Law Reform' (2008) 15 *Columbia Journal of European Law* 321, 334 and C Costello, 'Metock: Free Movement and Normal Family Life in the Union' (2009) 46 *Common Market Law Review* 587.

[48] In some cases *Metock* constituted the line of reasoning and in some others it was just quoted. In *Sahin* (Case C-551/07 *Sahin v Bundesminister für Inneres* EU:C:2008:755), the outcome of *Metock*

future.[49] Nevertheless *Metock* did not have a general application to all European citizens. Family rights in *Metock* were in fact tied to the cross-border movement of EU citizens: indeed the case reflects the transnational conception of European citizenship that is enshrined in Directive 2004/38/EC. Indeed, while in 2001 the CJEU itself proclaimed that 'Union citizenship is destined to be the fundamental status of nationals of the Member States, enabling those who find themselves in the same situation to enjoy the same treatment in law irrespective of their nationality, subject to such exceptions as are expressly provided for',[50] Directive 2004/38/EC emphasised the transnational/cross-border dimension of European citizenship.[51] It was only with *Zambrano* that the Court, relying directly on Article 20 TFEU, openly detached the protection granted to EU citizens and their third country national family members from the exercise of the right of free movement.

For the purpose of clarity, in order to understand the significant change that occurred in *Zambrano*, it is necessary to recall briefly the previously mentioned *Chen* case. One may remember that the Court in *Chen* was concerned with finding a link with EU law and, in the end it found it by relying on the current Article 21 TFEU, which protects the right to move and reside. Although no objective physical movement from one Member State to the other occurred,[52] a fictional cross-border element given by the mismatching of nationalities (the young daughter was an Irish national living on UK territory) was still present. It is exactly here that the main difference with *Zambrano* lies. As will be soon pointed out the Court

was used to allow a third country national pursuing asylum in Austria to derive her right of residence within the territory of the state after marrying a German national residing there. In *Ibrahim* (Case C-310/08 *London Borough of Harrow v Nimco Hassan Ibrahim and Secretary of State for the Home Department* EU:C:2010:80) and *Teixeira* (Case C-480/08 *Maria Teixeira v London Borough of Lambeth and Secretary of State for the Home Department* EU:C:2010:83), while granting under Art 12 of Reg 1612/68/EEC the right of residence in the host Member State of a child in education and therefore the right of the parents to reside, the CJEU used *Metock* to underline the fact that Dir 2004/38/EC did not repeal Art 12 Reg 1612/68/EEC because the scope of the Directive is to simplify and strengthen the right of residence (for a deeper account of this case see H Wray, 'Teixeira and Ibrahim: Looking back, looking forward or inward?' (2011) 2 *FMW: Online journal on free movement of workers in the European Union* 26). In *Chakroun* (Case C-578/08 *Chakroun v Minister van Buitenlandse Zaken* EU:C:2010:117) *Metock* was applied in a case involving Dir 2003/86/EC on the right of family reunification in order to forbid the discretion of Member States in deciding whether or not to introduce a distinction based on the time of marriage of the spouse. Finally in *McCarthy* (Case C-434/09 *Shirley McCarthy v Secretary of State for the Home Department* EU:C:2011:277) the Court used the reasoning of *Metock* on the applicability of Dir 2004/38/EC and on the fact that it meant to enhance freedom of movement and residence of Union citizens in order to forbid family reunification rights to Mrs McCarthy, who wanted to reunite with her Jamaican husband despite the fact that she had never moved to another Member State. This case will be analysed later in this chapter.

[49] See DA Arcarazo, 'Immigration in the European Union: Family Reunification after the Metock Case' (2009) 9 *University College Dublin Law Review* 64. The author wishes *Metock* to be applied also to cases involving family reunification just between third country nationals.

[50] Case C-184/99 *Grzelczyk v Centre Public d'Aide Sociale d'Ottignies—Louvain la Neuve* EU:C:2001:458.

[51] Costello, above n 47 at 616–17.

[52] See A Tryfonidou, 'Chen: Further Cracks in the Great Wall of the European Union' (2005) 11 *European Public Law* 527, 539.

in *Zambrano*, owing in particular to the *Rottman* case, which was decided some years after *Chen*, managed to untie the knot that still kept the concept of European citizenship attached to the idea of free movement by relying on the application of Article 20 TFEU.[53]

In *Zambrano*, the CJEU was faced with a situation involving the non-EU parents of two EU-citizen children, born and resident in Belgium and who had never left that Member State. Unlike the circumstances of *Chen*, in *Zambrano* the nationality matched the country of residence (the children involved were the son and daughter of Colombian nationals, were born in Belgium and acquired Belgian nationality). The question referred to in this case by the parents was significant: can third country national EU family members enjoy the right of residence within the territory of a Member State due to their blood link to European citizens even though the latter never exercised their right to move to another Member State? Eight Member States intervened[54] in the case and argued that the situation at stake had to be labelled as wholly internal so that EU law on citizenship was not applicable. Both AG Sharpston and the Court disagreed.

AG Sharpston suggested two feasible options to the Court.[55] In the first she challenged the legitimacy of the wholly internal rule in general, and in particular the circumstances at stake. She started by pointing out that, although in many citizenship cases a clearly identifiable cross-border element could be found,[56] there were some other cases in which the 'element of true movement is either barely discernible or frankly not existent'.[57] In the light of this backdrop, she questioned the real meaning of the core right of European citizenship, that is the 'right to move and reside'.[58] Reading the previous *Rottman* and *Chen* cases in conjunction, AG Sharpston concluded that European citizenship at Articles 20 and 21 TFEU conferred a right to reside, which was independent of the right to move.[59] The facts of *Zambrano* could not therefore constitute a purely internal situation, even though the two young Zambranos did not make use of their right to free movement.[60] The young Zambranos were citizens of the Union and, therefore, entitled to reside anywhere within the boundaries of the Union. However, given that the young Zambranos could not exercise their right of residence without the support of their parents, due to their young age, the refusal to grant a derivative right of

[53] S Lorenzon, 'Cittadinanza Europea e Principio di attribuzione delle competenze: 'integratione Europea alla prova del test di proporzionalita', in M Cartabia (ed), Dieci Casi Sui diricti in Europa: uno strumento didattico (Bdogna, ll mulino publishers, 2011) 176.

[54] Austria, Belgium, Denmark, Germany, Greece, Ireland, the Netherlands and Poland.

[55] AG Sharpston advanced also a third option in case the first two were not accepted. She foresaw that the solution of the case could have been given by the application of fundamental rights in subjects covered by unique or shared competence of the Community, even in cases in which that competence was not yet applied (para 163).

[56] *Zambrano* opinion, paras 75–76.

[57] ibid, para 77. At paras 78–79 she also gave some examples, such as *Garcia Avello*, *Chen* and *Rottman*.

[58] ibid, para 80.

[59] ibid, paras 94–96.

[60] ibid, para 97.

residence to Mr Zambrano would constitute an interference with their right of residence in their national state as Union citizens.[61]

With the second option she challenged the legitimacy of reverse discrimination. She started by defining the concept of reverse discrimination, which occurs when 'static factors of production will be left in a worse position than their mobile counterparts',[62] and wondered whether in the context of citizenship of the Union the application of reverse discrimination was an acceptable result.[63] After having considered some cases including *Carpenter*, *Chen* and *Metock* she concluded that all these cases offered a broad interpretation of Article 21 TFEU but ended up creating legal uncertainty.[64] Hence she proposed avoiding the temptation of stretching Article 21 TFEU in order to cover the situations of those that did not exercise freedom of movement[65] and to start interpreting Article 18 TFEU 'as prohibiting the reverse discrimination caused by the interaction between Article 21 TFEU and national law that entails a violation of a fundamental right protected under EU law where at least equivalent protection is not available under national law'.[66]

The Court dismissed both of AG Sharpston's reconstructions.[67] The reasoning of the Court focused solely on Article 20 TFEU. The Court, by quoting *Rottman*, introduced the new test of the 'genuine enjoyment of the substance of the citizenship rights' by stating that 'Article 20 TFEU precludes national measures which have the effect of depriving citizens of the Union of the genuine enjoyment of the substance of the rights conferred by virtue of their status as citizens of the Union'.[68] It then concluded that the deportation of Mr Zambrano would have had as a consequence the deprivation of the substance of the rights[69] conferred to the children by virtue of the citizenship of the Union because, due to their young age,

[61] ibid, para 102. AG Sharpston referred also to the concept of proportionality (paras 109–22).

[62] ibid, para 133.

[63] ibid, para 134.

[64] ibid, para 141.

[65] ibid, para 143.

[66] ibid, para 144. However, she underlined that Art 18 TFEU had to be used only under three cumulative conditions: 1) the claimant would have to be a citizen of the EU, resident in his Member State of nationality who had not exercised free movement rights under TFEU but whose situation was comparable to that of the other citizens of the Union in the same Member State who were able to invoke rights under Art 21 TFEU; 2) a violation of a fundamental right under EU law had occurred; 3) Art 18 would be only a subsidiary remedy if there were no adequate forms of protection (see paras 146–48).

[67] It has been pointed out how the reasoning of the Court is particularly short compared with the very well analysed opinion of Sharpston. On this point see E Guild, 'The Court of Justice of the European Union and Citizens of the Union: A Revolution Underway? The Zambrano judgment of 8 March 2011' EUDO comment 2011 available at eudo-citizenship.eu/citizenship-news/453-the-court-of-justice-of-the-european-union-and-citizens-of-the-union-a-revolution-underway-the-zambrano-judgment-of-8-march-2011; see also N Nic Shuibhne, 'Seven questions for seven paragraphs' (2011) 36 *European Law Review* 161.

[68] *Zambrano* judgment, paras 40–42.

[69] Some scholars showed perplexity in decrypting the real meaning of the phraseology 'substance of rights' used by the Court. Among others, see Nic Shuibhne, above n 67 at 161–62; V Eijken and S De Vries, 'A new route into the promised land? Being a European citizen after Ruiz Zambrano' (2011) 36 *European Law Review* 704, 713.

they should have been forced to follow their family and, therefore, to leave the Union.[70]

Suggesting the reasons why the Court decided to rely on Article 20 TFEU alone, rather than holding on to the same line of reasoning as *Chen* and extending Article 21 also to mere situations of pure residence, might sound a bit speculative. However, without attempting a definitive answer, some interesting considerations can be made. It is worth noting that also in this pronouncement the Court had to deal with the concerns of the Member States over third-country national immigration. The Court indicated Member States' concerns at recital 37, where it pointed out the content of their submissions:[71] 'all governments which submitted observations to the Court and the European Commission argue that a situation such as that of Mr Ruiz Zambrano's second and third children, where those children reside in the Member State of which they are nationals and have never left the territory of that Member State, does not come within the situations envisaged by the freedoms of movement and residence guaranteed under European Union law. Therefore, the provisions of European Union law referred to by the national court are not applicable to the dispute in the main proceedings.' These words show the Member States' intention to protect their sovereignty over immigration from possible friendly interpretations on family rights pursued by the CJEU. Following the first solution proposed by AG Sharpston to recognise an independent right of residence, detached from the right movement, through a combined interpretation of Articles 20 and 21 TFEU would have probably put an end to wholly internal situations and, therefore, shrunk further the area of Member States' sovereignty over immigration. It is perhaps for this reason that the Court decided not to go down this line but to create a sort of exception[72] to the wholly internal rule. As in *Rottman*, also in *Zambrano* purely internal circumstances can be encompassed within the umbrella of EU law[73] when the threat to the status of European citizenship is too high to leave the situation outside the protection of EU law:[74] in *Rottman* the risk was to lose the European citizenship status, in *Zambrano* the risk was to lose the effective enjoyment of the substance of citizenship rights. In other words, since in this case the substance of citizenship rights was in jeopardy, a purely internal situation could become exceptionally encompassed within the protection of EU law

[70] *Zambrano* judgment, paras 41–44.

[71] Belgium, Denmark, Germany, Ireland, Greece, the Netherlands, Austria and Poland made submissions to the CJEU.

[72] Many scholars defined *Zambrano* as an exception to the principle of the wholly internal rule. Among others see N Nic Shuibhne, 'Case Law: (Some) Of The Kids Are All Right' (2012) 49 *Common Market Law Review* 349, 365; K Hailbronner and D Thym, 'Case C-34/09, Gerardo Ruiz Zambrano v Office national de l'emploi (ONEM)' (2011) 48 *Common Market Law Review* 48 1253, 1260–62.

[73] Since none of the children exercised the treaty right to move and reside in a Member State other than the one of which they were nationals it was crucial for the Court to determine whether a connecting factor, apart from the free movement one, could be established. On this point see Nic Shuibhne, above n 72 at 365.

[74] A Hinarejos, 'Citizenship of the EU: clarifying genuine enjoyment of the substance of citizenship rights' (2012) 71 *Cambridge Law Journal* 279, 280.

owing to the application of Article 20 TFEU which, alone, could grant the right of residence to the EU citizens and to their third country national family members. To sum up, the more limited approach of the Court in comparison to the first solution proposed by Sharpston was probably endorsed in order to respect Member States' concerns over immigration.[75] The choice of the Court to create an exception to the wholly internal rule indeed does not turn the status of EU citizenship into an automatic source of residence rights for third country national family members but Member States' sovereignty still remains protected in all the situations that do not clearly fall within the *Zambrano* exception.

Despite the more limited Court's reading compared to the approach proposed by Sharpston it is worth noting that the decision of the Court somehow managed also to push forward the idea of European citizenship as a source of self-stemming rights and, in this case in particular, as a source of independent family residence rights. In her opinion AG Sharpston openly asked: '[I]s Union citizenship merely the non-economic version of the same generic kind of free movement rights as have long existed for the economically active and for persons of independent means? Or does it mean something more radical: true citizenship, carrying with it a uniform set of rights and obligations, in a Union under the rule of law in which respect for fundamental rights must necessarily play an integral part?'[76] In *Zambrano* the pendulum seems to have swung more toward the second position. As a matter of fact the right of residence of the third country national family member is granted as an ancillary right linked to the status of European citizenship, when the former right is functional to the scope of preserving the substance of citizenship's rights.[77] In *Zambrano* an ancillary relationship between family residence rights and the enjoyment of the substance of the rights of EU citizenship existed because the EU children were dependent on the third country national family member and, therefore, they could have never enjoyed their status of EU citizens without the presence of their father within the Belgian territory.[78] The dependency relationship, applied together with the enjoyment of the substance of citizens' rights

[75] Since *Zambrano* Belgium has attempted to change its national legislation with regard to EU static citizens. A legislative proposal of 2012 introduced more burdensome rights for static nationals when compared to other Union citizens, but made an exception for minor children and their parents. On this point see N Cambien, 'Union Citizenship and Immigration: Rethinking the Classics?' (2012) 5 *European Journal of Legal Studies* 10, 23.

[76] *Zambrano* opinion, para 3.

[77] For the sake of clarity it is worth pointing out that the rights granted to the third country national family members in *Chen* and *Zambrano* were slightly different. In the case of *Chen*, the EU law granted the child's third country national caregiver the derivative right to reside in the host Member State as long as the former was covered by sickness insurance and both the child and the third country national parent had sufficient resources not to become a burden on the Member State. In *Zambrano*, however, the Court granted the father of two European children of the same nationality of the state of application the right of residence in the Member State as the refusal would have forced the children to leave the territory of the European Union. For the same reason the father was also granted a work permit because, without it, the risk would have been the lack of sufficient resources for himself and the family (*Zambrano* judgment, para 44). On these two different paths see Eijken and De Vries, above n 69 at 714.

[78] *Zambrano* judgment, para 43.

test, turned the concept of EU citizenship, without free movement being involved, into the source from which protection of the family unit stems.[79]

In conclusion, it seems the reasoning adopted by the Court in *Zambrano* was shaped around the pursuit of citizenship rights of static citizens, although highly influenced and, in a way, limited by Member States' concerns over losing their sovereignty over immigration. Overall, the outcome of this judgment struck a balance in favour of EU citizenship's rights rather than immigration concerns. The precedent of *Zambrano* could have pushed the boundaries of the Member States' national immigration laws in new ways.[80] However, only the case of *CS*[81] ended up upholding the reasoning of *Zambrano*. The case concerned a Moroccan citizen who was convicted of criminal offences in the UK and issued an expulsion order. She argued that the UK should not have expelled her since she was the primary carer of her son, a British citizen of five years of age. The Court, despite leaving the final assessment to the national court, specified at paragraph 32 of the judgment, in the light of *Zambrano*, that the expulsion of the child's mother, who was his primary carer, could result in a restriction of the rights conferred by the status of Union citizenship. As can be noted, the Court applied the *Zambrano* exception again only in a case involving a minor and only because he did not have any other option other than following his third country national carer. Indeed, as will soon be seen, the activity of the Court over the years has mainly focused on trying to narrow down *Zambrano* and its future implications as much as possible.

4. THE FIRST *ZAMBRANO* CURTAILMENT: *McCARTHY*[82]

Zambrano was welcomed by many scholars thanks to the solution that was proposed to the factual circumstances of the case. Some, however, hoped that one of the issues that the Court left unanswered, that is whether or not the new test should be limited to the simple parent–child physical dependency relationship,[83] might lead to a more extensive application in future judgments and put an end to the wholly internal rule. The Court managed to clarify its position in the following cases of *McCarthy* and *Dereci*. These two cases ended up curtailing the scope of *Zambrano* and did not put an end to the wholly internal rule. This section of

[79] C Barnard, 'Citizenship of the Union and the Area of Justice: (Almost) the Court's Moment of Glory' in A Rosas, E Levits and Y Bot (eds), *The Court of Justice and the Construction of Europe: Analyses and Perspectives on Sixty Years of Case Law* (New York, Springer, 2012) 510–11.

[80] J Shaw, 'Has the European Court of Justice Challenged Member State Sovereignty in Nationality Law?' (2011) 62 EUI working papers, available at eudo-citizenship.eu/citizenship-forum/254-has-the-european-court-of-justice-challenged-member-state-sovereignty-in-nationality-law>, 38.

[81] Case C-304/14 *Secretary of State for the Home Department v CS* EU:C:2016:674.

[82] Case C-434/09 *McCarthy v Secretary of State for the Home Department* EU:C:2011:277.

[83] A Lansbergen and N Miller, 'European citizenship rights in internal situations: an ambiguous revolution? Decision of 8 March 2011, Case C-34/09 Gerardo Ruiz Zambrano v Office national de l'emploi (ONEM)' (2011) 7 *European Constitutional Law Review* 287, 296.

the chapter will analyse the approach of the Court in the first *Zambrano* curtailing case of *McCarthy*.

Shirley McCarthy was a British national who was born and had always resided in the United Kingdom. She also held Irish nationality. The case stemmed from a refusal by the Secretary of State for the Home Department to issue a residence permit to her on the basis of EU law as an Irish national residing in the UK. That refusal was grounded on the basis that she was not a qualified person (a worker, self-employed person or self-sufficient person). The decision of applying for a residence permit from her home state on the basis of EU law was taken not because of doubts about her own entitlement to live in the UK but because her husband, George McCarthy, was a Jamaican national who was not entitled to live there. Mrs McCarthy was therefore hoping to be granted a residence permit in the UK through EU citizenship so that her husband would gain the automatically derived right to reside with her.

On the first question regarding the application of Article 3(1) Directive 2004/38/EC to Mrs McCarthy AG Kokott stated that this provision and therefore the entire Directive could not apply, given that the Union citizen had never moved from her state of origin.[84] She continued by stating that this right could not be derived from primary law either and, in particular, from Article 21 TFEU, given the fact that in her view this primary law provision does not protect the right of residence of Union citizens vis-à-vis the Member States of which they are nationals.[85] AG Kokott eventually wondered whether dual nationality instead could be the link to EU law on which to rely in order to obtain family reunification,[86] recalling the decision in *Garcia Avello.* Looking at the circumstances of the case she concluded that no discrimination arose from the dual nationality of a Union citizen in Mrs McCarthy's position.[87] Finally, addressing the second question on whether Mrs McCarthy resided legally within the host Member State for the purpose of Article 16 of Directive 2004/38/EC in circumstances where she was unable to satisfy the self-sufficiency requirements, she stated that allowing Mrs McCarthy to establish permanent residence in the UK as an Irish citizen without requiring to meet the conditions of movement and self-sufficiency 'would ultimately result in cherry picking which does not accord with the spirit and purpose of the provisions of EU law on free movement and the right of residence'.[88] AG Kokott concluded that Mrs McCarthy could not rely on EU law at all and that, therefore, the situation had to be considered as wholly internal.

The Court, while reaching the same decision, differentiated itself from AG Kokott's reasoning. The Court, as well as AG Kokott, did not consider that

[84] *McCarthy* opinion, para 30.

[85] ibid, para 31. Note that this position is exactly the opposite of that supported by AG Sharpston in her first solution offered in the *Zambrano* case.

[86] ibid, para 32.

[87] ibid, paras 37–38.

[88] ibid, para 56.

Article 3(1) of Directive 2004/38/EC could bring the situation of a citizen who never moved to another Member State within the scope of EU law, irrespective of that citizen's dual nationality.[89] However, unlike AG Kokott, the Court reformulated the second question and asked instead whether the rights of Mrs McCarthy could derive from Article 21 TFEU even though she never exercised her right of movement.[90] The Court started by stating that the situation of a Union citizen that 'has made no use of the right of freedom of movement cannot, for that reason alone, be assimilated to a purely internal situation'.[91] In order to support this statement the Court recalled the previous *Zambrano* case, which not only underlined that the concept of EU citizenship was destined to become the fundamental status of the nationals of the Member States but also pointed out 'that national measures which have the effect of depriving Union citizens of the genuine enjoyment of the substance of the rights conferred by virtue of that status' have to be dismissed.[92] The Court then considered Article 21 TFEU as a substantive core right encompassed within the status of European citizenship. As a matter of fact it stated that as Mrs McCarthy enjoyed the status of a Union citizen under Article 20(1) TFEU she 'may therefore rely on the rights pertaining to that status', even against her Member State of origin, 'in particular the right conferred by Article 21 TFEU to move and reside freely within the territory of the Member States'.[93] Nevertheless, in the circumstances at stake, the Court found that nothing indicated that the national measure at issue in the main proceedings had the effect of depriving Mrs McCarthy of the genuine enjoyment of the substance of her rights or hindering her right to move and reside freely within the EU.[94] The Court concluded saying that the national measure at stake, unlike *Zambrano*, did not have the effect of obliging Mrs McCarthy to leave the territory of the European Union.[95]

Comparing *McCarthy* to *Zambrano* one can note that the Court ended up curtailing the latter's scope. As a matter of fact the Court in *McCarthy*, on the one hand, confirmed the principle created in *Zambrano* by applying it but, at the same time, 'stripped it out' by finding that there was no deprivation of the genuine enjoyment of the rights attached to EU citizenship in the circumstances at stake.[96] This conclusion was delivered without real consistency with the previous

[89] *McCarthy* judgment, paras 31–43.

[90] ibid, para 44. Note that, unlike *Zambrano*, the Court formulated its discussion under Art 21 and not Art 20. Art 21, in this case, was meant to protect the potential right of free movement of Mrs McCarthy that, in the view of the applicant, could be hindered in the event that her husband had to be sent back to Jamaica.

[91] ibid, para 46.

[92] ibid, para 47.

[93] ibid, para 48.

[94] ibid, para 49.

[95] ibid, para 50. The Court, in order to support its argument, contrasted it with the previous two cases of *Garcia Avello* and *Grunkin and Paul*. It stated that in both cases the serious inconvenience that stemmed from the dual nationality situation was liable to constitute an obstacle to free movement. This was not the case in *McCarthy*. On this point see Nic Shuibhne, above n 72 at 358.

[96] Lansbergen and Miller, above n 83 at 298–99. Some argued that the argument over the unconditional right to reside should have been faced referring also to the principles of international law.

Zambrano case. As a matter of fact in *McCarthy* the Court relied on international law in order to bolster the fact that the national measure would not force Mrs McCarthy to leave the territory of the Union but this reasoning was not endorsed in *Zambrano*.[97] In the light of the factual circumstances of these two cases it is difficult to understand why the Court reserved to them such different treatment. For instance, in the last part of the reasoning where the differences between *Garcia Avello* and *Zambrano*, on the one hand, and *McCarthy* on the other were underlined,[98] the Court was not capable of proposing a convincing explanation of the reasons why the national measure provoked a serious inconvenience to free movement for the Union citizens concerned in *Garcia Avello* and *Zambrano* and did not create such inconvenience for the enjoyment of the substance of citizenship rights in *McCarthy*.[99] As Nic Shuibhne underlined, the fact that Mrs McCarthy might have had to be forced to live in the UK without her husband, move to another Member State in order to invoke family reunification rights according to the more favourable EU free movement legislation or leave the territory of the Union to go to Jamaica are all situations in which the substance of citizenship rights could have been violated.[100]

The reasons that may have pushed the Court to engage in this U-turn can be read between the lines of this judgment. Although neither in the judgment nor in the opinion it is possible to find any expressed reference to the submissions presented by the UK or by any of the Member States that joined its complaints, it seems that both the Court and AG Kokott intentionally decided not to go down the broad route opened by *Zambrano* in order to preserve the Member States' sovereignty in the field of legal immigration. As a matter of fact the Court in

It would have been possible to argue simply that all nationals have the right to reside in the state by virtue of international law. See on this point H Oosterom-Staples, 'To What Extent Has Reverse Discrimination Been Reversed?' (2012) 14 *European Journal of Migration and Law* 151, 170. See also Nic Shuibhne, above n 75 at 367; P Van Elsuwege and D Kochenov, 'On The Limits of Judicial Intervention: EU Citizenship and Family Reunification Rights' (2011) 13 *European Journal of Migration and Law* 443, 454. Authoritative doctrine, however, specified that *McCarthy*, although curtailing *Zambrano*, did not contradict it. This doctrine underlined the importance of European citizenship as a focal source of several substantive rights that the applicant could claim before his own Member State on the condition, nevertheless, that the applicant was a minor. See S Coutts, 'Case C-434-09: Shirley McCarthy v Secretary of State for the Home Department', EUDO comment 2011, available at eudo-citizenship.eu/eu-citizenship.

[97] *Zambrano* judgment, para 50.

[98] *McCarthy* judgment, paras 51–53.

[99] A Wiesbroke, 'Disentangling the Union Citizenship Puzzle? The *McCarthy* case' (2011) 36 *European Law Review* 860, 869. Some criticism was raised on this point. Because of the open formulation of the test, its exact meaning will have to be formulated on a case-by-case basis. See on this point S Mantu, 'European Union Citizenship anno 2011: Zambrano, McCarthy and Dereci' (2012) 26 *Journal of Immigration Asylum and Nationality Law* 40, 52.

[100] See Nic Shuibhne, above n 72 at 368. In the first option her right to family life would be hindered, in the second option, although her right to free movement could theoretically be exercised, there could be some practical inconveniences that would prevent her from enjoying it. In the last circumstance, having to leave the territory of the Union automatically hinders the substance of EU citizenship rights.

McCarthy curtailed Zambrano to an exception,[101] stating that a situation such as the *McCarthy* one would not be at risk of seeing Mrs McCarthy's substance of citizenship right violated or of seeing her right to free movement among Member States hindered, by referring to the old theory on internal and external situations starting with *Morson and Jianhan*.[102] The overall outcome of the case confirms how the interest of the Court was to strike a balance in favour of the protection of Member States' sovereignty over immigration. It is very likely that, once it realised the potentially vast effect that *Zambrano* could have had in cases involving static EU citizens and third country nationals, the Court resolved to shrink as much as possible its consequences[103] in order to avoid conflicts and possible non-compliance by Member States. However, it is also worth noting that, despite the strong Member States' rationale that imbues this judgment, the Court engraved some space for developing a stronger idea of EU citizenship as a source of self-stemming rights by including free movement, even future and potential, to the substantive core right encompassed within the status of European citizenship.[104] We are still waiting to see the potentialities of this specification considering that the same point was reiterated in the following *Iida*[105] case but did not trigger any concrete factual consequence.

Overall, this case shows how the potentialities of *Zambrano* were soon curtailed by the Court, which transformed its test into an exception, probably due to pressure from Member States. The next case will show how this curtailment was eventually completed.

5. THE COMPLETION OF THE *ZAMBRANO* CURTAILMENT THROUGH THE SPECIFICATION OF THE SUBSTANCE OF RIGHTS TEST: *DERECI*[106]

The second case that had an impact on *Zambrano* was *Dereci*. *Dereci* started with a series of refusals to grant residence permits to third country national family members of Austrian nationals who had never exercised EU free movement rights. In rejecting all of the applications the Ministry for Home Affairs ruled out the application of EU law on the basis that the situation was purely internal. Nevertheless

[101] ibid, para 47. Nic Shuibhne pointed out that the language used by the Court was particularly ambiguous. Hence, it is difficult to understand immediately that the *Zambrano* test is considered an exception to the wholly internal rule. See Nic Shuibhne, above n 72 at 366.

[102] *McCarthy* judgment, para 45.

[103] A Dashwood, 'Judicial Activism and Conferred Powers—Is the CJEU Falling into Bad Habits?' paper presented at the 10th IEL (Institute of European Law) Annual Lecture, Birmingham University, 27 June 2012. He stated that the post-*Zambrano* cases 'provide a neat illustration of how a court may find that it has to scramble back from an activist decision, by inventing limits to the rights it has conjured out of nowhere in an earlier case'.

[104] Wiesbroke, above 99 at 866.

[105] Case C-40/11 *Yoshikazu Iida v Stadt Ulm* EU:C:2012:691.

[106] Case C-256/11 *Murat Dereci and Others v Bundesministerium für Inneres* EU:C:2011:734.

the referring court sought a preliminary ruling from the CJEU in order to get the scope of *Zambrano* clarified.[107]

AG Mengozzi agreed with the referring court that it was 'necessary to gain a better understanding of the implications of the judgment in *Ruiz Zambrano*'.[108] He started by ruling out the application of Directive 2004/38/EC to any of the situations of *Dereci*.[109] After a brief exposition of the points of *Zambrano* and *McCarthy*,[110] he found that none of the cases at hand were characterised by a risk of deprivation of the genuine enjoyment of the substance of the rights[111] because the enjoyment of the substance of the rights test does not include 'the right to respect for family life'.[112] Moreover, with regard to the issue of family life, he then recalled the old free movement logic in order to bolster the view that no rights of residence could be granted to the third country national applicants since their EU sponsors did not exercise any of the freedoms of movement laid down in the TFEU. He concluded that Article 20 should only be applied when a right of free movement has been exercised unless 'the situation of the Union citizen is not accompanied by the application of national measures which have the direct effect of depriving him of the genuine enjoyment of the substance of the rights attaching to his status as a Union citizen or as impeding the exercise of his right to move and reside freely within the territory of the Member State'.[113]

The Court developed its reasoning in a much deeper way. Whilst the advocate general simply referred to the substance of the right test without defining its content, the Court instead explicitly specified it. It started from questioning whether the provisions concerning the citizenship of the Union precluded the national state from refusing a residence permit to a third country national family member of a EU citizen who had never exercised his right to move.[114] First, as well as AG Mengozzi, it ruled out the application of Directive 2004/38/EC[115] and, recalling *McCarthy*, stated that 'a Union citizen, who has never exercised his right of free movement and has always resided in a Member State of which he is a national, is not covered by the concept of 'beneficiary' for the purposes of Article 3(1) of Directive 2004/38/EC, so that that directive is not applicable to him'.[116] Second, as in *McCarthy*, the Court addressed the applicability of the EU citizenship treaty provisions. Basing its reasoning on Article 20 TFEU, it reiterated the formulation of *McCarthy* that the non-exercise of movement rights did not imply

[107] For a more detailed summary of the case see Nic Shuibhne, above n 72 at 358–60.
[108] *Dereci* opinion, para 17.
[109] ibid, paras 32 et seq. AG Mengozzi stated that Dir 2004/38/EC was not applicable to any of the situations of *Dereci* simply because none of the applicants exercised their right to freedom of movement.
[110] ibid, paras 18–30.
[111] ibid, para 33.
[112] ibid, para 37.
[113] ibid, para 50.
[114] *Dereci* judgment, para 37.
[115] In reality the Court ruled out also the application of Dir 2003/86/EC (see paras 46–49).
[116] ibid, paras 54 et seq.

assimilation to a purely internal situation[117] and reconfirmed the *Zambrano* genuine enjoyment test.[118] However, unlike AG Mengozzi and the previous two abovementioned cases, the Grand Chamber then stated overtly what was just vaguely implied in *Zambrano* and *McCarthy*: the deprivation of the genuine enjoyment of the substance of citizenship rights is triggered when a Union citizen 'has, in fact, to leave not only the territory of the Member State of which he is a national but also the territory of the Union as a whole'.[119] The fact that it might appear desirable for the family to live together is not enough to support the view that the European citizens will be forced to leave the territory of the Union if the right of family reunification was not granted.[120] Finally, with regard to the right to respect for family life, in line with AG Mengozzi, the Court recalled Article 51(2) of the Charter of Fundamental Rights and pointed out that the respect of the right to family life should be assessed only if the circumstance of the case fell within the EU competences. It then stated that it was up to the national court to determine whether or not the circumstance would fall within the umbrella of EU law and, consequentially, whether or not Article 7 of the Charter had to be applied.[121]

Despite the lack of clarity that this judgment still left on the specificity of the rights that amount to the substance of EU citizenship, the Court in *Dereci* has the merit of having made clear when a national measure should be considered violating substantive EU citizenship rights. The Court underlined that a national measure has to be considered violating the substance of EU citizenship rights when it triggers the departure of the EU citizen not just from the Member State but also from the territory of the Union as a whole. This position clarified finally the *Zambrano* principle and curtailed it even more. Indeed, if in *McCarthy* it seems that the Court proposed a reading of the test based on the age of the EU citizen—where being a minor would entail a violation of the genuine enjoyment of the substance of EU citizenship rights whereas the same violation would not occur if the one enjoying the EU citizenship status was an adult—the Court in *Dereci* dismissed totally this line of interpretation and made clear that the outcome of a case should be based on whether the denial of residence rights to third country nationals would force the European citizen to leave the territory of the Union.[122] This approach implies that potentially also in a case in which a EU minor is involved and he is not forced to leave the territory of the Union by a national measure applied to his third country national relative, this case will not be protected by the

[117] ibid, para 61.

[118] ibid, para 64.

[119] ibid, para 66.

[120] ibid, para 68.

[121] ibid, para 72. On the other hand, if the national court takes the view that that situation is not covered by EU law, it must undertake that examination in the light of Art 8(1) ECHR.

[122] S Adam and P Van Elsuwege, 'Citizenship rights and the federal balance between the European Union and its Member States: Comment on Dereci' (2012) 37 *European Law Review* 176, 182. The authors underlined how this criterion is more consistent, considering the fact that there is no automatic connection between the age of a person and the 'genuine enjoyment' of his rights: in principle,

more favourable EU treaty provisions on EU citizenship but would fall within the competence of the Member State.

The *Dereci* case was subject to a lot of criticism with regard to its interpretation of the enjoyment of the substance of EU citizenship rights. It was argued that the *Zambrano* test was interpreted very strictly by the Court and that this interpretation limited its application to cases of absolute dependence of the citizen upon a third country national.[123] Moreover, since the Court in *Dereci* interpreted the substance of citizenship rights in such a restrictive way this test, against the hopes of many scholars, did not put an end to the phenomenon of reverse discrimination but simply shrunk the area of what accrues to be an exception to purely internal situations.[124] *Dereci*'s shortcomings seem to be, once again, a symptom of the fact that the Court, throughout its reasoning, tried to find a solution that would please the Member States. Unlike *McCarthy*, this time the judgment documented Member States' complaints. Paragraph 40 of *Dereci*'s judgment states reports that the Austrian, German, Irish, Dutch, Polish and UK governments submitted that the principles laid down in the *Zambrano* case should apply only to very exceptional circumstances in which EU citizens are at risk of leaving the territory of the Union or not being able to exercise their right of free movement and residence within the territory of the Member States.[125] The Court completely embraced their position by specifying overtly that the deprivation of the genuine enjoyment of the substance of citizenship rights is triggered when a Union citizen has not just to leave the territory of the Member State but also the territory of the Union as a whole.[126] Being forced to leave the territory of the Union embodies in fact a much higher threshold under which the Court decided that EU law could not be of any help and the sovereignty of the Member States had to be preserved. The solution proposed by the Court, indeed, ended up drawing safe and strict borders for the circumstances that could pierce the veil of the purely internal situations. As Shaw pointed out, the Court's approach in *Dereci* appears to be close to the guidance issued by the UK Border Agency on the applicability of *Zambrano* and this confirms that the Court was probably, after *Zambrano*, trying to reconcile its previous approach to the more stringent one endorsed by the national authorities.[127]

It is worth noting that the Court seems to have made an attempt to develop the concept of EU citizenship as a source of self-stemming rights by reiterating

a minor child with the nationality of a Member State may, under certain circumstances, be able to conduct an autonomous life in the Union without the presence of his parents, whereas certain adults may require the support of other persons.

[123] Hinarejos, above n 74 at 281. See also D Kochenov and R Plender, 'EU Citizenship: from an incipient form to an incipient substance? The discovery of the treaty text' (2012) 37 *European Law Review* 369, 395. The authors underlined that the substance of rights test should not be milder or stricter than the cross-border situation test (the functional relationship between free movement and family reunification).

[124] Mantu, above n 99 at 53.

[125] *Dereci* judgment, para 40.

[126] ibid, para 66.

[127] Shaw above n 80 at 39. See also Mantu above n 99 at 51.

the idea that the situation of a Union citizen who has not made use of the right to freedom of movement cannot, for that reason alone, be assimilated to a purely internal situation[128] or the fact that EU citizens should be able to rely on the rights pertaining to their status of EU citizens against the Member States via Article 20 TFEU.[129] However, these attempts seem to be just empty statements. An example of this emptiness is the reference that the Court makes to the right to family life only to exclude it from the protection of the genuine enjoyment test. This is arguably a limitation, rather than an enhancement, to the development of the idea of EU citizenship as the fundamental status of the nationals of the Member States.[130]

In less than a couple of years, the hopes of those who believed that the problem of the wholly internal situation could have been finally overcome owing to the *Zambrano* judgment eventually faded. The Court in *McCarthy* and *Dereci* managed to strip out the immense potential of *Zambrano* and tie up its test as tight as could be for the sake of protecting Member States' sovereignty over immigration. The discussion of the following cases shows how the strict approach of the Court has consolidated in more recent years.

6. THE POST-*DERECI* CASES: A CONFIRMATION OF THE STRICT APPROACH OF THE COURT ON THIRD COUNTRY NATIONAL FAMILY RESIDENCE RIGHTS

In late 2012, the Court of Justice delivered another judgment on the position of third-country national family members of EU citizens. This case challenged the application of the *Zambrano* test. The joined cases of *O and S v Maahanmuuttovirasto* and *Maahanmuuttovirasto v L*[131] involved, once again, static EU citizens and their third country national family members. However, the main question here was slightly different from the ones asked by the Court in the previous cases as it concerned the right to reside of a third country national who was not related to the EU citizen directly but via his third country national spouse.[132] In *O and S*, Ms S was a citizen from Ghana who migrated to Finland and lived there on the basis of a national permanent residence permit. In 2001, she married a Finnish national with whom she had a child in 2003 who had Finnish nationality. In 2005 Ms S and her husband got divorced and she was granted sole custody over the child. In 2008 Ms S married Mr O, a national of Côte d'Ivoire. In 2009 Ms S and Mr O had a child, who was granted Ghanaian nationality. Since then, Mr O lived with Ms S and her two children. In 2009 Mr O applied for a residence permit on the basis of the marriage which was, however, rejected on the grounds that he did not have secure means of subsistence. In the case of *L*, Ms L was a national of

[128] *Dereci* judgment, para 61.
[129] ibid, paras 62–63.
[130] Oosterom Staples, above n 96 at 168.
[131] Joined Cases C-356/11 and C-357/11 *O and S v Maahanmuuttovirasto* EU:C:2012:776.
[132] *O and S* judgment, para 35.

Algeria who resided lawfully in Finland owing to a national permanent residence permit obtained through her marriage to a Finnish national. Ms L and her Finnish husband had a child who was granted Finnish nationality. Ms L and her first husband divorced in 2004 and in October 2006 Ms L married Mr M, a national of Algeria who arrived legally in Finland as an asylum seeker. At the end of October 2006 Mr M was returned to his country of origin and Ms L applied for him to be granted a residence permit in Finland on the basis of their marriage, which was rejected.

As well as AG Bot,[133] the CJEU immediately excluded the possibility that Directive 2004/38/EC could find application over the circumstances at stake. Indeed, since the EU citizens concerned never made use of their right of free movement, they were not covered by the concept of 'beneficiary' under Article 3(1) and, hence, Directive 2004/38/EC could not apply to either of them or to their third country national family members.[134] Following in the steps of AG Bot, after having ruled out the relevance of Directive 2004/38/EC, the Court then focused on the application of Article 20 TFEU. The Court recalled *Zambrano* repeating that the simple fact that an EU citizen never made use of his right of free movement does not necessarily mean that the circumstances at stake have to be assimilated to a purely internal situation.[135] EU citizens can rely on the rights pertaining to their status, even against their state of nationality, if the national measure has the effect of denying the genuine enjoyment of the substance of citizenship rights.[136] The Court also recalled *Dereci* by stating that such denial occurs when the national measure forces the Union citizen not just to leave the territory of the Member State of which he is a national but also the territory of the Union as a whole.[137] Once again, contrarily, AG Bot's decision of assessing directly the non-applicability of Article 20 TFEU to the circumstances at stake, the Court pointed out that it is for the referring court to establish whether the refusal of granting the right of residence to the third country national family member entails a denial of the genuine enjoyment of the substance of the rights conferred by the status of EU citizenship.[138] In order to do so[139] the Court engaged in a thorough analysis of the factors that the national court should have taken into account in order to deliver its decision. In particular the national court should have considered that the mothers of the Union citizens held permanent residence permits in Finland and, therefore,

[133] *O and S* opinion, paras 32–34.
[134] *O and S* judgment, para 42.
[135] ibid, para 43.
[136] ibid, paras 44–45.
[137] ibid, para 47.
[138] ibid, para 49 (opinion paras 40–45).
[139] While in *Zambrano* and *McCarthy* the assessment on whether the national measure violated the genuine enjoyment of the substance of citizenship rights was already made by the CJEU, in *Dereci* the CJEU stated that such assessment was a matter for the national court to decide but it did not offer any criteria in order to pursue it. See *Dereci* judgment, para 74.

there was no obligation for them or for the EU citizens to leave the territory of the Union.[140] Moreover the custody of the children and the fact that the latter are part of reconstituted families were also circumstances that the national court should have been taken into account. Indeed, the decision of Mr S and Ms L to leave the territory of the Union would have deprived the EU children of their contacts with their biological fathers. On the contrary, if they decided to stay in Finland, such a decision would have ended up harming the relationship of the third country national children with their biological fathers.[141] The CJEU also added other factors to which the national court should have paid attention such as the fact that cohabitation was not decisive in its assessment[142] and the fact that blood relationship was not the only one upon which the *Zambrano* test should rely.[143] The CJEU also openly stated that the national court should have also taken into account that the third country national step-fathers were not those on whom the EU children were 'legally, financially or emotionally dependent', since it is precisely the dependency relationship that can force the EU citizen to leave the territory of the Union as a whole.[144] It also specified that, from the information available, it seemed that this dependency relationship in the circumstances at stake did not subsist.[145] The Court finally concluded stating that Article 20 TFEU should not have been interpreted as precluding a Member State from refusing to grant a third country national a residence permit in the circumstances of these cases, provided that this refusal did not entail, for the EU citizen concerned, the denial of the genuine enjoyment of the substance of the citizenship rights.[146]

It is evident that this judgment completely confirms the approach adopted by the Court since *McCarthy*. Indeed the Court decided to choose a strict approach with regard to the application of the *Zambrano* test. Once again, as in previous cases, Member States' concerns over the loss of their sovereignty on immigration due to a too liberal interpretation of Article 20 TFEU seem to have been the pivotal factors in the Court's reasoning. In their submissions, the Finnish, Danish, German, Italian, Dutch and Polish governments argued that the open interpretation of Article 20 TFEU offered by the *Zambrano* case could be utilised only in exceptional situations in which the application of a national measure would lead to the denial of the genuine enjoyment of the substance of the rights accruing to the concept of EU citizenship.[147] The Court answered these claims positively and upheld the position of the Member States, highlighting that the information available suggested that such a dependency relationship did not exist in the circumstances at hand.

[140] *O and S* judgment, para 50.
[141] ibid, para 51.
[142] ibid, para 54.
[143] ibid, para 55.
[144] ibid, para 56.
[145] ibid, para 57.
[146] ibid, para 58.
[147] ibid, paras 37–38.

However, it is also worth noting that this case shows glimpses of the Court's resilience in not giving up its aim of enhancing Article 20 TFEU as a source of independent rights. First of all, the Court stated that the exceptional circumstances covered by the *Zambrano* test could also encompass cases in which there is no blood relationship between the EU citizen and the third country national seeking a right of residence. This clarification is quite remarkable because, in the future, it could lead to granting the right of residence to third country nationals that perhaps are not linked to the EU citizen by 'official' family bonds. This could happen as long as the denial of their right of residence within the territory of the Member State concerned hinders the genuine enjoyment of the substance of citizenship rights accruing to the EU citizen involved, due to the dependence of the latter upon the former, and forces the EU citizen to leave the territory of the Union. Moreover, the Court for the first time also clarified in more detail the relationship of dependency that should subsist, in order for the *Zambrano* test to be applicable and for the circumstances of the case to fall within the realm of EU law, between the EU citizen and the third country national. The Court described the idea of dependency as legal, financial or emotional. The fact that the Court used 'or' suggests that these conditions are not cumulative but alternative. As seen when discussing the issue of blood relationships between EU citizens and third country nationals, if this is the interpretation that will be endorsed for the future, the right of residence for third country nationals could potentially be opened not just to core family members but also to those upon whose legal, financial or emotional support the EU citizen relies such as legal guardians, non-registered partners, third country national family members not encompassed within the category of beneficiaries according to Directive 2004/38/EC, including step-parents, and perhaps even friends.[148]

Despite the willingness of the Court to develop such an open approach toward dependency and the possibility of granting family residence rights to third country nationals not directly connected to EU citizens this open trend has not, so far, been followed up. This is probably due to the fact that such approach encroaches on Member States' interests in preserving their own sovereignty over immigration as it leads up to granting a right of residence to any third country national on the sole basis of Article 20 TFEU outside the provisions and limitations of secondary law.[149] As a result, in the majority of the follow-up cases concerning EU citizens and third country nationals where a dependency relationship occurred the Court never again found the circumstances at stake good enough to fulfil the *Zambrano* test[150] and, practically, turned the application of the *Zambrano* test into a mere fiction. In the *Ymeraga and Others* case[151] the applicant, Mr Ymeraga, arrived in

148 C Berneri and S Peers, 'Iida and O and S: further developments in the immigration status of static EU citizens' (2013) 27 *Journal of Immigration, Asylum and Nationality Law* 162, 173.

149 *O and S* opinion, para 45.

150 The only exception is the recent CS case.

151 Case C-87/12 *Kreshnik Ymeraga and Others v Ministre du Travail, de l'Emploi et de l'Immigration* EU:C:2013:291.

Luxembourg at the age of 15 to live with his uncle. After his situation was regularised he acquired Luxembourg citizenship. Later on his parents and two brothers applied for a residence permit as family members of a citizen of the Union. The application was refused but, on appeal, the national court decided to refer the matter to the CJEU. The latter, after excluding the applicability of Directive 2003/86/EC and 2004/38/EC,[152] in a brief analysis without any reference to the specific circumstances of the applicant found that there were no relevant elements, apart from the intention of Mr Ymeraga to live with the family, to support the view that a refusal to grant the right of residence to the third country national family members may have the effect of denying the genuine enjoyment of the substance of citizens' rights.[153]

The same line was taken in the following *Iida* case.[154] Mr Iida had initially been granted a residence permit in Germany in connection with a family reunion (marriage to a German citizen from which a child of Japanese, American and German nationality was born). After their marital separation, he was instead given a residence permit in Germany because of his employment there. However, since the subsequent extension of the permit was discretionary, Mr Iida decided to apply for a residence card as a family member of an EU citizen on the basis of Directive 2004/38/EC, despite the fact that the child and ex-spouse moved to Austria. The German authorities refused his application, and following his challenge to that decision, the national court referred the case to the CJEU. The Court considered that Mr Iida could not fall within the category of 'beneficiaries' of Directive 2004/38/EC.[155] The Court then explored whether Mr Iida could be granted protection by means of Articles 20 and 21 TFEU. It quoted the previous *Chen*, *Eind* and *Dereci* judgments[156] and pointed out that the common factor that characterised the situations in these judgments was an 'intrinsic connection with the freedom of movement of a Union citizen which prevents the right of entry and residence from being refused to those nationals (third country nationals) in the Member State of residence of that citizen, in order not to interfere with that freedom'.[157] Given the circumstances at stake, namely that Mr Iida was not seeking the right to reside in the new Member State of his daughter and wife, he had always resided in Germany in accordance with national law and his national permit was renewable (and he could 'in principle' obtain EU long-term resident status),[158] the Court found that there were no valid arguments to support the view that Mrs Iida and her daughter were denied the genuine enjoyment of the substance of the rights deriving from their status as EU citizens or were impeded in the exercise of their right to move

152 *Ymeraga* judgment, paras 24–27.
153 ibid, para 39.
154 Case C-40/11 *Yoshikazu Iida v Stadt Ulm* EU:C:2012:691.
155 *Iida* judgment, 54–56.
156 ibid, paras 69–71.
157 ibid, para 72.
158 ibid, paras 73–75.

and reside freely within the territory of the Member States.[159] Despite the fact that in this case some actual factors had been listed in order to explain the lack of applicability of the *Zambrano* test, the application of this test to the circumstances at stake is still fictional. The Court, for instance, did not consider at all the fact that perhaps the strong affective relationship between father and daughter (emotional dependence) could push the latter to leave the territory of the Union to stay with him, if he had to leave (he was also not granted the residence permit in accordance to Directive 2003/109/EC by Germany).

Finally, another failed attempt of relying upon Article 20 TFEU can be found in the *Alokpa*[160] case. This case concerned the refusal by Luxembourg to grant a residence permit to a Togolese national, the mother of two children of French nationality living in Luxembourg. The Court, after having ruled out the applicability of Directive 2004/38/ EC[161] and leaving the referring Court to ascertain whether the children and mother could reside in Luxembourg according to Article 21,[162] engaged with the discussion of whether Article 20 instead could grant her the right to reside in Luxembourg. Following the opinion of AG Mengozzi,[163] the Court in principle[164] concluded that the *Zambrano* exception would not apply in this case because Ms Alokpa's children would not be forced to leave the territory of the Union as a whole as they could still move to France, where she could get a derivative right of residence there as their primary carer.[165] Although the last assessment was left to the national court the CJEU, refrained from making any comment on the possibility that, despite the French nationality of the children, there could be still be a real possibility of them leaving the territory of the Union as a whole if, for example, their mother was not able to find a job or provide for them in France.

It is also worth highlighting how the Member States' influence[166] in the outcome of this case can be perceived from the Court's reasoning. Indeed, its reasoning is mainly dedicated to pointing out the ancillary function of family residence rights to the EU primary right of free movement[167] and the fact that only in specific and limited circumstances can the right of residence not be refused to a third country national family member if free movement is not involved[168] and the fact that the situation at stake, like that at the origin of *Ruiz Zambrano*, was 'purely internal' and had 'to be rejected from the outset'.[169]

[159] ibid, para 76.

[160] Case C-86/12 *Alokpa and Others v Ministre du Travail, de l'Emploi et de l'Immigration* EU:C:2013:645.

[161] ibid, para 24.

[162] ibid, paras 29–31. This is the application of the principle developed in the *Chen* case.

[163] *Alokpa* opinion, paras 55–56.

[164] The Court left it to the national court to ascertain if that was true on the facts the case.

[165] *Alokpa* judgment, paras 34–35.

[166] Submissions were issued by the Belgian, Czech, German, Greek, Lithuanian, Luxembourg, Netherlands and Polish Governments, as well as by the European Commission.

[167] *Alokpa* judgment, para 22.

[168] ibid, para 32.

[169] *Alokpa* opinion, para 11.

To conclude, the post-*Dereci* cases seem to have crystallised the strict application of the *Zambrano* test, turning it into a threshold that is very difficult to fulfil given the facts. The more recent cases of *Ymeraga*, *Iida* and *Alokpa* have also shown how the *Zambrano* test seems to have turned into a mere fictional test, as the Court has not really engaged in analysing the factors that could potentially trigger its application. This approach seems to have been taken in order to preserve Member States' sovereignty over immigration, to the detriment of the development of an enhanced concept of EU citizenship as a source of self-stemming rights.

7. CONCLUSIONS

As seen in this chapter, the Court has recently been involved in several judgments debating the right of EU static citizens to live in their state of origin with their third country national family members. The reasoning of the Court at times has lacked clarity and consistency. For instance, it is difficult to understand why *McCarthy* refers to free movement as a substantive EU citizenship right whereas *Dereci* does not mention this feature at all and, finally, in *Iida* free movement is mentioned again. It is also difficult to understand why *Dereci* is mentioned in *Iida* as a free movement case, considering that the right of free movement was not involved. It is also not easy to understand the reasons that moved the Court to refer to international principles in order to confirm that Mrs McCarthy had a right to live in the UK, despite the presence of her third country national husband, whereas this reference was not adopted for Mr Zambrano's children. The inconsistencies in the case law of the Court caused quite a few people, including practitioners and academic experts in the field, to share the view of AG Sharpston, according to whom 'lottery rather than logic would seem to be governing the exercise of EU citizenship rights'.[170]

The inconsistencies in this stream of case law provide evidence that the Court struggles to find solutions that would meet Member States' concerns over immigration without prejudicing its aim of protecting EU citizenship as a source of independent rights. In *Zambrano*, for example, the Court did not read Article 20 and 21 TFEU in conjunction to cover situations in which the EU citizen never exercised his right of free movement, as AG Sharpston originally suggested but, instead, preferred to rely only on Article 20 TFEU, basically creating an exception to circumstances that otherwise should have been governed by Member States' national legislation. Indeed, as seen above, this choice did not turn the status of European citizenship into an absolute source of residence rights and left Member States' sovereignty over immigration protected in all the situations that do not clearly fall within the exception. However, both in *Zambrano* and in some of the past *Zambrano* cases it is evident how the Court tried to find solutions of

[170] *Zambrano* opinion, para 88.

compromise between Member States' immigration concerns and the development of the concept of EU citizenship. For example, with regard to concerns over immigration, the Court in *McCarthy* ended up referring to the old theory on internal and external situations and confirmed *Zambrano* as a simple exception to Member States' sovereignty. However, the Court also tried to put flesh on the bones of the *Zambrano* test by identifying the substance of the EU citizenship rights with the right of free movement. In *Dereci* the Court took into account the Member States' claims by limiting the *Zambrano* test to the circumstances of when the EU citizen has to leave the territory of the Union as a whole and not just the single Member State. The Court also reiterated the idea of protecting the substance of citizens' rights stemming from the status of EU citizenship and the idea that citizens can rely on the rights pertaining to that status against the Member States by Article 20 TFEU.[171]

Overall, it seems that after *Zambrano* the Court has proposed solutions that have swung the pendulum in favour of protecting Member States' concerns over immigration rather than enhancing the development of the concept of EU citizenship. In the stream of cases involving EU static citizens the Court seemed to have preferred to opt for a very high threshold to reach since, as things now stand, the Court finds that the *Zambrano* test is met only in case of forced departure from the entire territory of the Union. Moreover, as pointed out by the most recent cases of *Iida*, *Ymeraga* and *Alokpa*, the Court seems to have decided to exclude the application of the *Zambrano* test even in circumstances in which the EU citizen could potentially have to leave turning the test into a mere fiction.

Some elements from the analysis proposed above suggest that strong Member State opposition[172] may have pushed the Court, which initially regarded EU law 'as mature enough for mutation, growth and plasticity',[173] to take a step back.[174] The reasons supporting the preference of the Court for prioritising the Member States' stances over immigration seem to be twofold. First of all, as mentioned before for cases concerning moving citizens and third country nationals the Court, despite its tendency to follow a communitarian approach, is always particularly careful in challenging certain areas of the law about which Member States have shown

[171] *Dereci* judgment, paras 62–63. Note that the attempt of developing the concept of EU citizenship was weakened by the express exclusion of the right to family life from the core substance of rights pertaining to the citizenship status.

[172] Many Member States opposed the *Zambrano* interpretation and pushed for a strict post-*Zambrano* jurisprudential approach. In *Zambrano* eight Member States intervened, in *McCarthy* five, in *Dereci* eight, in *O and S* six, in *Ymeraga* six and in *Iida* and *Alokpa* eight.

[173] Kochenov and Plender, above n 123 at 388.

[174] CJ Carrubba and M Gabel, 'Do Governments Sway European Court of Justice Decision-making?: Evidence from Government Court Briefs' IFIR Working Paper Series 2005 available at www.ifigr.org/workshop/fall05/gabel-workshop.pdf. In this paper the authors elaborated an empirical test of Member State influence on CJEU decisions over the time span of three years and demonstrated that the Court does take into account the concerns and the views of Member States in order to ponder its decisions.

themselves to be particularly sensitive,[175] such as immigration, especially when securitisation is at stake. As seen in the previous chapter, Gunnar Beck in his book highlights the elements that can be taken as evidence of the fact that a particular issue is of high political importance for a Member State. Good indicators of political sensitivity are the general willingness of Member States to intervene in support of one another and the numbers of Member States intervening. As pointed out in the analysis presented in this chapter, many Member States complained and intervened in the cases that have been analysed, amounting to eight in *Zambrano*,[176] five in *McCarthy*,[177] eight in *Dereci*,[178] six in the *O and S* case,[179] six in *Ymeraga*,[180] eight in *Iida*[181] and eight in *Alokpa*.[182] As reported above, the majority of their complaints consisted in arguing why the circumstances of the case at stake fell within the boundaries of their competence.

Moreover, another factor that may have influenced the interpretation the Court is budgetary,[183] which again is an area of high political sensitivity upon which the Court refrains from acting. The political uncertainty triggered by the economic crisis affecting Europe over the last few years has exacerbated this issue. As Spaventa underlines, 'the debate about "who pays for what" has become very prominent'[184] in the current historical circumstances. It is very likely that the Court took the budgetary implications well into account when deciding to curtail the effects of *Zambrano*, probably once again in order to prioritise securitisation and avoid the costly domino effects of a vast number of third country national family members' immigrating triggered by an enhanced concept of EU citizenship covering the substance of citizenship rights. By doing so, however, the Court ended up altering the legal trajectory of EU citizenship for the sake of protecting Member States' sovereignty over immigration.

To conclude, it is worth pointing out that the fact that the Court disseminated here and there in its judgments some elements of openness towards a further development of the concept of EU citizenship should not take anyone by surprise. It is a well-known habit of the Court since the very beginning of the European integration process to take advantage of the political fixation of the Member States on the direct and material consequences of the case to build up precedents without

[175] G Beck, *The Legal Reasoning of The Court of Justice of the EU* (Oxford, Hart Publishing, 2012) 352.

[176] Belgium, Denmark, Germany, Ireland, Greece, the Netherlands, Austria and Poland.

[177] UK, Denmark, Estonia, Ireland and the Netherlands.

[178] Austria, Denmark, Germany, Ireland, Greece, the Netherlands, Poland and the UK.

[179] Finland, Denmark, Germany, Italy, the Netherlands and Poland.

[180] Luxembourg, Belgium, Czech Republic, Denmark, Germany and Poland.

[181] Germany, Belgium, Czech Republic, Denmark, Italy, the Netherlands, Poland and the UK.

[182] Luxembourg, Belgium, Czech Republic, Germany, Greece, Lithuania, the Netherlands and Poland.

[183] Beck, above n 175 at 351.

[184] E Spaventa, 'Striving for Equality: Who "Deserves" to Be a Union Citizen?' paper, 2014, available at http://ssrn.com/abstract=2518955 11.

leading to any political concern.[185] Indeed establishing important legal principles without applying them to the cases at hand[186] is the way through which the Court has always managed patiently to expand its jurisdiction. Looking at the cases that have been analysed in this chapter one should not lose hope that the Court will still want, one day, to broaden its jurisdiction through the concept of EU citizenship by applying the innovative *Zambrano* test and some of its further more open specifications in future cases. However, this will happen only when the Member States' opposition to third country national immigration becomes less vehement.

[185] KJ Alter, 'Who are the "Masters of the Treaty"?: European Governments and the European Court of Justice' (1998) 52 *International Organization* 121, 131.

[186] ibid.

5

Conclusion

THIS FINAL CHAPTER brings together the findings of this book and aims to open up a discussion for future research on the opportunity for the CJEU to act in ways that would provide better protection to families composed of EU citizens and third country national family members.

This book has looked at the development of the phenomenon of family reunification between EU citizens and third country nationals. Chapter 1 pointed out how, after the signing of the Treaty of Rome, the main concern of the EU became the development of a common market and, in particular, of the idea of free movement of workers. This aim was pursued through the drafting of generous secondary free movement legislation, such as Council Regulation 15/1961/EEC, 38/1964/EEC and 1612/1968/EEC, which granted EU workers specific rights among which was also included the right to family reunification. However, after the oil crisis the socio-economic background underpinning the activity of the Union mutated. As seen in Chapter 2, Member States began to endorse strict immigration policies towards illegal and legal immigration of third country nationals. The Member States' stricter approach towards immigrants was accompanied by the continuing EU interest in the promotion of free movement of EU persons, and the development of the concept of EU citizenship as a source of self-stemming rights, as shown respectively by Chapter 3 and Chapter 4. The analysis in these two chapters showed how the legislation and, even more evidently, the reasoning of the Court was shaped by the interplay of these trends. Focusing on the approach of the Court more closely it seems that, overall, both in cases concerning EU moving and static citizens, despite the more open approach towards third country nationals of the cases concerning moving citizens,[1] the Court's activity has been highly influenced by Member States' concerns over immigration. Chapter 4 showed how the consequences of the Court's decision to take into account Member States' concerns over immigration ended up jeopardising the right of families to live together in cases concerning EU static citizens. As things stand now, in cases involving EU static citizens the Court has decided to curtail the potentiality of the *Zambrano* test to a mere exception and ended up protecting family reunification rights between EU citizens and third country nationals only in the remote case that the obstruction of these rights would force the EU citizen to leave the territory of the Union as a

[1] E Spaventa, 'Earned Citizenship: Understanding Union Citizenship Through its Scope', paper, 2014, available at http://ssrn.com/abstract=2497941, 15.

whole. Up until now this test has proved to work only in cases involving EU minors dependent on third country national parents who do not have even the slightest possibility of resettling in another Member State. Moreover, Chapter 3 showed that, to a certain extent, Member States' concerns over immigration have also been taken into account in cases concerning free-moving EU citizens. Indeed, as seen, when free movement is involved the Court grants residence family rights only when the principal free movement right of the EU sponsor would be obstructed by a potential denial of the right of residence with him or her to the third country national family member. If the application of the deterrence principle seemed to have reduced to a mere fiction with *Metock*, the more recent cases such as *O and S* have shown that the deterrence test is not dead and that it is still able to jeopardise family reunification applications.

In the light of these findings it seems that the contribution of the Member States, rather than being of support to these kind of mixed families, has been more one of obstacle. The cases examined show how applicants tried to overcome Member States' rejections to grant them residency rights by bringing their issues to national courts in the hope that their rights would be protected against the host state immigration authorities. The rejections issued by the host state immigration authorities suggest that some Member States are suspicious towards not just third country nationals but also EU citizens coming from other Member States that would like to rely on their free movement legitimate Rights in a host European country. This Member States' anti-immigrant approach seems to have broadened over the years. If up until some years ago the fear of the 'other' targeted primarily third country nationals it now includes fellow EU citizens. Events like the outcome of the Brexit referendum and talk of other states following the same path are clear evidence of this trend.

If this is where we stand now, is there a hope for families composed of EU citizens and third country nationals to rely on a friendly set of EU norms that would allow them to live together without the fear of falling within random and frankly nasty exceptions? This is an important question that opens up future research paths. Without pretending to give definitive and detailed answers at this point in the book, in these last few paragraphs I would like to point towards what I see as a possible way of improving the situation.

However, before moving on to look at what I see as the next steps to be taken, I would like to highlight two points. First of all, I would stress that the move that I foresee is jurisprudential and not legislative. This is because the current state of affairs in Europe realistically prevents me from seeing Member States finding solutions via legislation in a hurry. I believe that Member States are unlikely to make any move towards improving the situation of families composed of EU citizens and third country nationals because the antagonism against free movement spread throughout Europe at the moment is too high. The alternative is then either to wait for the Member States to act, which may never happen, or to hope for a creative interpretation of the Court. I believe that it is necessary to ask the Court to act without waiting for the Member States for several reasons. First of all, historically and precisely in periods of stalemate of the European project the Court decided to be bold and, despite the lack of support from the Member States, to keep on promoting European integration. The increasing national disillusion towards the EU calls for the Court to be audacious in protecting rights and in keeping on bolstering a real free movement of workers. Indeed, if the Court is not the one that acts, nobody will do so in its place. Furthermore, if Member States are unlikely to act, it makes sense to ask the Court to do it instead, in order to fill gaps that are unreasonable to keep. For instance, the Family Reunification Directive has shown that one of its scopes is protecting family life and fundamental rights[2] of third country nationals that want to reunite with their family members. If this is the case for third country nationals, why should EU citizens be excluded from being granted family life protection with their third country national relatives?

Finally, the second point I would like to highlight is why I suggest the Court should stop taking Member States' concerns into account in family reunification cases. This may look like forcing the Court in a direction that it has never completely chosen since the first cases concerning families composed of EU citizens and third country nationals have arisen. Indeed, throughout this book it has been highlighted how Member States' concerns over immigration by third country nationals shaped the legislation, reasoning and outcome of cases on family reunification. I do not make this suggestion light-heartedly since I do believe that Europe should be one in which anyone should be able to make his voice heard. However, I believe what Europe is witnessing now is unique and never seen before in this magnitude. There is a generally spread perception, confirmed by the recent events of Brexit, that the European project has failed and that the EU is not capable of bringing anything good to Member States' nationals, only from stringent rules to follow. The consequence of this general malaise and lack of trust towards the EU can be clearly perceived looking at how Member States are reacting in front of the current immigration crisis. Rather than sticking together, Member States have started to give individual answers dictated mostly by fear. All of a sudden, securitisation at its apex is pursued: walls are built and third country nationals sent back home without a clear and uniform plan of action. Against this current backdrop I believe that at least the Court should fly high, be bold and audacious. This means that, unlike it did in the past, only the rights of the people and not political considerations over competence, sovereignty and securitisation should move its decisions.

The way in which I suggest the Court could act is by recognising that the concept of EU citizenship does not simply cover the right to move of EU citizens but also their right to reside. This move has already been suggested by AG Maduro

[2] Second preamble of Dir 2003/86/EC. See also S Sanchez Iglesias, 'Fundamental Rights Protection for Third Country Nationals and Citizens of the Union: Principles of Enhancing Coherence' (2013) 15 *European Journal of Migration and Law* 137, 144: 'A different approach could undermine the consistency of the concept of citizenship with the enactment of a whole body of law—specifically the Family Reunification Directive—through which the status of foreigners has begun to be comprehensively regulated regardless of inter-state movement'.

in *Metock* and AG Sharpston in *Zambrano*. In particular AG Maduro highlighted how Directive 200/38/EC no longer simply covers free movement but also intends to secure 'the stability and permanence of residence'.[3] AG Sharpston instead particularly focused on Articles 20 and 21 TFEU and suggested that it is now time for the Court to officially recognise the existence of a free-standing right of residence.[4] In a previous piece[5] I suggested this new recognition should happen legislatively by splitting Article 20(2)(a) TFEU into two parts. The provision would read that citizens of the Union should enjoy: 'a) the right to move freely within the territory of the Member States; and b) the right to reside freely within the territory of the Member States'. Moreover, I also suggested that the same principle should be translated into Directive 2004/38/EC by deleting from Article 3(1) the locution 'other than that of which they are a national', where 'of which' stands for 'Member State'. However, for the reasons mentioned above, I believe now that this step should be made jurisprudentially. Moreover, this jurisprudential move would sit well within the previous jurisprudential background, being a natural conclusion of a path already paved by cases such as *Garcia Avello*, *Rottman*, *Chen* and *Zambrano* itself.[6]

This new approach would benefit families composed of EU citizens and third country nationals in two ways:

1) Situations in which a free movement element is present

   The approach that recognises EU citizenship as covering also the right of residence could help the Court to eventually disentangle its reasoning from the recent revival of the strong application of the concept of deterrence and, therefore, could grant better protection to families. As seen before, recently the deterrence test has been surprisingly reapplied in a strict way.[7] In the *O and B* case, the Court decided that not granting family reunification is not an obstacle to free movement when the EU sponsor has decided not to move to the host Member State permanently. In the *S* case the Court gave a strict reading of the *Carpenter* judgment and stated that it is for the national court to assess whether not allowing a third country national his right of residence in the host Member State would really hinder the right of movement of the EU sponsor. Adopting the idea that EU citizenship is a status that grants a certain bundle of rights including residence could hopefully trigger a realignment of the case law to the original intentions of the Legislator. As hinted in Chapter 3 when analysing the *Singh* case, it was the Court that introduced

[3] *Metock* opinion, para 13.

[4] *Zambrano* opinion, para 101.

[5] C Berneri, 'Protection of Families Composed by EU Citizens and Third Country Nationals; Some Suggestions to Tackle Reverse Discrimination' (2014) 16 *European Journal of Migration and Law* 249, 273.

[6] See *Zambrano* opinion, paras 93–97.

[7] This seems to be due to the fact that the application of EU citizenship rights is going through a reactionary phase. See Spaventa, above n 1 at 13.

the idea of interpreting family reunification rights as functional to the right of free movement in accordance with the market access model originally developed in the free movement of goods cases. This interpretation was probably not in the original plans of the European Legislator because it is very likely that the first family residence provisions inserted in the free movement legislation of the sixties, given the historical contingencies of the time, were drafted as bonus rights to be automatically granted once the primary right of free movement was exercised by the European sponsor. Hence, as suggested already, the utilisation of the *Singh* interpretation of the ancillary relationship between free movement and family reunification might have simply been a device to address Member States' concerns, which developed after the oil crisis, over immigration of third country nationals. Over the years, however, it has been seen how the application of the deterrence test has diluted and eventually become a fictional test. This is because, as pointed out in *Metock*, the Court interpreted the role of family reunification provisions as functional not just to the primary right of movement but also to the right of residence of the EU sponsor in the host Member State. However, the subsequent cases of *O and B* and *S* reutilised an old interpretation of deterrence and applied it strictly. This shows either that the Court did not have in mind to introduce a pivotal chance but simply to grant a positive outcome in the circumstances of *Metock* or, more sadly, that perhaps some initial embryonic steps towards a real change were made intentionally but have now been intentionally curtailed. Either way, it is desirable that the Court will officially spell out once and for all that residence should be protected as equally as movement. Just in this way the third country national family members covered by Article 3 Directive 2004/38/EC and their EU sponsors will be granted complete protection in all situations they may find themselves in.

2) Situations in which a free movement element is not present

If a reading of EU citizenship as covering also EU residence rights is to be applied, the immediate advantage would be finding a solution to the serious problem of reverse discrimination for EU static citizens that want to reunite with their third country national family members. Discrimination is characterised as reverse[8] when an unexpected group of people is treated

[8] There is a vast literature on the phenomenon of reverse discrimination. Among others see in particular C Ritter, 'Purely internal situations, reverse discrimination' (2006) 31 *European Law Review* 690; C Dutricourt and S Thomas, 'Reverse discrimination and free movement of persons under Community law: all for Ulysses, nothing for Penelope?' (2009) 34 *European Law Review* 433; S O'Leary, 'The past, the present and the future of the wholly internal rule' (2009) 44 *Irish Jurist* 13; N Nic Shuibhne, 'Free Movement of Persons and the Wholly Internal Rule: Time to Move On?' (2002) 39 *Common Market Law Review* 731; M Poiares Maduro, 'The scope of European remedies: The case of purely internal situations and reverse discrimination' in C Kilpatrick, T Novitz and P Skidmore (eds), *The Future of European Remedies* (Oxford, Hart Publishing, 2000) 117; E Cannizzaro, 'Producing "Reverse Discrimination" Through the Exercise of EC Competences' (1997) 17 *Yearbook of European Law* 29; A Tryfonidou, 'The outer limits of Article 28 EC: Purely internal situations and the development of the Court's approach through the years' in C Barnard and O Odudu (eds), *The Outer Limits of European Law* (Oxford, Hart Publishing, 2009) 197.

> less favourably than a group of persons that is normally treated less beneficially.[9] In cases concerning EU citizens and third country national family members reverse discrimination occurs when some EU citizens are granted family reunification with their third country national family member because they can claim a link with EU law whereas other EU static citizens that cannot claim the same link with EU law, despite finding themselves in similar circumstances, see the very same right denied. This problem is very serious when it involves families composed of EU citizens and third country nationals because, as we have seen in the previous jurisprudential accounts, it is 'capable of generating results that are curiously random'.[10] In *Metock*, for instance, all the static union citizens were left to suffer the consequences of reverse discrimination. However, given that the reasoning of the Court in this case is very much based on the fact that the EU citizen's right of residence could also be deterred if the third country national is not allowed to join him, it does not really make sense to distinguish the residence of a non-national EU citizen from the residence of a national EU citizen any more. In *Zambrano* the problem of reverse discrimination can also be found toward those EU static citizens whose situation does not fall within the application of the test. The fact that after *Zambrano* the Court reversed and decided to curtail even more the application of a test that it created, as pointed out in Chapter 4, is indicative of the fact that lottery and not consistency is determining who should be entitled and who should not be entitled to enjoy its application. At the moment the majority of static citizens are left out from the application of this test and this is a source of injustice. Applying EU citizenship as a status that protects also the right of residence could finally put an end to wholly internal rules situations and to the need to find fictitious EU links when free movement is not at stake.

This book has explained the development of the phenomenon of family reunification, both from a legislative and jurisprudential point of view, between EU citizens and third country nationals up until 2016. It has been shown that Member States' concerns over immigration have played a role in determining the shape of the legislation and, particularly, in shaping the reasoning and the outcome of some judgments to the detriment of families composed of EU citizens and third country nationals. For the protection of these families it has been suggested how the Court could act, by interpreting the concept of EU citizenship as encompassing also the right of residence and how this move would be beneficial both to cases involving EU moving and EU static sponsors.

In order for this new approach of the Court to be successful the institution will necessarily have to grow bold and distance itself from some Member States'

[9] G Davies, *Nationality Discrimination in the European Internal Market* (The Hague, Kluwer Law International, 2003) 19. On reverse discrimination see also A Tryfonidou, *Reverse Discrimination in EC Law* (The Hague, Kluwer Law International, 2010) 14.

[10] *Zambrano* opinion, para 135.

anti-immigration stances. Immigration cases involving divided families often present emotionally difficult situations. Compelling circumstances of individual applicants normally push the Court to be audacious in upholding its expansive interpretations.[11] The Court should apply this audacity in family reunification cases in order to protect the unity of those families whose EU sponsor has never moved—and which could be unjustly reverse discriminated compared to those whose sponsor moved to another Member State—and of those families whose sponsor exercised his right of movement but which still suffer the application of a strict deterrence test. Only in this way will real free movement and residence Rights, not just of economic actors but of human beings, be achieved and, perhaps, this will help the European integration process to survive.

[11] G Beck, *The Legal Reasoning of The Court of Justice of the EU* (Oxford, Hart Publishing, 2012) 424.

Bibliography

Books

Bade, KJ, *Migration in European History* (Oxford, Blackwell Publishing, 2003).

Barnard, C, *The Substantive Law of the EU: the Four Freedoms* (Oxford, Oxford University Press, 2010).

Beck, G, *The Legal Reasoning of the Court of Justice of the EU* (Oxford, Hart Publishing, 2012).

Bosma, U, Lucassen, J and Oostindie, G, *Postcolonial Migrants and Identity Politics: Europe, Russia, Japan and the United States in Comparison* vol 18 (New York, Berghan Books, 2012).

Buzan, B, Waver, O and de Wilde, J, *Security: a New Framework for Analysis* (London, Lynne Rienner Publishers, 1998).

Castles, S and Kosack, G, *Immigrant Workers and Class Structure in Western Europe* (Oxford, Oxford University Press, 1973).

Castles, S, de Haas, H and Miller, MJ, *The Age of Migration: International Population Movements in the Modern World* (New York, Palgrave Macmillan, 1993).

Cesarani, D and Fulbrook, M, *Citizenship, Nationality and Migration in Europe* (London, Taylor & Francis, 2002).

Cesary, J, *The Oxford Handbook of European Islam* (Oxford, Oxford University Press, 2014).

Codinanzi, M, Lang, A and Nascimbene, B, *Citizenship of the Union and Freedom of Movement of Persons* (Leiden, Martinus Nijhoff Publishers, 2008).

Craig, P and de Burca, G, *EU Law: Text, Cases and Materials* (Oxford, Oxford University Press, 2011).

Dauvergne, C, *Making People Illegal. What Globalization Means for Migration and Law* (Cambridge, Cambridge University Press, 2008).

Davies, G, *Nationality Discrimination in the European Internal Market* (The Hague, Kluwer Law International, 2003).

Dollat, P, *La Citoyenneté Européenne: Théorie et Status* (Bruxelles, Bruylant, 2008).

Eisele, K, *The External Dimension of the EU's Migration Policy: Different Legal Positions of TCN in the EU: A Comparative Perspective* (Leiden, Brill Nijhoff, 2013).

Eliav-Feldon, M, Isaac, B and Ziegler, J, *The Origins of Racism in the West* (Cambridge, Cambridge University Press, 2013).

Foster, NG, *Foster on EU Law* (Oxford, Oxford University Press, 2011).

Freeman, GP, *Immigrant Labor and Racial Conflict in Industrial Societies: The French and British Experience 1945–1975* (Princeton NJ, Princeton University Press, 1979).

Gassert, P and Steinweis, AE, *Coping with the Nazi Past: West German Debates on Nazism and Generational Conflict* (New York, Berghan Books, 2006).

Geddes, A, *Immigration and European Integration: Towards a Fortress Europe?* (Manchester, Manchester University Press, 2000).

Groenendijk, K, Guild, E and Minderhoud, P, *In Search of Europe's Borders* (Leiden, Martinus Nijhoff, 2002).

Guild, E and Niessen, J, *The Developing Immigration and Asylum Policies of the European Union: Adopted Conventions, Resolutions, Recommendations, Decisions and Conclusions* (The Hague, Kluwer Law International, 1996).

Guild, E, *The Legal Elements of European Identity, EU Citizenship and Migration Law* (The Hague, Kluwer Law International, 2004).

Guild, E, *Security and Migration in the 21st Century* (Cambridge, Polity Press, 2009).

Guild, E, Peers, S and Tomkin, J, *The EU Citizenship Directive* (Oxford, Oxford University Press, 2014).

Handoll, J, *Free Movement of Persons in the EU* (New York, Wiley, 1995).

Huxley, J, *We Europeans* (London, Penguin, 1935).

Ippolito, F and Sanchez, S, *Protecting Vulnerable Groups: The European Human Rights Framework* (Oxford, Hart Publishing, 2015).

Kreins, JM, *Histoire du Luxembourg: des origines à nos jours* (Paris, Presses Universitaires de France, 1996).

La Torre, M, *European Citizenship: An Institutional Challenge* (The Hague, Kluwer Law International, 1998).

Leman, J, *From Challenging Culture to Challenged Culture: The Sicilian Cultural Code and The Socio-Cultural Praxis of Sicilian Immigrants in Belgium* (Leuven, Leuven University Press, 1987).

Lequin, Y, *Histoire des étrangers et de l'immigration en France* (Paris, Larousse, 1992).

Lister, M and Pia, E, *Citizenship in Contemporary Europe* (Edinburgh, Edinburgh University Press, 2008).

Lucassen, L, Feldman, D and Oltmer, J, *Paths of Integration: Migrants in Western Europe (1880–2004)* (Amsterdam, Amsterdam University Press, 2006).

MacMaster, N, *Racism in Europe: 1870–2000* (New York, Palgrave, 2001).

Marin, RR, *Immigration as a Democratic Challenge: Citizenship and Inclusion in Germany and the United States* (Cambridge, Cambridge University Press, 2000).

Martens, A, *Les Immigrés: Flux et reflux d'une main-d'oeuvre d'appoint, La politique belge de l'immigration de 1945 à 1970* (Louvain, Presses Universitaires de Louvain, 1976).

Mehan, E, *Citizenship and the European Community* (London, Sage Publications, 1993).

Messina, AM, *The Logics and the Politics of Post-WWII Migration to Western Europe* (Cambridge, Cambridge University Press, 2007).

Milward, AS, *The European Rescue of the Nation State* (London, Routledge, 1992).

Minter, S, *Irregular Immigration; An Economic Analysis of Policies in the EU* (Tübingen, Mohr Siebec, 2015).

Mitsilegas, V, Monar, J and Rees, W, *The European Union and Internal Security: Guardian of the People?* (Basingstoke, Palgrave Macmillan, 2006).

Moccia, L, *Diritti Fondamentali e Cittadinanza dell'Unione Europea* (Milano, Franco Angeli Publishing, 2010).

O'Leary, S, *The Evolving Concept of Community Citizenship* (The Hague, Kluwer Law International, 1996).

OECD, *Recruiting Migrant Workers: Germany* (OECD Library, 2013).

Papagianni, G, *Institutional and Policy Dynamics of EU Migration Law* (Leiden, Martinus Nijhoff Publishers, 2006).

Peers, S, *EU Justice and Home Affairs Law* (Oxford, Oxford University Press, 2011).

Rist, RC, *Guestworkers in Germany: The Prospects for Pluralism* (New York, Praeger Publishers, 1978).

Rudolph, J, *Politics and Ethnicity: A Comparative Study* (New York, Palgrave Macmillan, 2006).

Tapinos, G, *L'immigration étrangère en France 1946–1973, Travaux et Documents* Cahier No 71 (Paris, Presses Universitaires de France, 1975).

Torpey, J, *The Invention of the Passport* (Cambridge, Cambridge University Press, 1999).

Triandafillydou, A and Gropas, R, *European Immigration: A Source Book* (Oxford, Ashgate, 2014).

Tryfonidou, A, *Reverse Discrimination in EU Law* (The Hague, Kluwer Law International, 2009).

Van de Berghe, G, *Political Rights for European Citizens* (Aldershot, Gower Publishing Company Limited, 1982).

Van Walsum, SK, *The Family and the Nation: Dutch Family Migration Policies in the Context of Changing Family Norms* (Cambridge, Cambridge Scholar Publishing, 2008).

Urwin, DW, *The Community of Europe, A History of European Integration since 1945* (New York, Longman, 1995).

Book chapters

Antokolskaia, M, 'The "better law" approach and the harmonization of family law', in KB Woelki (ed), *Perspective for the Unification and Harmonization of Family Law in Europe* (Oxford, Hart Publishing, 2003) 159–82.

Barnard, C, 'Citizenship of the Union and the Area of Justice: (Almost) the Court's Moment of Glory' in A Rosas, E Levits and Y Bot (eds), *The Court of Justice and the Construction of Europe: Analyses and Perspectives on Sixty Years of Case Law* (New York, Springer, 2012) 505–22.

Besana, C, 'Accordi Internazionali ed Emigrazione della Manodopera Italiana tra Ricostruzione e Sviluppo' in Sergio Zaninelli and M Taccolini (eds), *Il lavoro come fattore produttivo e come risorsa nella storia economica italiana: atti del Convegno di studi, Roma, 24 novembre 2000* (Milano, Vita e pensiero, 2002) 3–31.

Borruso, P, 'Note sull'emigrazione clandestina italiana 1876–1976' in M Sanfilippo (ed), *Emigrazione e Storia d'Italia* (Cosenza, Luigi Pellegrini Editore, 2003) 243–66.

De Lary, H, 'Bilateral Labour Agreements Concluded by France' in *Migration for Employment: Bilateral Agreements at a Crossroads* (Paris, OECD Publishing, 2004) 43–54.

De Lobkowicz, 'Intergovernmental Cooperation in the Field of Migration—From the Single European Act to Maastricht' in J Monar and R Morgan (eds), *The Third Pillar of the European Union, Cooperation in the fields of justice and home affairs*, Proceedings of an International Conference organised by the College of Europe, Bruges, the Institut für Europäische Politik, Bonn, and the European University Institute, Florence, Conférences de Bruges—Bruges Conferences—vol 5 (Brussels, European University Press, 1994) 99–122.

Liebig, T, 'Recruitment of Foreign Labour in Germany and Switzerland' in *Migration for Employment: Bilateral Agreements at a Crossroads* (Paris, OECD Publishing, 2004) 157–186.

Esser, H and Korte, H, 'Federal Republic of Germany' in T Hammar (ed), *European Immigration Policy: A Comparative Study* (Cambridge, Cambridge University Press, 1985) 165–205.

Groussot, X, 'Principled Citizenship' and the Process of European Constitutionalization—From a Pie in the Sky to a Sky with Diamonds' in U Bernitz, C Cardner and X Groussot (eds), *General Principles of EC Law in a Process of Development* (Alphen aan den Rijn, Wolters Kluwer, 2008) 315–42.

Habermas, J, 'Citizenship and National Identity: Some Reflections on the Future of Europe' in R Beiner (ed), *Theorising Citizenship* (Albany, NY, State University of New York Press, 1995) 255–81.

Kadelbach, S, 'Union Citizenship' in A von Bogdandy and J Bast (eds), *Principles of European Constitutional Law* (Oxford, Hart Publishing, 2006) 453–99.

Kostakopoulou, D, 'European Union Citizenship: The Journey Goes On' in A Ott and E Vos (eds), *Fifty years of European Integration: Foundations and Perspectives* (The Hague, TMC Asser Press, 2009) 271–90.

Maduro, M Poiares, 'The scope of European remedies: The case of purely internal situations and reverse discrimination' in C Kilpatrick, T Novitz and P Skidmore (eds), *The Future of European Remedies* (Oxford, Hart Publishing, 2000) 117–40.

Martiniello, M, 'The new migratory Europe: Towards a proactive immigration policy', in CA Parsons and TM Smeeding (eds), *Immigration and the Transformation of Europe* (Cambridge, Cambridge University Press, 2006) 298–326.

Miles, R, 'The Articulation of Racism and Nationalism: Reflections on European History' in J Solomos and J Wrech (eds), *Racism and Migration in Western Europe* (Oxford, Berghan Books, 1993) 35–52.

Moch, LP, 'Foreign Workers in Western Europe: The "Cheaper Hands" in Historical Perspective' in J Klausen and L Tilly (eds), *European Integration in Social and Historical Perspective: 1850 to the Present* (New York, Rowman & Littlefield, 1997) 103–16.

Peers, S, 'EU Justice and Home Affairs Law (non-civil)' in P Craig and G de Burca (eds), *The Evolution of EU Law* (Oxford, Oxford University Press, 2011) 269–97.

Rath, J, 'The ideological representation of Migrant workers in Europe: a matter of racialization?' in J Solomos and J Wrech (eds), *Racism and Migration in Western Europe* (Oxford, Berghan Books, 1993) 215–32.

Romero, F, 'Migration as an issue in European interdependence and integration: the case of Italy' in AS Milward, F Lynch, R Ranieri, F Romero and V Soresen (eds), *The Frontier of National Sovereignty: History and Theory, 1945–1992* (London, Routledge, 1993) 33–57.

Rudge, P, 'European Initiatives on Asylum' in D Joly and R Cohen (eds), *Reluctant Hosts: Europe and its Refugees* (Aldershot, Avebury, 1989) 212–15.

Shaw, J, 'The Constitutional Development of Citizenship in the EU Context: With or Without the Treaty of Lisbon', in I Pernice and E Tanchev (eds), *Ceci n'est pas une constitution—constitutionalism without constitution?* (Baden-Baden, Nomos Verlagsgesellschaft, 2009) 104–18.

Shaw, J, 'Citizenship: Contrasting Dynamics at the Interface of Integration and Constitutionalism' in G de Burca and P Craig (eds), *The Evolution of EU Law* (Oxford, Oxford University Press, 2011) 575–610.

Solomos, J, 'Racism and Anti-Racism in Great Britain: Historical Trends and Contemporary Issues', in BP Bowser, *Racism and Anti-Racism in World Perspective* (Thousand Oaks, Sage Publications, 1995) 157–80.

Spaventa, E, 'The Free Movement of Workers in the Twenty-first Century' in D Chalmers and A Arnull (eds), *The Oxford Handbook of European Union Law* (Oxford, Oxford University Press, 2015) 459–75.

Steinert, JD, 'L'accordo di emigrazione italo-tedesco e il reclutamento di manodopera italiana negli anni cinquanta' in J Petersen (ed), *L'emigrazione tra Italia e Germania* (Bari, Piero Lacaita Editore, 1993) 139–68.

Tosi, L, 'La tutela internazionale dell'immigrazione' in P Bevilacqua, A De Clementi and E Franzina (eds), *Storia dell'immigrazione italiana, vol 2, arrivi* (Roma, Donzelli Editore, 2001) 439–56.

Tryfonidou, A, 'The outer limits of Article 28 EC: Purely internal situations and the development of the Court's approach through the years' in C Barnard and O Odudu (eds), *The Outer Limits of European Law* (Oxford, Hart Publishing, 2009) 197–224.

Tsoukala, A, 'Looking at migrants as enemies' in D Bigo and E Guild (eds), *Controlling Frontiers: Free Movement into and Within Europe* (Aldershot, Ashgate Publishing, 2005) 161–92.

Verbunt, G, 'France' in T Hammar (ed), *European Immigration Policy: A Comparative Study* (Cambridge, Cambridge University Press, 1985) 127–64.

Weiler, JHH, 'To Be a European Citizen—Eros and Civilization' in JHH Weiler (ed), *The Constitution of Europe: Do the new clothes have an emperor and other essays on European integration* (Cambridge, Cambridge University Press, 1999) 324–57.

Weiler, JHH, 'Europa: Nous coalisons des États nous n'unissons pas des hommes' in M Cartabia and A Simoncini (eds), *La Sostenibilita' della democrazia nel XXI secolo* (Bologna, Il Mulino Publishers, 2009) 51–82.

Wihtol de Wenden, C, 'The case of France', in G Zincone, R Pennix and M Borkert (eds), *Migration Policy Making in Europe* (Amsterdam, Amsterdam University Press, 2001) 61–94.

Journal articles

Acierno, S, 'The *Carpenter* judgment: fundamental rights and the limits of the Community legal order' (2003) 28 *European Law Review* 398–407.

Adam, S and Van Elsuwege, P, 'Citizenship rights and the federal balance between the European Union and its Member States: Comment on Dereci' (2012) 37 *European Law Review* 176–90.

Alter, KJ, 'Who are the "Masters of the Treaty"?: European Governments and the European Court of Justice' (1998) 52 *International Organization* 121–47.

Arcarazo, DA, 'Immigration in the European Union: Family Reunification after the Metock Case' (2009) 9 *University College Dublin Law Review* 64–88.

Aziz, M, 'Implementation as the Test Case of European Union Citizenship' (2009) 15 *Columbia Journal of European Law* 281–98.

Barret, G, 'Family Matters: European Community Law and Third Country National Family Members' (2003) 40 *Common Market Law Review* 369–421.

Bartolini, S and Biondi, A, 'Life as Human Rights Court: Challenges and Developments in the EU Courts Activity in 2014' (2016) 22 *European Public Law* 3–24.

Berneri, C and Peers, S, 'Iida and O and S: further developments in the immigration status of static EU citizens' (2013) 27 *Journal of Immigration, Asylum and Nationality Law* 162–73.

Berneri, C, 'Protection of Families Composed by EU Citizens and Third Country Nationals; Some Suggestions to Tackle Reverse Discrimination' (2014) 16 *European Journal of Migration and Law* 249–75.

Bierbach, JB, 'European citizens' third-country family members and Community law' (2008) 4 *European Constitutional Law Review* 344–62.

Boyd, M, 'Family and Personal Networks in International Migration: Recent Development and New Agendas' (1989) 23 *International Migration Review* 638–70.

Cambien, N, 'Case C-127/08, Blaise Baheten Metock and Others v Minister for Justice, Equality and Law Reform' (2008) 15 *Columbia Journal of European Law* 321–42.

Cambien, N, 'Union Citizenship and Immigration: Rethinking the Classics?' (2012) 5 *European Journal of Legal Studies* 10–37.

Cannizzaro, E, 'Producing "Reverse Discrimination" Through the Exercise of EC Competences' (1997) 17 *Yearbook of European Law* 29–46.

Carlier, JY, 'Case C-200/02, Kunqian Catherine Zhu, Man Lavette Chen v Secretary of State for the Home Department' (2005) 42 *Common Market Law Review* 1121–31.

Castles, S, 'The Guest-Worker in Western Europe—An Obituary' (1986) 20 *International Migration Review* 761–78.

Coppel, J and O'Neill, A, 'The European Court of Justice: Taking Rights Seriously' (1992) 29 *Common Market Law Review* 669–92.

Costello, C, 'Metock: Free Movement and Normal Family Life in the Union' (2009) 46 *Common Market Law Review* 587–622.

Currie, S, 'Accelerated justice or a step too far? Residence rights of non EU family members and the court's ruling in Metock' (2009) 34 *European Law Review* 310–26.

Davies, G, 'Freedoms unlimited? Reflections on Mary Carpenter v Secretary of State' (2003) 40 *Common Market Law Review* 537–43.

Davies, G, '"Any Place I Hang My Hat?" or: Residence is the New Nationality', (2005) 11 *European Law Journal* 43–56.

Dougan, M, 'The Constitutional Dimension to the Case Law on Union Citizenship' (2006) 31 *European Law Review* 613–41.

De Burca, G, 'After the EU Charter of Fundamental Rights: The Court of Justice as a Human Rights Adjudicator?' (2013) 20 *Maastricht Journal* 168–84.

Douglas Scott, S, 'A Tale of Two Courts: Luxembourg, Strasbourg and the Growing European Human Rights Acquis' (2006) 43 *Common Market Law Review* 629–65.

Dutricourt, C and Thomas, S, 'Reverse discrimination and free movement of persons under Community law: all for Ulysses, nothing for Penelope?' (2009) 34 *European Law Review* 433–54.

Eijken, V and De Vries, S, 'A new route into the promised land? Being a European citizen after Ruiz Zambrano' (2011) 36 *European Law Review* 704–21.

Elsmore, M and Starup, P, 'Union Citizenship—Background, Jurisprudence, and Perspective: The Past, Present, and Future of Law and Policy' (2007) 26 *Yearbook of European Law* 57–113.

Elsmore, M, and Starup, P, 'Case C-1/05, Yunying Jia v Migrationsverket' (2007) 44 *Common Market Law Review* 787–801.

Groenendijk, K, 'Family Reunification as a Right under Community Law' (2006) 10 *European Journal of Migration and Law* 215–30.

Hailbronner, K and Thym, D, 'Case C-34/09, Gerardo Ruiz Zambrano v Office national de l'emploi (ONEM)' (2011) 48 *Common Market Law Review* 1253–70.

Hansen, R, 'Migration to Europe since 1945: its History and its Lessons' (2003) 74 *The Political Quarterly* 25–38.

Harbacevica, S and Reich, N, 'Citizenship and family on trial: a fairly optimistic overview of recent court practice with regard to free movement of persons' (2003) 40 *Common Market Law Review* 615–38.

Hinarejos, A, 'Citizenship of the EU: clarifying genuine enjoyment of the substance of citizenship rights' (2012) 71 *Cambridge Law Journal* 279–82.

Heisler, BS, 'Sending Countries and the Politics of Emigration and Destination' (1985) 19 *International Migration Review* 469–84.

Huysmans, J, 'The European Union and the Securitization of Migration' (2003) 38 *Journal of Common Market Studies* 751–77.

Jacobs, FG, 'Citizenship of the European Union—A Legal Analysis' (2007) 13 *European Law Journal* 591–610.

Jadoul, L and Vanneste, F, 'Casenote under case C-60/00. Mary Carpenter v Secretary of State for the Home Department (ECJ July 11, 2002) (2003) 9 *The Columbia Journal of European Law* 447–55.

Kochenov, D, 'Ius Tractum of Many Faces: European Citizenship and the Difficult Relationship between Status and Rights' (2008) 15 *Columbia Journal of European Law* 169–237.

Kochenov, D and Plender, R, 'EU Citizenship: from an incipient form to an incipient substance? The discovery of the treaty text' (2012) 37 *European Law Review* 369–96.

Kofman, E, 'Female "Birds of Passage" a Decade later: Gender and Immigration in the European Union' (1999) 33 *International Migration Review* 269–99.

Kostakopoulou, D, 'Ideas, Norms, and European Citizenship: Explaining Institutional Change' (2005) 68 *Modern Law Review* 233–67.

Kostakopoulou, D, 'European Citizenship: Writing the Future' (2007) 13 *European Law Journal* 623–46.

Kruma, K, 'A Hopeful Transmission: Searching for Citizenship Beyond State' (2015) 17 *European Journal of Migration and Law* 361–93.

Lansbergen, A and Miller, N, 'European citizenship rights in internal situations: an ambiguous revolution? Decision of 8 March 2011, Case C-34/09 Gerardo Ruiz Zambrano v Office national de l'emploi (ONEM)' (2011) 7 *European Constitutional Law Review* 287–307.

Maas, W, 'Unrespected, Unequal, Hollow?: Contingent Citizenship and Reversible Rights in the European Union' (2009) 15 *Columbia Journal of European Law* 265–80.

Mantu, S, 'European Union Citizenship anno 2011: Zambrano, McCarthy and Dereci' (2012) 26 *Journal of Immigration Asylum and Nationality Law* 40–56.

Mattli, W and Slaughter, A, 'Revisiting the European Court of Justice' *International Organization* (1998) 52 177–209.

McDonald, JR, 'Labour Immigration in France, 1946–1965' (1969) 59 *Annals of the Association of the American Geographers* 116–34.

Martin, PL and Miller, MJ, 'Guestworkers: Lessons from Western Europe' (1980) 33 *Industrial and Labor Relations Review* 315–30.

Nic Shuibhne, N, 'Free Movement of Persons and the Wholly Internal Rule: Time to Move On?'(2002) 39 *Common Market Law Review* 731–71.

Nic Shuibhne, N, 'Margins of Appreciation: national values, fundamental rights and EC free movement law' (2009) 34 *European Law Review* 230–56.

Nic Shuibhne, N, 'The Resilience of EU Market Citizenship' (2010) 47 *Common Market Law Review* 1597–1628.

Nic Shuibhne, N, 'Seven questions for seven paragraphs' (2011) 36 *European Law Review* 161–63.

Nic Shuibhne, N, 'Case Law: (Some) Of The Kids Are All right' (2012) 49 *Common Market Law Review* 349–80.

Nic Shuibhne, N, 'Limits Rising Duties Ascending: The Changing Legal Shape of Union Citizenship' (2015) 52 *Common Market Law Review* 889–938.

O'Leary, S, 'The past, the present and the future of the wholly internal rule' (2009) 44 *Irish Jurist* 13–46.

Oliver P and Henning Roth, W, 'The Internal Market and the Four Freedoms' (2004) 41 *Common Market Law Review* 407–41.

Oosterom-Staples, H, 'To What Extent Has Reverse Discrimination Been Reversed?' (2012) 14 *European Journal of Migration and Law* 151–72.

Palombella, G, 'Whose Europe? After the Constitution: A Goal-Based Citizenship' (2005) 3 *International Law Journal of Constitutional Law* 357–82.

Peers, S, 'Free Movement, Immigration Control and Constitutional Conflict' (2009) 5 *European Constitutional Law Review* 173–96.

Peers, S, 'EC Immigration and Asylum Law Attracting and Deterring Labour Migration: The Blue Card and Employer Sanctions Directives' (2009) 11 *European Journal of Migration and Law* 387–426.

Penninx, R, 'International Migration in Western Europe Since 1973: Developments, Mechanism and Controls' (1986) 20 *International Migration Review* 951–72.

Pinyol-Jimenez, G, 'The migration security nexus in short: instruments and actions in the European Union' (2012) 4 *Amsterdam Law Forum* 36–57.

Ritter, C, 'Purely internal situations, reverse discrimination' (2006) 31 *European Law Review* 690–711.

Sanchez Iglesias, S, 'Fundamental Rights Protection for Third Country Nationals and Citizens of the Union: Principles of Enhancing Coherence' (2013) 15 *European Journal of Migration and Law* 137–53.

Sauvy, A, 'Evaluation des besoins de l'immigration française' (1946) 1 *Population* (French edition) 91–98.

Schiltz, C, 'Akrich: A Clear Delimitation without Limits' (2005) 12 *Maastricht Journal of European and Comparative Law* 241–52.

Sawyer, C, 'Civis Europeanus sum: the citizenship rights of the children of foreign parents' (2005) *Public Law* 475–82.

Shaw, J, 'The Interpretation of European Union Citizenship' (1998) 61 *Modern Law Review* 293–317.

Shaw, J, Between Law and Political Truth? Member State Preferences, EU Free Movement Rules and National Immigration Law (2015) 17 *Cambridge Yearbook of European Legal Studies* 247–86.

Shore, C, 'Whither European Citizenship?: Eros and Civilization Revisited' (2004) 7 *European Journal of Social Theory* 27–44.

Smismans, S, 'The European Union's Fundamental Rights Myth' (2009) 48 *Journal of Common Market Studies* 45–66.

Spaventa, E, 'From Gebhard to Carpenter: Towards a (Non-) Economic European Constitution' *Common Market Law Review* (2004) 41 743–73.

Spaventa, E, 'Case C-109/01, *Secretary of State for the Home Department v H Akrich*, judgment of the Full Court of 23 September 2003, [2003] ECR I-9607' (2005) 42 *Common Market Law Review* 225–39.

Spaventa, E, 'Seeing the Wood Despite the Trees?: On the Scope of Union Citizenship and Its Constitutional Effects' (2008) 45 *Common Market Law Review* 13–45.

Toner, H, 'Comments on Mary Carpenter v Secretary of State, 11 July 2002 (Case C-60/00)' (2003) 5 *European Journal of Migration and Law* 163–72.

Tryfonidou, A, '*Mary Carpenter v Secretary of State for the Home Department*: The Beginning of a New Era in the European Union?' (2003) 14 *King's College Law Journal* 81–86.

Tryfonidou, A, 'Chen: Further Cracks in the Great Wall of the European Union' (2005) 11 *European Public Law* 527–41.

Tryfonidou, A, 'Jia or "Carpenter II": the edge of reason' (2007) 32 *European Law Review* 908–18.

Tryfonidou, A, 'Family Reunification Rights of (Migrant) Union Citizens: Towards a More Liberal Approach' (2009) 15 *European Law Journal* 634–53.

Van Der Brink, MJ, 'EU Citizenship and EU Fundamental Rights: taking EU Citizenship Rights Seriously?' (2012) 39 *Legal Issues of Economic Integration* 273–89.

Van Elsuwege, P and Kochenov, D, 'On The Limits of Judicial Intervention: EU Citizenship and Family Reunification Rights' (2011) 13 *European Journal of Migration and Law* 443–66.

Weiler, JHH, 'A Quiet Revolution The European Court of Justice and its Interlocutors' (1994) 26 *Comparative Political Studies* 510–34.

White, RCA, 'Free Movement, Equal Treatment and Citizenship of the Union' (2005) 54 *International and Comparative Law Quarterly* 885–905.

Wiesbrock, A, 'Disentangling the Union Citizenship Puzzle? The *McCarthy* case' (2011) 36 *European Law Review* 860–72.

Wiesbrock, A, 'Granting Citizenship-related Rights to Third Country Nationals: An Alternative to the Full Extension of European Citizenship?' (2012) 14 *European Journal of Migration and Law* 63–94.

Wollenschläger, F, 'A New Fundamental Freedom Beyond Market Integration: Union Citizenship and Its Dynamics for Shifting the Economic Paradigm of European Integration' (2011) 17 *European Law Journal* 1–34.

Wray, H, 'Teixeira and Ibrahim: Looking back, looking forward or inward?' (2011) 2 *FMW: Online journal on free movement of workers in the European Union* 26–37.

Zimmerman, KF, 'Tackling the European Migration Problem' (1995) 9 *The Journal of Economic Perspectives* 45–62.

Online papers

Caldognetto, ML, 'Per una storia dell'emigrazione dal Montefeltro al Lussemburgo: temi, problemi, prospettive' (2010) 32 Studi Montefeltrani, Pesaro, Societa' di Studi Storici per il Montefeltro available at www.cdmh.lu/resources/pdf/_base_documents/9983156792.pdf.

Canovi, A, 'L'Immagine degli Italiani in Belgio: Appunti Geostorici' (2011) 5 Dossier: Italia altre. Immagini e Comunita' Italiane all'Estero available at www.studistorici.com/2011/01/29/canovi_numero_5/.

Carrubba, CJ and Gabel, M, 'Do Governments Sway European Court of Justice Decision-making?: Evidence from Government Court Briefs' IFIR Working Paper Series 2005, available at www.ifigr.org/workshop/fall05/gabel-workshop.pdf.

Cerna, L, 'The EU Blue Card: preferences, policies and negotiations between Member States' (2013) 1 *Migration Studies* available at migration.oxfordjournals.org/content/early/2013/07/26/migration.mnt010.full.

Collett, E, 'The Proposed European Blue Card System: Arming for the Global War on Talent?' Migration Policy Institute 7/1/2008 available at www.migrationinformation.org/feature/display.cfm?ID=667.

Coutts, S, 'Case C- 434-09: Shirley McCarthy v Secretary of State for the Home Department' EUDO comment 2011 available at eudo-citizenship.eu/eu-citizenship.

Cumoli, F, 'Dai campi al sottosuolo. Reclutamento e strategie di adattamento al lavoro dei minatori italiani in Belgio' in (2009) 5 *Storicamente* available at www.storicamente.org/07_dossier/emigrazione-italiana-in-belgio.htm.

De la Rica, S, Glitz, A and Ortega, F, 'Immigration in Europe: Trends, Policies and Empirical Evidence' discussion paper No 7778 IZA 2013 available at www.econ.upf.edu/~glitz/ImmigrationEurope2013.pdf.

Ette, A, 'Germany's Immigration Policy, 2000–2002. Understanding Policy Change with a Political Process Approach' (Bremen: COMCAD, 2003) available at www.uni-bielefeld.de/tdrc/ag_comcad/downloads/workingpaper_3.pdf.

Guild, E, 'The Court of Justice of the European Union and Citizens of the Union: A Revolution Underway? The Zambrano judgment of 8 March 2011' EUDO comment 2011 available at eudo-citizenship.eu/citizenship-news/453-the-court-of-justice-of-the-european-union-and-citizens-of-the-union-a-revolution-underway-the-zambrano-judgment-of-8-march-2011.

John, A, 'Family Reunification For Migrants and Refugees: a Forgotten Human Right?' *A comparative analysis of family reunification under domestic law and jurisprudence, international and regional instruments, ECHR case law and the EU* (2003) available at www.fd.uc.pt/hrc/working_papers/arturojohn.pdf.

Kollwelter, S, 'Immigration in Luxembourg: New Challenges for a New Country' Migration Policy Institute available at www.migrationpolicy.org/article/immigration-luxembourg-new-challenges-old-country.

Mattes, M, 'Gender and Migration in Germany: the case of female labour migration from the 1950s to the 1970s' (2009) available at migrationeducation.de/fileadmin/uploads/MattesGenderMigration_01.pdf.

Micelli, F, 'L'emigrazione dal Friuli Venezia Giulia in Belgio' available at www.ammer-fvg.org/ita/paesi/index_tree_d.asp?CCat_ID=BE&CCatS_ID=&Cont_ID=262.

Prontera, G, 'L'emigrazione italiana verso la Repubblica Federale Tedesca. L'accordo bilaterale del 1955, la ricezione sulla stampa, il ruolo dei centri di emigrazione di Milano e Verona' (2008) 4 *Storicamente* available at www.storicamente.org/07_dossier/migrazioni-prontera.htm.

Sartori, F, 'Population and Social Conditions' Eurostat 2012 table 4 available at ec.europa.eu/eurostat/documents/3433488/5585336/KS-SF-12-045-EN.PDF/241b75f4-2dfb-4aca-b0ff-1b6c34a78dc8.

Shaw, J, 'Has the European Court of Justice challenged Member State Sovereignty in Nationality Law?' (2011) 62 EUI working papers available at eudo-citizenship.eu/citizenship-forum/254-has-the-european-court-of-justice-challenged-member-state-sovereignty-in-nationality-law.

Spaventa, E, 'Striving for Equality: Who "Deserves" to Be a Union Citizen?' paper 2014 available at http://ssrn.com/abstract=2518955.
Valentova, M and Berzoza, G, 'Attitudes towards immigrants in Luxembourg: do contacts matter?' CEPS/INSTEAD working paper (2010) available at www.ceps.lu/pdf/3/art1547.pdf.
Werner, H 'From the German "Guestworker" Programmes of the Sixties to the Current "Green Card" Initiative for IT Specialists' (2001) 43 Institut für Arbeitsmarkt- und Berufsforschung der Bundesanstalt für Arbeit (IAB) available at www.ilo.org/wcmsp5/groups/public/---ed_protect/---protrav/---migrant/documents/publication/wcms_201876.pdf.
Wieclawski, 'The Eastern Enlargement of the European Union: Fears, Challenges and Reality' (2010) *Globality Studies Journal* available at https://gsj.stonybrook.edu/wp-content/uploads/2010/03/0015Wieclawski.pdf.

Other electronic sources

European Agenda on Migration—Legislative Documents available at ec.europa.eu/dgs/home-affairs/what-we-do/policies/european-agenda-migration/proposal-implementation-package/index_en.htm.
Eurostat 'First residence permits issued in the EU-28 by reasons, 2008, 2009, 2010, 2011, 2012, 2013 and 2014.png' available at ec.europa.eu/eurostat/statistics-explained/index.php?title=File:First_residence_permits_issued_in_the_EU-28_by_reasons,_2008,_2009,_2010,_2011,_2012,_2013_and_2014.png&oldid=259903.
Thomas, A, 'Asylum seekers continue to be stigmatized by the British Press', 31 October 2012, available at www.theguardian.com/media/2012/oct/31/asylum-seekers-stigmatised-british-press.
UN High Commissioner for Refugees, interview of Antonio Guterres 20 March 2012 available at www.un.org/apps/news/newsmakers.asp?NewsID=107.
Warren, R, 'Why are refugees going to Germany, and Will they stay?' BuzzFeed News 2015 available at https://www.buzzfeed.com/rossalynwarren/why-are-refugees-going-to-germany-and-will-they-stay?utm_term=.xkBxMraxR#.byYB6PqBr.

Green papers, policy papers, reports

Comité Intergouvernemental créé par la Conference de Messine, Rapport des Chefs de délegation aux Ministres des Affaires Etrangères Bruxelles (Spaak Report) 21 April 1956 available at www.cvce.eu/obj/rapport_des_chefs_de_delegation_aux_ministres_des_affaires_etrangeres_bruxelles_21_avril_1956-fr-52a08e74-02f5-4912-a667-2ea34b9dcdea.html.
Dimensioni e caratteristiche del fenomeno occupazionale della popolazione immigrata in provincia di Latina available at www.progettostima.it/public/articoli/29/Files/Rapporto%20finale%2009%2006%202010.pdf.
European Council 2002 Conclusions of the Presidency Seville 21–22 June available at www.cvce.eu/en/obj/seville_european_council_presidency_conclusions_21_and_22_june_2002-en-f96751f6-9eed-4390-99a8-3174841a1b2d.html.

Green Paper on the right to family reunification of third-country nationals living in the European Union (Directive 2003/86/EC) COM (2011) 735 final.

Guild, E, 'EU Policy on Labour Migration: A First look at the Commission's Blue Card Initiative' CEPS Policy Brief 145/2007 available at papers.ssrn.com/sol3/papers.cfm?abstract_id=1334076.

Hayes, B, 'From the Schengen Information System to SIS II and the Visa Information (VIS): the proposals explained' (2004), available at http://www.statewatch.org/news/2005/may/analysis-sisII.pdf.

Pascouau, Y and McLoughlin, S, 'EU Single Permit Directive: a small step forward in EU migration policy', European Policy Centre Policy Brief 24/1/2012 available at www.epc.eu/pub_details.php?cat_id=3&pub_id=1398.

Pastore, F and Sciortino, G, *Tutori Lontani: il Ruolo degli Stati d'Origine nel Processo di Integrazione degli Immigrati* (2001) Ricerca svolta su incarico della Commissione delle politiche di integrazione degli immigrati presso Centro Studi di Politica Internazionale (Cespi) available at www.cespi.it/PASTORE/tutori-lontani.PDF.

Sauvy, A, *Le rapport Sauvy sur le problème de l'économie et de la population en Wallonie*, Liège, 1962, Conseil Economique Wallon.

Western Europe's Migrant Workers (1974) report 28.

Conference papers and speeches

Dashwood, A, 'Judicial Activism and Conferred Powers—Is the CJEU Falling into Bad Habits?' paper presented at the 10th IEL (Institute of European Law) Annual Lecture, Birmingham University, 27 June 2012.

Guild, E, 'The European Union after the Treaty of Lisbon. Fundamental Rights and EU Citizenship' Global Jean Monnet/European Community Studies Association, World Conference 25–26 May 2010 available at aei.pitt.edu/15107/1/Guild_Jean_Monnet_speech_e-version.pdf.

Hallstein, W, 'Halfway to Europe Unity', EU speech held on occasion of the 10th anniversary of the signature of the Rome Treaty, published in *Die Zeit*, 17 and 24 March 1967.

Peacock, A, *The oil crisis and the professional economist*, Sir Ellis Hunter memorial lectures, lecture delivered at the University of York on 11 December 1974 (York, University of York publication, 1975).

Index

www.ingramcontent.com/pod-product-compliance
Lightning Source LLC
Chambersburg PA
CBHW071256180926
51613CB00001B/46
9781509904785